ADVANCES IN INTERNATIONAL COMPARATIVE MANAGEMENT

Volume 13

Advances in International Comparative Management

Joseph L. C. Cheng and Richard B. Peterson, Series Editors

ADVANCES IN INTERNATIONAL COMPARATIVE MANAGEMENT

Edited by   JOSEPH L. C. CHENG
Department of Business Administration
University of Illinois at Urbana-Champaign

RICHARD B. PETERSON
School of Business Administration
University of Washington

VOLUME 13

JAI PRESS INC.
Stamford, Connecticut

ISBN: 0-7623-0589-4

ISSN: 0747-7929

Manufactured in the United States of America

3 2280 00675 0863

CONTENTS

PART I. RESEARCH FORUM

PART II. ARTICLES

LIST OF CONTRIBUTORS

Kevin Au	Faculty of Business Administration Chinese University of Hong Kong
Brian Bemmels	Faculty of Commerce and Business Administration University of British Columbia
Peter Buckley	Centre for International Business Leeds University Business School
Joseph L. C. Cheng	Department of Business Administration University of Illinois at Urbana-Champaign
John Child	Judge Institute of Management Studies University of Cambridge
Roger L. M. Dunbar	Stern School of Business New York University
Mauro F. Guillén	The Wharton School and Department of Sociology University of Pennsylvania
John R. Kimberly	The Wharton School University of Pennsylvania and INSEAD
Suresh Kotha	Department of Management and Organization University of Washington
Zhiang Lin	School of Management University of Texas at Dallas

Richard B. Peterson

Department of Management and
  Organization
University of Washington

Gordon Redding

INSEAD Euro-Asia Center
France

James A. Robins

Graduate School of Management
University of California at Irvine

Oded Shenkar

Fisher College of Business
The Ohio State University

EDITORIAL REVIEW BOARD

REVIEWER ACKNOWLEDGMENT

The editors would like to thank the following individuals who have assisted the AICM editorial board in reviewing manuscripts submitted for the present volume:

Peter Dorfman	New Mexico State University
Lorna Doucet	University of Illinois at Urbana-Champaign
Roberto Garcia	Indiana University
Jeffrey Krug	University of Illinois at Urbana-Champaign
Daniel Miller	Central Connecticut State University
John Milliman	University of Colorado at Denver
Bai Young Park	University of Illinois at Urbana-Champaign
Anju Seth	University of Illinois at Urbana-Champaign
Justin Tan	Chinese University of Hong Kong
David Thomas	University of Auckland
Ming Zeng	INSEAD

NOTICE TO AUTHORS

Advances in International Comparative Management (*AICM*) is a scholarly publication devoted to advancing the cross-national study of organizations and management. It publishes conceptual and empirical papers that deal with topics from any area within the management field, including strategic management, organization theory, organizational behavior, human resource management, business ethics, labor relations, and technology management, among others. The editors are particularly interested in manuscripts that go beyond the current "culture-free" versus "culture-dependent" debate to systematically incorporate the societal context into the study of organizations and management. This requires an analysis of specific relationships between organization/management practices and characteristics of the societal context that vary across nations, such as those pertaining to a country's cultural, institutional, economic, legal, and political systems. The organizations studied can be domestic or multinational, and the level of analysis can be macro or micro. To be accepted for publication, a paper must make a significant contribution to the field through some combination of new theoretical insights, managerial applications, methodology, or data.

AICM welcomes submission of the following types of manuscripts:

1. Comprehensive, state-of-the-art literature reviews that integrate diverse research streams and identify promising directions for future research.

2. Analytical essays that offer new conceptual models or theoretical perspectives and use those frameworks as a foundation for developing research propositions.
3. Empirical articles that report results from exploratory or hypothesis-testing studies based on quantitative and/or qualitative methodologies.
4. Methodological papers that refine existing methodologies or develop new ones for investigating particular issues or topics central to international comparative management research.

All manuscripts will be subject to a double-blind review process. Publication decisions are made by the editors based on recommendations from the reviewers and members of the editorial board. Reviewers' comments will be made available to the authors. Occasionally, *AICM* publishes invited papers from leading experts on special topics that are of interest to international comparative management scholars.

Contributors should prepare their manuscripts following the guidelines used by the *Academy of Management Journal*. Please send five (5) copies of the manuscript to: Professor Joseph Cheng, *AICM* Co-editor, Department of Business Administration, College of Commerce, University of Illinois at Urbana-Champaign, 1206 South Sixth Street, Champaign, IL 61820, U.S.A. Prospective contributors desiring further information may contact Joseph Cheng at 217-333-2963 (e-mail: jlcheng@uiuc.edu) or Michael Hitt at 409-845-5577 (e-mail: mhitt@cgsb.tamu.edu).

PREFACE

In this second volume under our editorship, we continue the innovation that we started for the research series in 1998—the *AICM* Distinguished Scholar Award and Research Forum. This new feature recognizes individuals who have made outstanding scholarly contributions to the cross-national or cross-cultural study of organizations and management. *AICM* will publish in the volume that honors the scholar a biographical profile highlighting his or her research activities and accomplishments. Additionally, the scholar will prepare an invited article for publication in the same volume. The editors will invite three to four leading researchers in the scholar's area of specialization to write commentaries. These commentaries, along with the scholar's invited article, will be published together as a Research Forum.

We are delighted to announce that Professor John Child of the University of Cambridge is the recipient of the 2000 Distinguished Scholar Award. As a result of co-sponsorship between *AICM* and the International Management Division (IMD) of the Academy of Management, the award is now renamed the AICM-IMD Distinguished Scholar Award. This co-sponsorship provides added recognition to the scholar, and furthers the goals of both *AICM* and IMD in advancing scholarly research in international comparative management studies. Professor Child will be receiving the award at the 2000 Annual Academy of Management Meeting in Toronto in August, where he will also make a research presentation based on his invited *AICM* article.

A world-renowned scholar in organization theory and international management, Professor Child has published 17 books, more than 50 refereed journal articles, and numerous book chapters (more about Professor Child later in the research forum section). He has prepared an article, titled "Theorizing about Organization Cross-nationally," to serve as the anchor piece for this volume's research forum. At our invitation, four other scholars who are familiar with Child's work have written commentaries on his paper. They are all leading researchers in the areas of organization studies and international business/management: Professor Peter Buckley of Leeds University, Professor John Kimberly of University of Pennsylvania, Professor Gordon Redding of INSEAD, and Professor Oded Shenkar of Ohio State University. In addition to commenting on Child's invited paper, we also asked the commentators to extend his ideas and discuss their implications to their own research and area of specialization.

The present volume also publishes four other articles selected through a double-blind review process among the manuscripts ($n = 46$) submitted. Together, they cover an interesting set of topics in international management studies with a comparative focus, including: organizational control in international joint ventures, institutional and cultural effects on subsidiary operations, corporate governance practices, and employees' choice of dissatisfaction behavior display. These articles, along with the five Research Forum papers, present a rich diversity of theoretical and methodological approaches. They also represent the state of the art and some of the best thinking in the field.

This volume marks the last publication with Dick Peterson serving as co-editor of *AICM*. After a long and distinguished academic career which spans over 30 years, Dick retired on January 1, 2000 from his post at the University of Washington. He has been a strong advocate of and contributor to the international comparative management field. He has made numerous and important contributions to *AICM*, first as an editorial board member and then as associate editor and co-editor. Dick will continue his involvement with *AICM* by switching roles to become an editorial board member. Starting with the next volume, Professor Mike Hitt of Texas A&M University will join Joe Cheng as the new *AICM* co-editor. He is a past president of the Academy of Management and former editor of the *Academy of Management Journal*, and has served on the *AICM* editorial board since 1997. We all look forward to working with Mike in his new role as co-editor.

We hope you will enjoy the exciting works published in the present volume.

Joseph L. C. Cheng
Richard B. Peterson
Series Co-editors

PART I

RESEARCH FORUM

INTRODUCTION AND INTERVIEW WITH JOHN CHILD, RECIPIENT OF THE 2000 AICM-IMD DISTINGUISHED SCHOLAR AWARD

Joseph L. C. Cheng and Richard B. Peterson

John Child is the Diageo Professor of Management Studies at the Judge Institute of Management Studies, University of Cambridge. He is currently on leave from Cambridge, serving as Distinguished Visiting Professor and Co-director of the Chinese Management Center at the School of Business, University of Hong Kong. Born and raised in England, Professor Child received a B.A. with First Class Honors in 1962, an M.A. in 1965, a Ph.D. in 1967, and an Sc.D. in 1984, all from the University of Cambridge. In 1996 he was awarded a Honorary Doctorate of Economics by the Helsinki School of Economics.

A world-renowned scholar in organization theory and international management, Professor Child has published 17 books, more than 50 refereed journal articles, and numerous book chapters. Among the books he has authored or co-authored are: *British Management Thought—A Critical Analysis* (1969), *Man and Organization* (1973), *Lost Managers: Supervisors in Industry and Society*

Advances in International Comparative Management, Volume 13, pages 3-25.
Copyright © 2000 by JAI Press Inc.
All rights of reproduction in any form reserved.
ISBN: 0-7623-0589-4

(1982), *Organization of Innovation: East-West Perspectives* (1987), *New Technology in European Services* (1990), *Societal Change Between Market and Organization* (1993), *Management in China During the Age of Reform* (1994), *Management in China During the 1990s: International Enterprises* (1996), *Strategies of Cooperation* (1998), and *The Management of International Acquisitions* (2000). He has lectured at leading universities around the world and received research grants from funding agencies in the UK, Germany, Hong Kong, and the United States.

Before starting his academic career in 1967, Professor Child worked as a systems analyst at Rolls-Royce Limited for two years after completing his doctoral studies at Cambridge. This experience has had a profound impact on his future research in organization studies, particularly his pioneer work on strategic choice. While primarily known as a leading academic scholar, Professor Child has over the years served in a number of administrative positions with distinction, including: Chairman, Cailvale Limited (1973-1976); Dean, Faculty of Management and Modern Languages at Aston University (1986-1989); Dean and Director, China-EC Management Institute in Beijing, China (1989-1990); and Director, Strategic Partnerships International Limited (1996-present). He was the Editor in Chief of *Organization Studies* (1992-1996) and has served on the editorial boards of several other journals, including the *Administrative Science Quaterly*, *Academy of Management Journal*, *Journal of Enterprise Management*, *Hong Kong Journal of Business Management*, and *Organization Science*.

INTERVIEW

The editors felt that our readers would benefit from learning something more about Professor Child before reading his invited article. Hence, co-editor Joseph Cheng interviewed Professor Child to gain his responses to a set of questions concerning: his academic training and career choice, early involvements in international comparative research, recent studies on economic reform and joint ventures in China, and his assessment of the field including theoretical and methodological challenges facing international comparative management researchers. The interview was conducted in person in Hong Kong in January of 1999.

Cheng: How did you become an academic? Also, were there any life experiences that influenced your career decision?

Child: To a degree (forgive the pun) I was following in my father's footsteps. He studied for his master's dissertation in history at Wisconsin. He would have gone on to do a Ph.D., but the war intervened. I sat the history exams to enter Cambridge University but then switched to take my first degree in economics. That was 1959 to 1962. Then I stayed on for three more years to do a Ph.D. By then I'd already shifted more toward a sociological perspective because in the middle of my economics undergraduate course, the Faculty of Economics introduced options in sociology. This was a very contentious decision at the time, with many purist economists saying "over my dead body." I thought that sociology offered a more realistic view of business and commerce than neoclassical economics which hardly acknowledged that firms and organizations even existed. This view was powerfully reinforced by an industrial tour open to first-year undergraduates during the first Christmas vacation. This tour took in visits to some six companies in the English Midlands, during which a small group of students not only visited factory floors but also had the opportunity to engage with CEOs and other senior managers. It was a marvelous experience organized by Professors Austin (E.A.G.) Robinson at Cambridge and Professor Sargant Florence at Birmingham University. It left me even more dissatisfied with economics, and encouraged me to take up all the new sociology options, as well as subjects like industrial relations, that seemed to have more to do with the real world of industry and behavior within it.

When I received my bachelor's degree in 1962 I wasn't sure whether I wanted to pursue a career in industry or become an academic. It was relatively easy just to stay on and study for a Ph.D. Because I had been awarded a double first-class honors, I was offered a postgraduate scholarship and found an excellent supervisor in Cambridge—John Goldthorpe. I undertook a study that aimed to examine the turmoil in management education then resulting from the critique of the comfortable "one best way" approach by the pioneers of the empirically based contingency approach, particularly Burns and Stalker, Joan Woodward and, later, Lawrence and Lorsch. My Ph.D. started off intending to examine the flux in British management education as a result of this revolution in thinking. And so I did an interview and questionnaire-based survey of 35 higher-education colleges, all offering what was then the standard British postgraduate qualification in management studies—the Diploma in Management Studies.

However, research is a journey of discovery. As things turned out, what started as a historical introduction to the study began to take over the whole enterprise as I unearthed more and more fascinating material on the historical development of thinking on management at the hands of the so-called management movement. These were the business people, managers and academics who from the very first years of the twentieth century wrote and spoke on the emerging occupation of management. They were concerned to develop a body of relevant technical knowledge for the emerging occupational group and at the same time to claim legitimacy for its use of business assets without owning them. Bear in mind that concern was beginning to grow over the issue of corporate governance, expressed in terms of the "divorce of ownership from control." So the notion of managerial professionalism, based on a combination of superior training in relevant knowledge and a sense of social responsibility, was advanced very early on as a justification for this growth of managerial power in large corporations. These claims colored the views about organizational behavior and leadership, and about the fundamental nature of relationships at work, that became incorporated into textbooks and other teaching materials on the subject. This historical part of the research eventually comprised the larger volume of a two-volume thesis. It was later published in 1969 as a book titled *British Management Thought* (Child, 1969).

By 1965 the Ph.D. was all but completed and I was still uncertain about my choice of career. I had now studied at Cambridge for six years. Was I going to stay on in this superb and wonderfully agreeable university for the rest of my life? Or was it now time to get out of the "gilded cage" into the "real" world? In the end I felt that it was now or never, so I went to work for Rolls-Royce for a couple of years. And it was really that experience which led me further into organizational studies because I became involved with systems analysis. It just so happened that at the time Rolls-Royce initiated a company-wide "systems survey." The company was at the time diversified into the manufacture of aircraft engines, cars, and diesel engines. I was in the oil engine division, which made diesels and employed some 2,600 people. The systems survey was triggered by a policy decision to undertake a major upgrade of the company's computer facilities, a very large investment at the time. Top management said we better look at all our information and operating systems to see how these could be improved to take advantage of the projected new computing power. In effect, this became an exercise in company-wide organizational redesign. So I found myself working with one other guy, a young engineer, Clive Singleton-Turner...

Cheng: So you were actually practicing organization design at the time!

Child: Yes! Although I didn't fully recognize it as such at the time, because to start with I was pretty over-awed by the computing side of the exercise. The brief the two of us had was to come up with a full systems design for the oil engine division's direct customer-related activities. The division had no marketing function. It had six different departments, all of which could be speaking to the same customer with different voices...it was a real mess. So we soon saw our purpose as being to sort out the confusion by reorganizing the direct customer-related activities as a unified system, and we worked on the data information and file requirements for this. The end-result was to design and establish a new function.

As I said, the task was pretty daunting because the only way to accomplish our brief was to come up with a new design for a function that didn't exist. And there were some major sensitivities between the six separate departments which reported to four different functional heads. We were going to bring them under one unified function, or at least argue for this.

Cheng: This other guy you worked with also had a Ph.D.?

Child: No, he didn't. I think he just had an undergraduate engineering degree. Actually, I hadn't yet been awarded my Ph.D. when we started on this. Anyway, here we were wondering what the hell are we going to do.

There is really only one option in this situation, you have to go out and talk to the people in the various departments. That's what we did. We said, "what do you think?" In other words, "what problems do you experience, how would you like things to improve, and what do you suggest?" Clive and I were just one team out of three working on the systems survey in the oil engine division. There was another team working on systems for the engineering function. And there was a guy, who was brought in from IBM because Rolls Royce was using IBM hardware, whose task was to look into production. Now here's the interesting contrast. This guy had a strong systems background—he was a professional. But what happened? He didn't bother to talk to anybody. He came up with his textbook solution (as we saw it) and said, "here we are, guys, here's the best solution and this is what you're going to do." Well, they threw it out. Clive and I, anxious at feeling so ignorant, had gone round talking with almost everybody. We came up with a plan that owed a lot to other people's ideas, and those people felt they owned it. The reorganization was implemented even though the company's investment in new computers was delayed for other reasons. And that was one of the most important experiential lessons I have learned. If you're going to bring about change, you have to talk with the people involved. They're valuable sources of knowledge. But it's not only that, they need to have a sense of ownership because they're the guys that are going to live with it. They have the power to say "yes" or "no". So that was one very important lesson for me from my time in Rolls-Royce. The other lesson concerns strategic choice.

Cheng: Great! Let us talk about strategic choice.

Child: Yes, strategic choice. Perhaps I should start by trying to dispel a myth for which my good friend Lex Donaldson must bear some responsibility, though I'm sure what he has written on the matter was done in good faith (e.g., Donaldson, 1985). The myth goes something like this. The Aston Program of organizational research, which I joined after Rolls-Royce, had by the late 1960s made excellent progress in developing the contingency perspective. This perspective, in contrast to most others in organizational analysis, provides knowledge that is useful for practicing managers. The Aston program's findings suggest that if managers are, say, going for growth and want their organizations to remain effective, they have to adjust the structures of those organizations in identifiable ways. If managers are going to operate their companies in particular environments or adopt certain technologies, this also requires that the organization of those companies be configured in certain ways in order to remain fully effective.

This was potentially useful knowledge. But, according to the myth, there came along a third generation recruit to the Aston Program, who joined it six years into its life. This guy, John Child, imported the insidious Cambridge habit of criticism for its own sake. Students in Cambridge University, especially the undergraduates, are encouraged to think critically through the tutorial system in which they are brought face-to-face with distinguished academics in very small groups, often just pairs. The students are expected to examine research studies and conventional wisdom critically, though their criticism must be well-founded and preferably accompanied by a constructive alternative. Lex perceives that having joined the Aston group, instead of just accepting its assumptions as they were, I started to challenge them in a somewhat ungracious manner! It's true that I began to ask, "what's the theory behind what we're doing?" My perception was that the breakthrough achieved by the original Aston group lay in its operationalization of organizational structure and its context, rather than in any new theory. The group had drawn eclectically from pioneering writers like Max Weber, Henri Fayol, Lyndall Urwick, Peter Blau, Alvin Gouldner, and Joan Woodward (see Pugh, Hickson, Hinings, Macdonald, Turner, & Lupton, 1963). The group's achievement was a very significant one—there's no doubt about that—but it had not articulated its own explicit theoretical underpinning. I recall asking Derek Pugh (leader of the Aston group), "what is the theory behind the Aston program?" And his answer was, "it will emerge in time."

Well, there was actually a latent theory behind the Aston Program. It was broadly consistent with a contextually deterministic contingency approach, whereby environment leads to organizational structure and structure in turn shapes organizational behavior. I felt this was not adequate. This feeling was not simply smart Cambridge criticism trying to undermine worthy Aston achievement, though the social action perspective within sociology that I had absorbed as a student certainly had an intellectually formative influence on what I came up with. No, the main reason for believing that there was something missing actually came directly from my recent industrial experience.

The Rolls-Royce company-wide systems survey generated a lot of discussion about change. It was an initiative that was supposed at the end of the day to come up with proposals for potentially fundamental change. Working in the middle of this process, you come to realize that arriving at a solution is not really a matter of a rational decision reached after weighing up contingencies. There is some of that in it, of course, except that few if any people at the time have such a clear idea of what the contingencies are and even less about their organizational implications. And you also discover, as all the studies of decision making on open-ended issues show, that the people involved tend to take fixed positions motivated largely by concern about who is going to win or lose from what could be decided. So there's an intense political process going on which also affects the outcome. This means that the outcome may be less than optimum from a purely technical point of view. On the other hand, this downside may be more than balanced by a positive motivational factor if the outcome is one people are prepared to buy into and live with. It may be an outcome that is workable, rather than a better technical solution that nobody will accept. And that really was the trigger for my thoughts on strategic choice. Aston is fine…so far as it goes.

The whole contingency view is fine, so far as it goes. But it's not enough if we're trying to explain how things actually happen and can be made to happen; how organizational design actually comes about.

And it's not just a matter of organizational politics intervening. Even in terms of contingency analysis, there are often genuine choices because you can get conflicting contingencies. It's not usually black and white. Organizations are founded on contradictory principles, which is why Herb Simon was right in saying that classical theory enunciated contradictory principles but perhaps wrong in suggesting that these principles were consequently unhelpful. There's an inherent contradiction, for example, in the organizational principles conducive to adaptation in a fast-moving hyper-competitive environment and to maintaining cohesion within a large company. The organizational features supportive of creativity and innovation may not sit easily with running a large show. Nowadays, of course, what we do is break it all up and create networks, so as to have the benefits of small units within an overall large empire that retains financial and other muscle. Back in the 1960s we didn't think in terms of these new and evolving organizational forms, though Burns and Stalker's book, *The Management of Innovation*, had started to point the way toward more organic models.

So, my time at Roll-Royce acquainted me with the uncertainty that stemmed from incomplete knowledge and the open-endedness that was created by multiple contingencies. These mean that choices have to be made. This is emphasized by organizational politics in which different groups argue for their own preferred outcomes, each paradoxically maintaining that there is no choice! At the same time, decision making under uncertainty encourages a political process. So the concept of strategic choice that appeared in the journal *Sociology* in 1972 was not simply a challenge to orthodoxy for the sake of it (Child, 1972, 1997). It was not the mischief of somebody coming from Cambridge University with a love for debate. It's actually founded on direct organizational experience. I suspect Lex Donaldson may have thought that I had subconsciously transposed the model of a Cambridge common-room debate to the very different hard reality of business. That embedded in my view of strategic choice was an image of people sitting around with nothing better to do than argue endlessly about organizational design solutions when it was obvious what was required. The reality that I experienced is that few things are obvious at the time!

Cheng: You've answered this question about career choice and relevant life experiences very fully. Your description of your work at Rolls-Royce and how it tied in with your academic work is very interesting.

Child: Well, the career decision, or indecision, was more a matter of serendipity. I had originally intended to stay for five years in industry before making up my mind because I was still in my mid-20s. One can look back through life and see it as a series of chance occurrences and opportunities. And that was the case with deciding to leave Rolls-Royce. It was triggered by finding I was kicking my heels a bit having done the systems analysis work with nothing special to do next because new investment was brought to a standstill by a government imposed credit squeeze at the time. That was the trigger to think well, maybe I should look elsewhere.

Cheng: When was that?

Child: That was toward the end of 1966. The Aston people advertised a research position just at that time. But I was in real doubt, "should I make this move?" And I talked to somebody named Don Conlon, who I'd interviewed during my Ph.D. and then met again when he ran a junior managers course for Roll-Royce and two other companies. He worked in the then Wolverhampton College of Technology. I remember asking, "can I come and see you? I've got an important decision to make. I need your advice." We lived quite close together and he gave me half a day, taking me though the pros and cons. At the end of the afternoon, I decided I would apply for the Aston job. So that's how I joined the Aston Program. I sometimes need to recall that the huge service Don did for me could be just as important in turn for the young people who knock on my door or send an e-mail, especially when I feel that I cannot possibly afford the time!

Cheng: So Aston was a research position, not a lecturer position.

Child: Yes, I did not go up the usual British academic career ladder. I started with a research fellowship at Aston, working with Derek Pugh. Derek then moved to the London Business School and I moved with him, in September 1968. And I became a senior research officer at the London Business School, though I also lectured there to the MBA program. I stayed at LBS for five years. Then I jumped from what was a limited-term contract research position to a chair professorship back at Aston University.

Cheng: At the age of 32!

Child: Yes, it now seems a long time ago! The offer surprised me at the time, but I didn't say no! So, finally to answer your question about specific life experiences affecting my career, I owe much to serendipity—to fortunate circumstance.

Cheng: Tell us about your first involvement in international research. When did you get involved and why? What was the research about?

Child: This arose from one of the principles of the Aston Program, which gave a very high priority to building and confirming knowledge through replication. In other words, are constructs stable across different samples, and do relationships appear to have some generality? This is a basic procedure in the "scientific" approach that sadly present-day career pressures militate against. The first Aston study covered 46 organizations in the English Midlands, and was therefore very focused in terms of location. The second major study, for which I was responsible, was called the National Study because it extended to the whole of Great Britain. It was no longer just confined to one region. Its purpose was to check the conclusions of the first study through replication, though it also went further by investigating organizational structuring in relation to performance and managerial behavior. On the replication side, the National Study confirmed many of the findings of the first study, but inevitably not all of them. It also gave rise to some important new insights. The next step in the process of replication was to undertake international comparisons. And the first people to do this were David Hickson and some colleagues with a study in Ohio. Reports on all this research—the original Aston study and subsequent ones—were published in the *Administrative Science Quarterly* between 1968 and 1973.

So the move to international studies at this stage was not motivated so much by a theory of cross-national comparative management as by an urge to test the limits of our previous findings. Are the relationships between organizational and contextual variables maintained as we move to different countries? Finding that there was a degree of consistency led to the view that the contextual factors shaping organization are culture-free; in other words the exigencies and hence organizational requirements of running, say, large auto plants are much the same wherever they are located. This view was set out by David Hickson, Bob Hinings, Charlie McMillan, and Joe Schwitter in an influential article that appeared in *Sociology* in 1974. It's pretty well the same theme on which Lex Donaldson has expanded more recently in his books. Now, about the same time I started to work with Alfred Kieser in Germany. We extended the Aston comparative methodology to a sample of West German firms. However, we were sensitive to the fact that the two countries, Britain and Germany, had important institutional differences. For example, Germany had its co-determination system, and its occupational formation and skill structure were also very different to those in Britain. There had also been some work identifying cultural differences in terms of attitudes to authority, and emphasis on order, control, and formalization. We had in mind the possibility that cultural preferences might be expressed through strategic choice.

So we carried out the Anglo-German comparison, finding certain significant differences between the two nations. This led us into a debate with David Hickson and others because we argued that some aspects of organization are not free of the cultural and institutional specifics of different national settings (Child & Kieser, 1979). But we did not want to dismiss the culture-free thesis in its entirety either—that would be throwing out the baby with the bathwater. Some aspects of organization were likely to be particularly sensitive to cultural differences and others to contingencies of a more universalistic nature.

This way of thinking was set out in my paper on "Culture, Contingency and Capitalism in the Cross-National Study of Organizations" that reviewed the scene in the 1981 volume of *Research in Organizational Behavior*

(Child, 1981). First, you have the cultural perspective which, of course, didn't all start with Hofstede. You had had important work by people like George England on comparative work values, and Karlene Roberts's 1970 landmark review in the *Psychological Bulletin* had adopted a primarily cross-cultural perspective. Hofstede, however, provided a powerful conceptual framework. Second, there were the contingency theorists. They were saying that "there are certain requirements on organizations imposed by contingencies of size, diversification, technology, employee capabilities, and so forth, wherever you are. That's the thing we ought to tell managers about because either they have a chance to work with these contingencies as in socio-technical systems design, or at least they can make strategic decisions about them." So you have contingency. Third, you have to remember that we were then still very much in the middle of the cold war. We were therefore very sensitive to the impact on organizations of the political economy within which they operated—was this capitalist or socialist? There was research coming out about Soviet and East European factories, and there was the beginning of interest in China especially a debate about whether the Cultural Revolution there had led to revolutionary new non-bureaucratic forms of organization. Those were the three "contextual" factors discussed in that article. My conclusion was that all three of them were relevant, in that they would primarily impact upon different facets of organizations and that culture could also play an important mediating role.

That's to say...you would have contingencies coming from task and scale factors, and so forth. But then it was a question of saying, "okay, maybe the technology sets up limits on how we can organize the work." But the limits still allowed for some choice. And that choice might be informed by a culturally preferred mode of organizing work, like the authority relationships between supervisors and work groups. So empowerment would come more naturally to somebody from the United States, because it suits a culture that emphasizes individualism and self-actualization. Empowerment and entrepreneurship would also be regarded as more legitimate within a capitalist system than a command socialist one. Yet, this was not to say that the socialist countries of the day were adopting the same organizational forms and policies. It was, for instance, evident that Hungary and Russia differed quite substantially, despite sharing many of the formal provisions of the command economy. So again perhaps culture and to some extent pre-communist development, were mediating the influences on organization coming from the economic and political system.

Cheng: You really need to look at the interaction among these factors.

Child: Yes. That was the conclusion I was reaching then. It is different to the view that culture pervades everything, that ultimately it's all down to culture and that the way we construct institutions and express political preferences reflects our culture. I don't believe that's entirely the case because the way we construct institutions can be enormously affected by the political regime. I mean, why is it that until 1989 you had a communist regime in East Germany? It's not due to the culture. And why not a communist regime in West Germany? It's because of the way they divided up Germany after the war between the East and the West. And the institutions that were established under the two different political systems had quite an impact after two generations on work attitudes and taken-for-granted organizational practices. West German companies investing in the former East Germany certainly discovered this and it created many difficulties for them. So it doesn't all come from cultures that are inherited and passed on over the ages. It's also a matter of institutional arrangements and the influence of accompanying ideologies, which are shaped by politics and may even be imposed by military force in extreme cases. A fascinating question is whether cultures that have been suppressed by political regimes even for several generations will then reassert themselves when the regime becomes more liberal. This seems to be happening in China today, though that same country also shows that values can change significantly between generations under the apparent influence of commercialism coming from abroad. Perhaps, after all, the cash-till is mightier than the sword!

Cheng: My impression is that many scholars in the United States have picked up on the contingency and cultural elements discussed in your 1981 *Research in Organizational Behavior* paper, but not as much has been done with the political/institutional dimension. Is this also true among the European organizational researchers?

Child: I think Europeans are probably more sensitive to the impact of political forces for a number of reasons. We've lived closer to Eastern Europe and been more conscious of the two systems. The transition after 1989-1990 has been a European event. Also the massive project of bringing together a European Union has very much kept our attention on political issues. You have to remember that the origins of the European unity project lay in a passionate desire never again to suffer the ravages of war between political systems—fascism and democracy. Also there was quite a lot of political diversity and experimentation in western Europe after the war. There have been socialist and social democratic governments as well as right wing and center ones. Even within a single country like the UK, we have shifted in a major way between the substantial nationalization of industry in the late 1940s and its privatization in the 1980s and 1990s. There have been quite high levels of institutional change and diversity in Europe, whereas in America you have maintained one system, and the Civil War confirmed that. It's been a relatively liberal system, at least the ideology has been. The government on the whole keeps out of business. So maybe the American people are not so sensitive to the possible impact of politics on how activities are organized because the system allows for free enterprise within certain rules and it has not been subject to fundamental changes and ideological challenges over the years.

Cheng: And yet if you are concerned about the transfer of management practices, we do need to know a lot more about how the political system and other macro societal-level variables affect organizations.

Child: Yes, and you see this obviously in China. There, it is very important in some sectors where it's still the case that government institutions and officials restrict a lot of your options. In fields like telecommunications, shipbuilding, or other strategic industries there's very much of a constraint on how you can organize your business activities. First of all, you have to have a partner whether you like it or not. And in bidding for a partner, you are also bidding for your market. Whereas this does not really apply in other sectors like fast-moving consumer goods. So the context of say Proctor & Gamble is very different to that of AT&T, and this has an important bearing on the forms of organization they can adopt in China.

Cheng: Tell us about your subsequent international research following the 1981 article.

Child: In the 1980s a lot of my work was on information technology and its application in services. The question there was, "is information technology having the same impact on work organizations in different countries?" We conducted a six-nation comparison with teams working in each country and coming together regularly. There were 36 case studies from the six countries. The cases were all from three sectors, two in each sector in each country. Retail banking, looking at counter terminals and to some extent ATMs. Retail stores, looking at electronic point of sale systems. And clinical chemistry laboratories in hospitals, looking at laboratory automation. So we had the same technologies in the same sectors across different countries (Child & Loveridge, 1990).

Cheng: What were the six countries and how were they selected?

Child: They were the UK, Sweden, Germany or West Germany as it then was, Italy, Belgium, and Hungary, selected partly on the basis of saying we think looking across these countries there are sufficient contrasts in culture and institutional features including the customary arrangements for decision making in industry. That was, if you like the formal rationale. But there is another consideration in collaborative research, and that's the teamwork. You chose to collaborate largely with people you already know or at least believe you can work with. So the six countries were also chosen on the basis of our personal network and common interests. We had to spend quite a lot of time on deciding what was going to be the frame for this study, what was going to be the methodology. We had debates between people who favored using questionnaires and people who favored in-depth case studies. We ended up doing in-depth case studies because we realized how much this was an exploratory area. We didn't know anything about it. This work carried on through quite a number of years in the 1980s. It was an extremely interesting experience in how to organize collaborative cross-cultural work, and also intellectually very enriching because we really did move forward through discussion and discovery of a quite intensive kind. Everybody met for several days every six months and as our findings became available we formed sector sub-groups with mixed national memberships that met more frequently.

Cheng: In what way did your experience with this IT project reinforce or further extend the view presented in your 1981 paper?

Child: The project confirmed that different perspectives can together contribute to our understanding of a major contemporary development in the nature of organization and of how it is being handled in different countries. For example, if you have to recognize the contingency side of it. You couldn't understand what was happening if you ignored relevant technological and economic changes. New technological capabilities were becoming available; competitive pressures were increasing, markets were evolving with developments such as deregulation in financial services and, in the case of hospitals, there were pressures for more cost-effective treatment. Not all of the economic contingencies applied to hospitals, but they certainly did to banks and retail stores. So managers and administrators were looking for the technology to provide better service delivery and cut costs.

But while there were fairly common contingencies in each sector across all the countries, the criteria being attached to the introduction of new technology were not the same. The relative emphasis given to service improvement versus cost reduction differed between the six countries. There were also different views on how the technology should be applied to the organization of work. In some countries, like the UK, cost reduction and work simplification tended to be quite prominent considerations. In other countries, especially Sweden, there was more interest in using the technology to help people learn and develop their own capacities. This meant, for example, using the technology to give people more information and so enable them to learn and take on more responsibilities, rather than using it to simplify their jobs and monitor what they do more closely. We concluded that an important factor determining which approach prevailed lay in how much institutionalized participation there was by concerned parties in the design and decision process. In Sweden, for instance, it was the practice, which had some legal backing, for quite a wide range of interested parties to join IT project teams: some of the targeted employee users, union representatives, and HRM people in addition to technical specialists and managers. So again, reference to contingencies was not enough to account for how IT was introduced and applied to organization. Culture and institutionalized practice had to be included in the model.

So yes, I think this research clarified the 1981 framework and suggested it was useful. However, the political economy dimension did not come across so strongly. Our research design did not fully allow for it. We did have a contrast in terms of political system between Hungary and the other European countries, but this did not have a great impact because by the mid-1980s Hungary had already introduced a lot of economic reform and marketization. Both retail banks and retail stores were already operating pretty well in a competitive market.

If we had included, say, China, the impact of contrasting political systems might have shown up more strongly. As a matter of fact, I carried out a case study in 1986 on the introduction and use of IT-based automated analyzers in the clinical chemistry laboratory of the main Beijing teaching hospital. The analyzers were the same as those we had looked at in Europe and were supplied through a World Health Organization development program. The attitude of the laboratory technicians toward the technology was dramatically different—much more positive than typically in Europe. And a prime reason for that lay in political events. The technicians had missed out on a systematic professional education because of the Cultural Revolution. So, now they had a chance to learn from the machines, especially the analytical procedures displayed on the computer monitors as various tests were carried out. There was also the prestige factor of having the most advanced equipment in the whole of China.

Cheng: Let us talk about your China research.

Child: My early work in China, from 1985 onward, focused on state enterprises looking at the reform process. How far was this percolating down to enterprises? Then as time went on colleagues and I became more conscious of the challenges facing foreign firms investing in China with the potential to contribute in a very important way to the country's development. The European Community MBA program with which I was working was increasingly being sponsored by European companies operating in China and many of the graduates were offered jobs by them. However, while the Chinese were saying officially, "we want you in because we need your technology and your management expertise," in reality Chinese personnel would often resist the transfer of knowledge and practice and all sorts of problems could arise (see Child, 1994).

So my work on China since around 1990 on has focused primarily on Sino-foreign joint ventures. Looking at their formation and management processes, and more recently looking at what we call management networks between the parent companies and their joint venture affiliates and, indeed, between the parents themselves. We also came to look at the impact of these factors on the performance of Sino-foreign joint ventures and the ability of their parents to learn from their joint venture experience.

The transfer of management practices by companies into a given national location like China allows one to compare transnational with national "effects." We concluded that whether the foreign firm is a multinational or not distinguishes the practices it brings into China more than its domestic country of origin—whether it is an American or Japanese company by origin. Another interesting contrast emerged within the main non-MNC group of companies investing in China, those from Hong Kong and other overseas Chinese communities like Singapore and Taiwan. We found that the Hong Kong firms were quite distinctive in their approach to management and organization. They adopted much shorter-term objectives for their joint ventures in China. Actually, for many of them the ventures were just extensions of their domestic operations with production facilities across the border in Shenzhen and Guangdong Province. They moved there to take advantage of cheaper costs and more space. This geo-physical aspect has important organizational implications because when you're operating a joint venture just across the border, distance takes on a different meaning. When you can make day trips to your affiliate, you're going to have a totally different pattern of contact and communication with it. You'll have much more personal contact and this can affect your management style. You don't have to rely so much on formal reporting. The Hong Kong firms could maintain their traditional Chinese family business style which is hands-on and centralized. So there were quite marked differences within the overseas Chinese group of investors in China, although they shared much the same cultural background. Geo-physical considerations definitely come into play even in this age of instant global electronic communications.

However, I have to say that the research in China has been concerned as much with the management of cross-national organization (international management) as with my previous focus on comparing different national management practices (comparative management). My current research on the internationalization of Hong Kong firms and post-acquisition management in several countries, is maintaining this focus on integrating and managing organization across national borders.

Cheng: I would like to ask you to step back and reflect on your more than 20 years of experience in doing international research. In what ways have these projects contributed to our knowledge about organizations?

Child: It will be easier for me to answer your question in terms of how have the projects contributed to my own developing view on the subject. First, they led me to ask whether we need different theories of organization for different contexts. I don't really think we do. It seems to me that we've got a sufficiently rich portfolio of concepts and perspectives to be able to make good sense of different international situations. Others may not agree. Nicole Biggart and Gary Hamilton, for example, have been very critical of applying Western economic and organizational theories to East Asia. They think we need a different theory for East Asia. I'm not convinced that's the case, though of course I admit that the region presents very different circumstances compared to, say, the United States. But the contrast could be interpreted as two different configurations of variables, or scores on dimensions, *already* identified by our existing theories. Arguing this way is not an instance of Western theoretical imperialism on my part, but rather a pragmatic statement in the best tradition of Deng Xiao Ping that's intended to avoid an unnecessary and confusing multiplicity of noncommunicating academic discourses.

Second, the projects suggest that the notion of "equifinality" is very apt. An international comparative perspective shows that organizations can perform similar tasks and achieve similar goals, but through different means. There is some choice and flexibility. How much depends on the extent to which effective organizational practices are situation-specific, and this is an issue on which international research can make a major contribution. For instance, we know that the Japanese approach is different to say the American approach, and that the British one is different to the German. So the question is whether each approach only works well in its home environment. Does the Japanese approach only work well in Japan? It is interesting that, although Japanese practices transferred abroad have had to be re-contextualized—modified to suit the context, they nevertheless represent a non-indigenous approach to doing things that can work very well elsewhere, usually giving very significant improvements in productivity and quality. So, working in the field for the past 20 years or more leads me toward the view that both theory and practice are transferable across countries and regions, though great sensitivity to the local context is required in both cases. And in order to achieve this sensitivity better, we need to take much more careful account of the context as you, Joe, have argued many times.

Third, international research is opening up our thinking on organization, which, let's face it, has got itself bogged down in a bit of a morass during the past 20 years. Such research encourages an open-ended view of organization: to be aware of it as a multifaceted and evolving phenomenon. It also presents us with the challenge of conceptualizing and assessing newer forms of organization, such as alliances, networks, and the transnational corporation, that are emerging to govern cross-border and global transactions. These are large and complex phenomena that require us to draw upon the insights of many rather than just one perspective. The international projects we have discussed indicate to me the insufficiency of adopting a narrow theoretical approach. In this way, international research is making an important contribution to organization theory by forcing that theory to take better account of current and emerging realities. I want to stress again, though, that this doesn't mean we have to invent new theories, so much as draw together insights from those we already have.

Let's think of this for a moment in terms of Burrell and Morgan's fourfold categorization of organizational studies according to the two dimensions: subjective/objective and radical/conservative (Burrell & Morgan, 1979). They and others have used this categorization to argue that different paradigms in organizational analysis are incommensurable. That, theoretically speaking, they are cases of chalk and cheese. Yet once we start to look at organizations crossing national boundaries in dynamic terms, at their ongoing processes such as the transfer of practice internationally or cross-cultural accommodation, then the boundaries between those four boxes actually appear extremely permeable. So the effective recontextualization of an "objective" organizational practice involves the "subjective" processes of interpretation and identification. Likewise, the self-imposed gulf between universalistic theories and context-specific theories doesn't wear very well in the light of international research. We've got to overcome this bounded type of thinking and face up to the fact that we're dealing with more complex and dynamic phenomenon than is allowed for by neat theoretical boxes which preserve their simple elegance by factoring out too much of the relevant reality.

Cheng: In your view, has international comparative research contributed to the advancement of basic knowledge about organizations? Not just knowledge about Chinese, British, or Japanese organizations, but some fundamental knowledge about organizations?

Child: Yes, I think so—at two levels: theoretical and conceptual. A good example of theoretical advance is the analysis of "business systems" at the hands of people like Richard Whitley, Nicole Biggart, Gary Hamilton, and Gordon Redding. The business system perspective has arisen directly from the question of "are there different kinds of capitalism?" It deals with the relation between the institutional context and business organization. It has shown how the organizational forms commonly found in different countries are shaped by the state (including regulations) and by intermediate institutions like the financial and banking system, and the education and training system. The countries may all be fundamentally capitalist, but there are different variants of capitalism each of which has some implications for the way business enterprises are organized. It would have been difficult to arrive at this fruitful perspective unless detailed comparative work had been undertaken on differences and similarities between national systems. The type of analysis offered by business systems theory advances understanding within organization theory as a whole, and takes forward the pioneering work on the subject of people like Max Weber.

    At the second level, let me mention an example of the type of conceptual advance arising from an international comparison that promises to advance basic knowledge about organizations. This is an article by Anne Tsui and Larry Farh appearing in a 1997 issue of *Work and Occupations*. They explore the overlap between Chinese notion of *guanxi* and the Western definition of relational demography. They find significant overlaps between the two in that both refer to the social ties that can exist between people and the effects they may have on behavior in organizations. Their mapping out of these overlaps points the way toward a broader synthesized concept of relationship that contributes to our understanding of organizations in general.

Cheng: What are some of the theoretical and methodological challenges facing researchers in the international comparative area? And, what kind of training do we need to provide for Ph.D. students and junior colleagues to help them overcome these challenges?

Child: Let's start with the challenges and then go on to the training.

The theoretical challenge is, as I said, how to better utilize the contributions offered by different perspectives. It's not going to be easy. It means saying: "Look, we're working on a broad international canvas here. Even if our focus is very narrow, even if we are focusing, say, on a certain aspect of work behavior such as the motivational impact of leadership style, it is rather unlikely that we can fully understand that behavior if we just apply one perspective to it." Now that may be true within a country as well as across countries, but the international dimension brings in some context-relevant theoretical dimensions that might not apply just domestically. So I think that's the challenge. We've got to recognize we're dealing with a complex field and also one that isn't standing still either. Because globalization means that there are some rapidly moving processes going on out there which are impacting on organization cross-nationally as we speak.

The methodological challenge is concerned with conceptual equivalence and, when it comes down to operational measures, there is the problem of language and meaning. While this is most acute in specifically cross-cultural research, I don't think we necessarily have to treat it as an insurmountable challenge. Sometimes we rely too much on cultural stereotypes that may exaggerate the non-equivalence of meaning. It was very interesting to find at the Inaugural Meeting of the Asia Academy of Management held in Hong Kong last month (December 1998) that some people were talking about China and Chinese organizational values as though they were somehow both monolithic and impenetrable. Yet others, local people, were saying: "Hey, it's not as simple as that. Values are not simply the same in Hong Kong and mainland China; mainland Chinese values are themselves changing between the generations. Things are not that homogeneous." Two interesting observations come out of this discourse. First, people were offering insights into differences among value systems and so implicitly acknowledging that we have a methodology for comparing them. Second, the differences could only mean that over time economic and institutional factors were impacting on Chinese values, over and above any cultural effects.

Actually, I think that many of the methodological challenges have been recognized for a long time now. But they continue as a matter of debate in the design and execution of international research. On the execution side, they point to the enriching feature of cross-national collaboration between researchers, but also the potential difficulty of realizing this through a pooling of different interpretations and perspectives among a diverse group of researchers.

Now the training: If we're training Ph.D. students and junior colleagues in the field of international management, a basic requirement is to give them international exposure. This can go back to what I just said. It suggests the utility of having Ph.D. students working with teams of researchers who themselves are collaborating across countries. Otherwise, if they are working on their own, Ph.D. students might be advised to think twice before embarking on international projects that involve fieldwork in other countries. It adds such great uncertainties about access, time expenditure, cost, and so forth. At Cambridge University, we've got many students from abroad including those with an interest in China. So a lot of the Ph.D. students do their field work in another country. Through international institutional linkages with the Chinese Management Center at Hong Kong University and other places, we already have colleagues who are working together and things become rather easier. They can offer external supervision, so if somebody is doing work in China they can have a supervisor from Hong Kong as well as their Cambridge supervisor. If they are working in association with a project in the region, the problem of access can be eased. Similarly, we have been able to offer some students from our overseas partners an opportunity to receive research training or to consult source materials in Cambridge. So cross-national university links help enormously.

Cheng: In terms of the disciplinary areas like economics, sociology, political science, anthropology, is any specific course work in any of these areas that you feel would most benefit a Ph.D. student or a junior colleague in conducting international research?

Child: There are a number of perspectives arising from a number of disciplines, particularly economics, sociology, anthropology, and cross-cultural psychology. If we're going to adopt a more holistic approach, then yes, it does suggest that some familiarity with these disciplines would be valuable. And students are unfortunately not going to be given this familiarity in most universities. This is a real challenge and to make matters worse some universities have closed down international business departments on the argument that since everything today has become international, so international business and management studies can be absorbed into general business and disciplinary curricula. This argument would be fine if it were really taken seriously, and if business and management studies were actually addressed from an international perspective, and if an interdisciplinary approach were adopted. But I suspect that it probably doesn't happen like that.

Cheng: Their assumption is that anyone can pick up the international dimension so we do not need a separate group for international business or international management. But in reality you do need a critical mass of colleagues in any area whether it is international business, or marketing, or whatever. We just won't have enough good ideas if there is not a critical mass of researchers.

Child: And another benefit of having that critical mass of international business people is that they can constantly remind their other colleagues about the international dimension. Otherwise it's easy for people to slip back into comfortable assumptions, traditional theoretical assumptions, and ignore it.

Cheng: What kind of research would you like to see more of in the journals? And why?

Child: We have at present a lot of what Lawrence Mohr called variance type research, especially as people increasingly use databases and secondary sources. Just look at recent issues of *JIBS* (*Journal of International Business Studies*). Yet it is fundamentally important for work also to be done on process as well as on variance and prediction. We need to know a lot more about how cross-national organizations work. How do they resolve their inherent tensions such as between globalization benefits and local responsiveness? How do key individuals hold such organizations together and make them function?

So I would like to see more process-oriented research. This would inevitably be case-type research, though it could be comparative as well. Some people say that comparative case studies fall between two stools: they are not sufficiently rich or holistic to justify the case method nor involve samples sufficiently large to permit statistical testing. I think that they can actually contribute importantly to theory development and at the same time produce insights specific enough to assist the practitioner. If you build in an element of comparison, say between even four to six cases, this can be quite productive in terms of suggesting propositions that might later be tested on the basis of more extensive surveys. So I would like to see more case-based process research published in the journals. Some of it should look at ongoing change situations. The study of change and crisis exposes phenomena and highlights how organizations as systems work. It also helps process research because things happen faster if there's a rapid change going on. An example of what I have in mind by change would be the establishment of operations by companies from one country in another country, or the bedding down of ISAs [international strategic alliances].

More process research, then, would usefully complement the present emphasis on variance studies. I appreciate there are difficulties. In particular, process research takes time and considerable fieldwork effort. It can't easily be delegated to research assistants. So it is not so attractive for younger faculty who are concerned to produce quickly in order to get their contracts renewed and tenure confirmed. But doesn't this suggest that we have somehow written the rules wrongly?

Cheng: What is your assessment of the future of cross-national organization research as an area of study in the management field?

Child: If we are at all sensitive to what is happening in the real world, if we're going to get outside our ivory towers, then cross-national organizational research must have a very important and bright future. It's quite clear that the most significant organizations in terms of their power to effect people's lives are cross-national in scope. Just look at the present rate of international mergers, acquisitions, and joint ventures. Just look at how since the mid-1980s foreign direct investment has far outstripped the growth in domestic investment. Cross-national research has a most exciting and important agenda in terms of all this global business restructuring and the accompanying experimentation into how to organize on a global scale. Just think of the huge challenges now faced by multinationals in finding new forms of organization that maintain an inherent cohesion while at the same time encouraging adaptation and innovation. They need to reconcile central direction with at the same time being open to learning from below and far afield. Their next significant innovation could crop up almost anywhere

Cheng: It can be from a very tiny place like Hong Kong!

Child: Exactly. So the issue of how to allow for, indeed encourage, that possibility organizationally is an enormously important challenge. The point I'm try-ing to make is that empirically this is a phenomenon that nobody can deny is increasing in importance. We can see it's taking organizations into new areas of design, particularly combined with other features that are promot-ing globalization like the new technologies. So there's a major new field of practice emerging which we identify by terms like network and virtual orga-nization. These are features that are particularly prominent in cross-national organization. If we take a broader view and recall how organizations are a terribly important tool for economic and human development, there's another huge challenge. That lies in the rapid international concentration of power underway, especially in certain key industries, and the move toward a "big business" system which raises fundamental questions about the gov-ernance and accountability of these organizations. So a great deal for cross-national organizational research to do, especially as we start from a position of relative ignorance.

I've always been passionately concerned about organizational power and accountability. It's one reason why it is vital to recognize that senior exec-utives exercise strategic choice, because they can then justifiably be held accountable for their actions. If all they can do is respond to external contin-gencies, then their responsibility is to that extent diminished. This is more than ever an issue given the growth in corporate transnationalism and the power this represents. The larger our organizations become in scale and scope, the more powerful they are. It then becomes more incumbent for we academics to try and help find ways for both their own people and the peo-ple in societies where they operate to have a say in their policies. Organiza-tions after all are social constructs. They're presumably there to serve a purpose for mankind. This is obviously a very big issue, and the centralized accumulation of assets and power are making it a much more acute prob-lem. Nowadays, we're no longer talking about small local organizations that it might be fairly easy to keep an eye on and so hold accountable. You're talking about organizations that are increasingly much more power-ful than many nation-states. This always used to be said of General Motors, but we're now getting many more General Motors, many more of them.

And it does raise such important issues to do with the concentration of power. Organizational theorists have something very important to say about this in terms of how to enhance effective participation and accountability...the ways to increase real empowerment, and so on.

Cheng: There seems to be a natural marriage between organizational theory and international business.

Child: Absolutely. But what I am now talking about is the social agenda of organizational theory. And the key issues in that social agenda today concern international business. Not just that business has become internationalized in the sense that there's more trade going on...we've had international trade for a long time. It's become internationalized in that we have created...or they have created international business institutions.

We need to know a lot more about these organizations. I'm not saying that big organizations are more important than small ones in every respect. The small ones are very important too, in their own ways, because for instance of their entrepreneurial capabilities. But in terms of affecting an increasing number of people in the world, having more impact on the world economic system, and becoming accumulations of potential power, the organization and governance of bodies deploying such huge resources is a matter of paramount importance. And organizational theorists should have a great deal to say about this because mechanisms for accountability and member participation are a matter of organizational design. If we don't have much to say on it at the moment, we'd better get down to work fast!

REFERENCES

Burrell, G., & Morgan, G. (1979). *Sociological paradigms and organizational analysis*. London: Heinemann.

Child, J. (1969). *British management thought: A critical analysis*. London: Allen & Unwin.

Child, J. (1972). Organizational structure, environment and performance: The role of strategic choice. *Sociology, 6*, 1-22.

Child, J. (1981). Culture, contingency, and capitalism in the cross-national study of organizations. In L. Cummings & B. Staw (Eds.), *Research in organizational behavior* (Vol. 3, pp. 303-356). Greenwich, CT: JAI Press.

Child, J. (1994). *Management in China during the age of reform*. Cambridge: Cambridge University Press.

Child, J. (1997). Strategic choice in the analysis of action, structure, organizations and environment: retrospect and prospect. *Organization Studies, 18*, 43-76.

Child, J., & Kieser, A. (1979). Organization and managerial roles in British and German companies: An examination of the culture-free thesis. In Lammers, C.J. and Hickson, D.J. (Eds.), *Organizations: Like and unlike*. London: Routledge and Kegan Paul.

Child, J., & Loveridge, R. (1990). *Information technology in European services*. Oxford: Blackwell.

Donaldson, L. (1985). *In defence of organization theory—a reply to the critics*. Cambridge: Cambridge University Press.

Hickson, D. J., Hinings, C. R., McMillan, C. J., & Schwitter, J. P. (1974). The culture-free context of organization structure: A trinational comparison. *Sociology, 8*, 59-80.

Pugh, D. S., Hickson, D. J., Hinings, C. R., Macdonald, K. M. Turner, C., & Lupton, T. (1963). A conceptual scheme for organizational analysis. *Administrative Science Quarterly, 8*, 28-315.

THEORIZING ABOUT ORGANIZATION CROSS-NATIONALLY

John Child

ABSTRACT

This essay argues that there are two fundamental issues the study of organizations cross-nationally must address if it is to progress. The first is whether we can find an analytical framework that constructively combines the present partial and some-times narrow perspectives on the subject. Following a review of these perspectives, the essay advances a framework that can help bring together the insights offered by different perspectives and direct attention toward potential interactions between them. The framework avoids an uncritical acceptance of the primacy of any one per-spective, together with its methodological or paradigmatic limitations. The utility of this framework is examined with reference to globalization, the most important cross-national development bearing upon organization today.

The second issue is whether we can increase conceptual consistency across theo-retical boundaries through moves toward greater operational synthesis. This is seen to require the deconstruction of concepts differentiated by culture and discipline into their underlying dimensions and their subsequent reconfiguration into more inte-grated constructs that permit comparisons across countries. This procedure is not only a methodological complement to the combination of theoretical insights, but it

Advances in International Comparative Management, Volume 13, pages 27-75.
ISBN: 0-7623-0589-4

is actually a necessary condition for effective comparative work to be undertaken at all.

Those interested in cross-national aspects of organization have for many years rued the slow progress of their field. Redding (1994) concluded from his "review of the reviews" that 30 year's work had made little impression on an area of study which "has suffered from the excessive repetition of sterile reporting, from theoretical poverty and from a lack of clear direction" (p. 331). Little has happened since then to dispel this sense of frustration and crisis. The field continues to suffer from the lack of a clear focus and unifying theoretical framework. This, in turn, gives rise to conceptual and operational fragmentation.

The blurring of focus results from the fact that the field has been defined both as the cross-national study of organization *and* the study of cross-national organization. These two approaches are often distinguished respectively as the "comparative" and "international" study of management or organization. The first approach has been the mainstream, concentrating on the similarities and differences between features of organization that might characterize various countries or cultural regions (e.g., Lammers & Hickson, 1979; Hampden-Turner & Trompenaars, 1993). However, the number of organizational entities that span national boundaries is increasing rapidly. Corporations are steadily extending the scope of their international operations, and there is a burgeoning of cross-border mergers and strategic alliances.[1] The public sector has also seen a significant increase in both cross-national and supra-national governmental agencies. A focus on corporations and other bodies that have become transnational in scope offers an alternative approach to studying organization in its international context (Ghoshal & Bartlett, 1998).

Which of these options offers the more fruitful path toward understanding the relevance of nationality for organization? One possibility is to concentrate on comparing national models of organization, assuming that they are embedded within distinct systems of business, culture, and innovation (Hofstede, 1991; Whitley, 1992a, 1992b; Amable et al., 1997). In addition to their intrinsic sociological interest, the national differences embodied in organization play a significant contextual role for the management of cross-national organizations. Another option is to concentrate on how organization transcends national boundaries, recognizing that in so doing it may be a powerful force for international homogeneity through the transfer of organizational and management practices (Child et al., 2000). At an empirical level, the subject-matter of both approaches is very similar. Those who maintain that globalization is subsuming national influences within transnational forces suggest that it will become increasingly necessary to marry these two focuses within an appropriate supporting theoretical framework. The present essay acknowledges the force of this view. It therefore considers cross-national organizational studies to embrace both the comparison of organizational forms between nations and the study of cross-national organization.

The presence of multiple theoretical frameworks further diffuses the focus of this field. As Roberts (1970) recognized 30 years ago, the difficulty of reaching agreement on the nature of the cross-national organizational beast to a large extent reflects a theoretical profusion, if not confusion. People are continuing to look at different parts of the elephant and its habitat through different theoretical lenses each with their own coordinates, as it were. These can range from the broad sweep of economics to the very specific focus of indigenous cultural psychology. Sometimes, scholars may even be directing their attention to the same parts of the beast and its habitat, but using the different filters supplied by apparently incompatible or non-contiguous concepts. Groups of scholars, each with their own theoretical and conceptual language, compete to define the field and their members hesitate to engage in mutual constructive discourse. As has been pointed out (Reed, 1996; Child, 1997), this description applies to the current fragmentation within organizational studies as a whole. Resolution of the problem is, however, a more daunting challenge for the study of organization cross-nationally because this brings into play an additional dimension of theoretical complexity due to the diversity of contexts that have to be considered.

Theoretical fragmentation leaves a number of methodological problems unresolved. Defining the field exclusively within the ambit of a single theoretical perspective, such as national culture, discourages research designs that allow for an examination of other potential influences on organization. Thus in so-called "cross-cultural" studies, attention to organizational variance between nations has not generally been complemented by an equivalent attention to variance within nations of the sort that might be suggested by theories of industrial economics. There has also been a long-standing and potentially confusing debate between those adopting interpretative and positivistic ontological assumptions about the possibility of achieving greater conceptual consistency and equivalence in operational measurement. Whereas economists using highly codified financial or physical data may not regard this as a serious problem, students of indigenous cultural psychology are very likely to. The dispute has particularly affected cross-national organization studies with the result that only rarely, as in the Aston Program (Hickson & Macmillan, 1981), has there been any consistency in the features of organization being compared cross-nationally. This lack of conceptual and operational consistency has impeded progress on such fundamental issues as ascertaining the validity of national stereotypes of organization.

Problems such as these reflect the absence of a comprehensive and synthesizing theoretical framework to guide the design of research on organization with a cross-national focus. Theoretical pluralism has so far led to confusion and paralysis rather than to enlightenment, which leads one to ask whether the "jungle" that confronts us can eventually be arranged into a tidy garden (Redding, 1994). This essay proceeds on the basis that some constructive arrangement is possible. Its underlying premise is that there is no problem in looking at different parts of an elephant as long as we also have an idea of how the parts fit together to describe the whole. If that is the case, we can compare black with white, blue with green elephants, or alternatively just their trunks, without forgetting that in other respects they continue to share the characteristics of being elephants. If, however, our lines of sight continue to be constrained by the fixed focal lengths of unduly bounded concepts and theories, we shall find it extremely difficult to move beyond limited and non-communicating perspectives to achieve this more holistic view.

The intention of this essay is therefore to take some small steps toward theoretical synthesis and a refocusing of the field. The term "synthesis" is used advisedly to indicate constructive combination rather than complete integration. The essay begins by rehearsing the main perspectives that are on offer to guide the study of organization cross-nationally. It then explores their potential synthesis within a unifying theoretical framework. An analysis of globalization, the major contextual development for cross-national organization, demonstrates the value of the framework and assists its development. The final section considers methodological issues in light of the theoretical synthesis being advocated. These concern the choice of designs for future research, and the underpinning of theoretical synthesis through increased conceptual consistency based on greater operational equivalence.

RELEVANT THEORETICAL PERSPECTIVES

There is a palette of theoretical perspectives relevant to cross-national organization studies. They almost all derive from Western scholarship, though contributions from anthropology and sociology have also been informed by research in other parts of the world. In fact, many of the founding fathers of Western social science adopted an internationally comparative approach in their attempts to construct general social theories and to trace the development of different civilizations.

A basic distinction can be drawn between two categories of theoretical perspective in terms of their sensitivity to nations or regions as analytically significant contexts. The first category consists of theories that are not sensitive to particular nations or regions as special contexts, but that refer instead to universal rationales. This universalism is seen to arise from ubiquitous economic and technological forces that are in turn motivated by universal human needs and drives. These generate certain operational contingencies that establish a functional imperative for organizational design and process, regardless of national setting. An extension of this perspective predicts an increasing convergence between modes of organization as countries develop industrial and postindustrial economies with similar political systems and personal lifestyles, a convergence that is seen to have accelerated under the impetus of late twentieth-century globalization. This first set of perspectives may therefore be called "low context" in the sense that they do not grant national context any analytical significance over and above the configuration of universals that happen to characterize a country at any point in its development.[2]

The other category consists of theoretical perspectives that grant theoretical primacy to national cultures, or national institutional systems, when accounting for national differences in organization. Because they grant explanatory primacy to specifically national rationalities, they may be termed "high context" perspectives. They posit national uniqueness in organizational structures, systems and behaviors, and ascribe such uniqueness to specifically national properties of a cultural and/or institutional nature. These perspectives expect national organizational differences to persist over time regardless of economic development.

"Low Context" Perspectives

A common feature of low context perspectives is that they minimize the impact of national distinctiveness. They contain a strong presumption of eventual convergence in management and organization as nations become increasingly engaged in an increasingly efficient global economy and are increasingly subject to the impact of technological change. These perspectives imply that, as new technologies break down barriers of communication and information, and (hopefully) dire poverty is reduced, people will increasingly come to express similar demands for organization and work to be arranged in ways that meet the fundamental psychological needs and aspirations they are assumed to share. This encourages the search for new forms of organization that reconcile efficiency and human needs more effectively than hitherto. Economics, technology, and psychology thus figure prominently among the low context perspectives.

Economic Universalism

Economic theory centers on the allocation of scarce resources through the pursuit of utility via the market mechanism. By extension, it purports to explain the formal organization of economic activities by firms as an economically rational response to market conditions. For example, Chandler (1977) accounts for the rise of the modern "multiunit business enterprise" by reference to the growth of markets, assisted by new production and transportation technologies, and the development of professional managers to coordinate activities previously conducted in the marketplace (Biggart, 1997). Williamson (1985) also refers to market factors as the primary condition for hierarchically controlled and coordinated firms to develop. These factors include the costs of coordinating market transactions and maintaining market contracts, as well as risks due to opportunism by market partners when the deal entails investing in specific-use assets. Most economists assume that their market-based theories are universally applicable and can account for which forms of business organization will be effective (that is, expected to survive in the long term), wherever the national location.

The credibility of economic universalism has grown since the advent of neo-liberal economics in Western countries and the introduction of economic reform in former state-socialist or state-militarist countries. It argues that, given the growth of the global economy and common human aspirations for betterment, "free market" economics will eventually prevail in all societies, and present a common context for management. Thus, the editors of the Heritage Foundation/ *Wall Street Journal*'s "1999 Index of Economic Freedom" state that "freedom is the surest path to growth" (Johnson et al., 1998, p. 14). The argument is that ultimately liberalization and financial transparency, as conditions for efficient markets, are required for sustained economic development. Institutions like the IMF and journals such as *The Economist* and *Wall Street Journal* praise non-intervention by governments, liberalization, transparency, and freedom of capital movements.

The success of China's economic reform as a result of (1) creating decentralized business systems that grant increasing strategic autonomy to managers and (2) opening to the outside world is cited in support of economic universalism (e.g., *The Economist*, 1992). It has also been argued that Asia's long period of economic success before the recent crisis can be ascribed to the pursuit of fundamentally similar economic principles to those that are successful in other parts of the world. According to this view, Asia's success has not been built on the discovery of a new form of capitalism but, rather, on a tried-and-true formula that is just as evident in Silicon Valley as in Hong Kong (e.g., Wong, 1998). The problems that have arisen in Asia are ascribed to aberrations from the efficient markets model, such as dubious financing and a lack of transparency, leading to poor economic judgment and a misallocation of resources. Thus, the dean of the Asian Development Bank Institute has commented that the Asian economic crisis stemmed from structural deficiencies and "imprudence" compared with global norms. Arguing against purely national solutions, he added that "we have also found that as important and valuable as cultural differences are, at bottom the similarities between us, especially in this day and age when communication is open and free, are more basic and fundamental" (Estanislao, 1999).

Much economic development theory adopts the perspective of economic universalism, especially modernization theory with its late-development and catch-up variants. This posits an eventual convergence among developed countries, including their forms of organization and management (Biggart & Hamilton, 1992). It is claimed that economic rationality dictates a need for professional management under world competitive conditions (Kerr at al., 1960). The canons of professional management include provisions that may be at variance with more traditional practices in developing nations, such as transparency of goals, rational resource allocation, systematic selection and human resource development, objective performance appraisal and reward.

The economic perspective regards the organization as a micro-level phenomenon. Economists therefore generally confine themselves to discussing broad alternative organizational phenomena, such as the choice between U- and M-form structures (Williamson, 1970), the organizational internalization of markets (Buckley & Casson, 1976; Williamson, 1985), and models for the organization of international business (Bartlett & Ghoshal, 1989; Ghoshal & Westney, 1993). Economic universalism continues to hold powerful sway in much contemporary work. For example, the debate on corporate governance is powerfully informed by agency theory and by criteria for efficient resource utilization including transparency and fiduciary accountability (Hawley & Williams, 1996; Shleifer & Vishny, 1997). Internal discussion in China about the restructuring of that country's leading large enterprises is today being conducted with reference not to specifically Chinese, or even socialist principles, but rather in light of theories on transactions costs and market forces (e.g., Qin, 1999). A third example concerns one of the most far-reaching developments in cross-national organization, the internationalization of firms. The predominant line of theorizing available to account for the stages through which activities are located abroad, and the choice of forms for organizing international operations, articulates these issues in terms of general principles governing risk, managerial exigency, and market opportunity (Johanson & Vahlne, 1977; Kogut, 1988).

Economic theory endeavors to apply principles in ways that rarely accord a positive value to national specifics. When these are taken into account, it tends to regard them as contingencies such as market imperfections that constrain economically optimum behavior, or opportunism that generates economically dysfunctional behavior. In other words, national conditions tend to be treated as constraints on the effective operation of the market system rather than as features that confer cultural preferences for, and differential degrees of institutional legitimacy on, particular ways of organizing.

Technology

Technological change and development has been regarded as the prime mover of capitalism (Schumpter, 1943; Toffler, 1971). Moreover, as Dicken (1998, p. 145) notes, "technology is, without doubt, one of the most important contributory factors underlying the internationalization and globalization of economic activity." The impact of technology extends not only to the location of productive activities but also increasingly to the ways in which these can be managed. This development is associated with the contemporary "shift from a technology based primarily on cheap inputs of energy to one predominantly based on cheap inputs of information derived from advances in microelectronic and telecommunications technology" (Freeman, 1988, p. 10). With the increasing importance of this "new technology," there is a convergence between the considerations advanced for organization by information theorists and those advanced by students of technology.

Much of the literature on information and communications technologies claims that these technologies offer path-breaking new ways of handling information which have implications for the design of effective organizations (Fulk & DeSanctis, 1995). It is argued, for example, that such technologies offer more effective ways of reconciling long-standing inherent organizational dilemmas such as the need for simultaneous control and flexible autonomy. Some elevate information to be the spirit of the age, and they argue that it carries a universal message for organization and management. An example is found in Applegate's (1995) writing on "designing and managing the information age organization." She takes the view that advances in information technology, when coupled with changes in workforce capabilities, can address the problems that previously stood in the way of transformation from bureaucratic to organic, if not virtual, organizations. Given an increasingly competitive and fast-moving world economic environment, Applegate believes that advances in information technology, and in related conceptions of information, knowledge and learning, have created an irresistible movement toward new forms of organization, a movement that she and others of a like mind indeed wish to foster.

If these IT solutions are so powerful, it follows that managers wherever they are located cannot neglect to apply the new technologies to their organization if they are to remain competitive. Insofar as technological solutions are being offered by technologists working from broadly similar design principles, this may well be a strong force for organizational convergence. An additional reason for expecting growing similarity lies in the increasing connectivity that modern information technologies provide around the world. This facility for disseminating and sharing information is also thought to increase homogeneity. In these ways, information theory—or at least the technologically deterministic strand of it—also offers a low-context perspective.

As modern communication and information technologies become ubiquitous, they are increasingly integrated into the ways that in contemporary organizations information is processed, people communicate and knowledge is managed. In other words, there is a increasing amalgamation between the design of such technological systems and that of organization itself. The key question that then arises is whether preferences for particular forms of organization are now coming to drive the use of technology or whether the technology itself has its own impact as an exogenous factor.

There is a long-standing dispute over this matter. Some have regarded technology in general, and production technology in particular, as constraining or even determining workplace organization and social relations (e.g., Woodward, 1965; Hickson et al., 1974). The implication of their perspective for the cross-national study of organization is that, whatever the national setting, the adoption of a given technology will have the same influential consequences for the design of a viable organization and for the way that social relations at work are consequently structured (Child, 1981). In other words, technological determinists argue that different production technologies determine particular organization structures and behaviors independently of the local context (Knights & Murray, 1994). As Hickson and his colleagues put it, "the technological equipment of an oil refinery requires much the same operatives and supervisors wherever it is" (1974, p. 64).

Others have, by contrast, concluded from close examination of the adoption of particular forms of technology that the decisions made at the time reflected managerial preferences for increasing control over the work process rather than any technological imperative (e.g., Noble, 1977). Child and Loveridge (1990) concluded from studies of IT in European services that it remained an open question whether the application of new technology will give rise to increasing similarities in the process of organizing across different countries. This is because there is considerable latitude in how organizational arrangements are constituted around the technology, and hence plenty of scope for their negotiation. Scarbrough (1996) concluded similarly, from a study of information systems (IS) projects in six financial organizations located in Scotland, that the possibilities presented by IT for organizational redesign are worked through the social construction of different classificatory systems. The organization was a "contested terrain across which different classificatory systems slug it out" (p. 200). Each system is fought for by interested parties whose desire is to "promote classificatory world-views in which their own expertise is central" (p. 200).

One might have expected the greater inherent flexibility of the new technology to have softened the deterministic stance. Some prophets of the new technology, however, continue to embrace a position of technological determinism even though their message may now be an optimistic one emphasizing how new technology can assist people to realize their potential (cf. Zuboff, 1988), rather than the earlier pessimistic message of alienation (cf. Blauner, 1964). This leads Dicken (1998, p. 145) to warn that "it is all too easy to be seduced by the notion that technology 'causes' a specific set of changes [and] makes particular structures and arrangements 'inevitable'."

Psychological Universalism/Methodological Individualism

This perspective assumes that all human beings share common needs and motivational structures. The desire to satisfy common needs forms the basis for similar structures of individual motivation. Insofar as such motivation drives people's behavior in organizations, it is argued that the design of work organization as well as managerial systems for control and reward must treat this as a major exigency. Even cross-cultural psychologists who recognize that human behavior varies across different cultural settings are primarily concerned to pursue the discipline's aim of arriving at universal generalizations. This means that they tend to regard the contextual specifics of different countries as anomalous rather than fundamental (Bond & Smith, 1996). For, according to Poortinga, "it is assumed that the same psychological processes are operating in all humans independent of culture" (1992, p. 13).

For the past hundred years, from scientific management through to contemporary industrial and social psychology, there has been a search for a generally applicable theory of motivation at work. Content theories attempt to identify the factors that actually motivate people, such as Maslow's (1943) hierarchy of needs model, Herzberg's (1959) two-factor theory, or McClelland's (1988) achievement motivation theory. Process theories attempt to identify the relationship among the dynamic variables that comprise motivation, and include expectancy theory (Porter & Lawler, 1968), equity theory (Adams, 1965), goal theory (Locke, 1968), and attribution theory (Heider, 1958). Cognitive social psychologists have also developed theories of chronic individual motive, emphasizing for instance uncertainty reduction (Sorrentino & Hewitt, 1984), the need for structure (Neuberg & Newsom, 1993), and the need for closure (Kruglanski & Freund, 1983).

Many of these psychological theories and concepts have become the standard fare of textbooks on management and organizational behavior. This not only indicates their wide acceptance; it also serves to propagate them further. They carry clear implications for organizational design, favoring empowerment, teamwork, and performance-related rewards. Many of them also speak for non-hierarchical structures, with open communications, in order to promote closer interpersonal relationships, to foster a common organizational culture, and through transparency to facilitate goal acceptance and a feeling of equity.

While these psychological theories differ in detail, they take individuals or groups as their focus, more or less in isolation from their cultural and social context. Thus people are regarded as essentially the same everywhere. They all need to eat, have security, enjoy social relations, and derive some meaning from their lives. Reducing the theoretical and methodological level to the individual encourages the assumption all people share a similar set of needs. The more basic needs are taken to be biological and physiological in nature. They are not subject to a high degree of social definition; whether you have sufficient to eat and enjoy shelter and security are to a large extent common necessities. The assumption of universal human needs has importantly informed the analysis of utility that underlies much economic theory.

Appropriate levels even of basic need fulfillment are in practice to some extent socially defined, as with acceptable levels of obesity or sexual activity. However, psychological universalism starts to run into serious problems when it addresses so-called higher-order needs that are of a cognitive rather than material nature, such as esteem and self-actualization. For these are expressed primarily through social norms and are thus subject to cultural definition. What constitutes achievement, for example, is defined for all but a few isolates in terms of cultural norms.

It is precisely because many needs are socially defined and reflect what is valued culturally, that the universal applicability of psychological theories has been heavily questioned. They have been criticized for their universalism—for assuming that the same theory can be applied to all people regardless of their social origins, upbringing, education, and culture. They have also been criticized for their imperialism. Hofstede (1980b) in particular has argued that these psychological theories actually reflect American cultural values, especially individualism, with their emphasis on achievement and self-actualization as the highest level needs. Some psychologists have themselves urged the need to develop theories of behavior and motivation that are indigenous to different societies rather than universalistic in nature (e.g., Yang, 1994). This critique derives, of course, from a high-context perspective, and it calls to mind Kluckhohn's (1951) recommendation that, even with reference to those values that express common human material or moral fundamentals, we speak about "conditional absolutes" because they may be subject to culturally nuanced definitions. If the general applicability of current psychological work-related theories can be questioned, then their prescriptions for organizational design have to be treated with caution.

"High Context" Perspectives

High context perspectives share the strong presumption that management and organization will retain and develop its own distinct characteristics that derive from cultural preferences and embedded institutions.

Cultural Theory

The cultural perspective places the previous "low context" theories into what it considers as their appropriate cultural context. Economic utilities, personal motivations, and the ways information is interpreted and used are seen to be culture-bound. This perspective maintains that thinking and behavior are significantly governed by cultural values. Culture therefore differentiates management across nations and other social collectivities.

The two best-known cultural perspectives that have been applied to management and organization are those of Hofstede (1980a, 1991) and Trompenaars (1993). While these two Dutchmen fiercely contest the validity of their respective cultural dimensions and methodologies, they agree on the following basic assumptions. Cultural values are deep-seated and enduring. They vary systematically between different societies. They condition what is acceptable organizational practice. And they predict inter-societal differences in economic performance (GDP).

The cultural perspective has for some time provided the dominant paradigm in comparative studies of organization. It is indicative that Hickson and Pugh (1995) chose to subtitle their review of the field "The Impact of Societal Culture on Organizations around the Globe." Even before Hofstede's seminal work, international studies of organization predominantly regarded culture as the key explanatory factor for cross-national differences, as reviews such as Roberts (1970) make clear. Attention to culture also has intuitive appeal to practicing international managers, for whom it serves as a convenient reference for the many frustrating difficulties they can experience when working with people from other countries, the source of which they do not fully comprehend.

Despite its appeal and influence, many questions remain to be answered about the cultural perspective. The first and most fundamental concerns the theoretical status of culture. Is culture all pervasive, as Sorge (1982) has argued, so that we need to reposition our economic and technological theories within a cultural space, as Boisot (1995) has advocated for information theory?[3] In other words, does culture take primacy over other factors not only in terms of predictive power but also in terms of structuring the systems of meaning, and shaping the rationales, that other theorists can legitimately employ? If that is the case, then the comparative study of organization across cultural boundaries employing concepts and equivalent operational measures derived from only one culture becomes hazardous in terms of validity criteria.

Cultural relativism thus raises the question of conceptual equivalence. Indigenous psychologists argue that the meaning attached to words, and the definitions of acceptable behaviors, is particular to the members of different societies. This questions the equivalence between cultures of any comparative concept and its operational measurement. Universalistic concepts and their standardized measurement of the kind that cross-cultural scholars like Hofstede have employed become suspect on the basis of this argument. This is a problem that Hofstede has himself recognized and which encouraged him and Bond to uncover the fifth dimension of "Confucian Dynamism" in East Asian societies (Hofstede & Bond, 1988). On the other hand, standard measures such as Hofstede's appear sufficiently robust to uncover replicable differences between societies that also accord with common experience. The issue of conceptual equivalence is fundamental to our ability to undertake valid cross-national studies of organization, and is discussed in the last section of this essay.

Moreover, we still do not have an adequate theory on the relevance of culture for organization. Key issues remain unclear, namely which organizational features are shaped by culture, how are they so influenced, and what the significance of culture is as compared to, say, economic, technological, and political factors. A satisfactory theory would have to address two levels of analysis. The first concerns the independence of culture as an explanatory variable. To what extent are cultures themselves shaped by national economic, technological, and political factors through the mediation of lifestyle, mass media, access to global information, and government-sponsored ideology? Can culture be regarded as an independent, let alone dominant, force? The common assumption that national differences can simply be expressed in cultural terms, and that nation can be used as the unit of analysis for culture (Gannon, 1994), is in reality a hypothesis that still requires testing. The second level concerns the identification of organizational attributes that are culturally specific in the sense that they vary systematically between cultures and can be shown to be impacted directly by culture. These considerations imply that "a test of national differences which are culturally intrinsic would require an examination of whether organizational characteristics continue to differ across nations when contingencies and economic systems are similar or controlled, and a demonstration that the remaining differences are explicable in terms of an adequate theory of national cultures" (Child, 1981, p. 305). In similar vein, one of the "recommendations for progress" that Redding (1994, p. 350) offered from his review of comparative management theory is to "enrich the current grand theory of Hofstede further by probing into the societal origins of his value clusters, and in terms of outcomes, trace more explicitly the patterns of their organizational consequences."

Cultural Information Theory

Information is a ubiquitous social phenomenon. Information theory takes the view that managing organizations primarily involves the processing and communication of information, whether this be in imparting a vision, reaching decisions, carrying out control and coordination, or managing knowledge. As a result, information theory is applied to a range of organizational levels, from strategic decision making down to the information-processing capabilities of individuals. Information has also been treated in a variety of ways from a cybernetic artifact to a cultural phenomenon.

Among cultural information theories, Boisot's (1986) is particularly fruitful for a comparative understanding of organizational forms. He identifies four institutionalized approaches to organizing transactions and relationships, in terms of the modes of information processing that characterize them. These modes are defined in terms of two primary dimensions of information: its codification and diffusion.[4] Boisot named the "space" that these create, the "culture-space," on the basis that there are marked cultural and/or institutionalized preferences to be found in different nations for particular positions on the two dimensions. Thus the relatively open, transparent "Anglo-Saxon" nations, with their highly codified legal and other systems, would be expected to favor a combination of high information codification and diffusion (availability). The four fundamental organizational forms to which this framework gives rise are bureaucracy, market, clan, and fief. On the assumption just made, Anglo-Saxon nations should exhibit a high preference for the organization of transactions through markets, and this is undoubtedly the case.

Boisot and Child (1988, 1996) have applied this framework to a comparison of Chinese and "Western" organizational forms. They concluded that whereas capitalist business involving private ownership and funding was significant in both societies (increasingly so even in the PRC), the mode of organization typifying that capitalism was different. This led them to suggest that the Chinese form should be labeled "network capitalism." This is an example of the application of cultural information theory cross-nationally for purposes of identifying broad organizational forms.

At the group or team level, information theory adopts a quite different focus depending on whether it is sensitive to the influence of cross-national culture or not. Abstracted from culture, emphasis is likely to be placed on the effective functioning of teams as information processing units, employing procedures such as agreeing objectives, preparing briefing papers, recording the results of discussions, and accumulating a relevant knowledge base. The intention is to structure team process in ways that will encourage them to transform the quality of available information, especially from tacit to explicit, and to codify that explicit knowledge so as to transform it into a property available to the organization as a whole (Nonaka & Takuechi, 1995). If, however, information theory is sensitive to cultural influences, it will recognize that accepted modes of group functioning, including the conduct of meetings, vary considerably across cultures. It will therefore pay a great deal more attention to the social composition of groups or teams within organizations, and to the processes whereby they can find a commonly acceptable way of proceeding, communicating, and (eventually) sharing identity (Tjorsvold, 1991; Drummond, 1997).

At the individual level, the cross-national sensitivity of information theory again varies. Much has focused on the cognitive capacities of individuals per se, including their ability to handle complex or incomplete information (Streufert & Swezey, 1986). Other work has, however, taken account of how, for instance, interpretative models vary in different cultures, and the implications this has for information-processing capabilities. An example is the contrast between the factorial-analytical orientation of the Western cognitive model and the synthetic-holistic orientation of the Chinese interpretative model (Liu, 1986). This type of distinction between the nationally specific information-processing modes of individuals assumes considerable significance for organizations in two respects. First, if there are national styles of information interpretation, they will shape the preferences of organizational members for particular forms of information processing and hence transactional governance. Second, they will color the character of whole organizations if they are strongly reflected in the decision-making and management style of leaders.

Institutional Theory

This perspective emphasizes that management and business have different institutional foundations in different societies. Key institutions are the state, the legal system, the financial system, and the family. Taken together, such institutions constitute the distinctive social organization of a country and its economy. The forms these institutions take and their economic role are seen to shape different "national business systems" or varieties of capitalism (Whitley, 1992a, 1992b;

Orru et al., 1997). Although the institutional perspective draws on a long socio-logical tradition, there is still not much agreement about, or understanding of, the processes whereby institutions are formed and in turn impact on organizations (Tolbert & Zucker, 1996). There is, however, much more consensus on the poten-tial analytical power that the perspective offers.

Institutional theory implies that nations have their own logic of social and eco-nomic organization, and that theories claiming universal application may in fact betray their own specific institutional origins. Thus, neoclassical economics is most appropriate to the nineteenth-century liberal capitalism it was first devel-oped to explain. Some institutionalists have argued that East Asian countries require their own economic theory because their dominant transactional logic is different (Biggart & Hamilton, 1992). For example, in China the logic and ratio-nale of hierarchy has been based upon the relational norms expounded by Con-fucius and legal codes such as those developed during the Tang Dynasty. This institutionalized relational logic shapes a society whose transactional order rests on social obligation to higher authority and to the community rather than on rules oriented to protecting the individual. Chinese capitalism is seen to be intrinsically different from Western capitalism because of this contrast in institutional framing over a long period of time (Gerth & Mills, 1946; Weber, 1964).

Institutional theorists stress the historical embeddedness of social structures and processes. This carries two particularly significant implications for the cross-national analysis of organization. First, "institutional theory proposes that social and economic organization is informed by historically developed logics, which are changed only with difficulty" (Biggart & Guillen, 1999, p. 742). In other words, institutions are likely to be "sticky" in the face of economic and tech-nological change. This means that, insofar as a country's constituent bodies (firms, public organizations, and so forth) are enabled, supported, and guided by national institutions, one would expect cross-national contrasts in the organiza-tional responses to handling such change. Second, as Biggart and Guillen also note, the social organization of a country "acts as a repository of useful resources or capabilities" (p. 742). In other words, social organization influences a coun-try's ability to undertake certain kinds of production or other economic activity efficiently and effectively. National institutions such as education systems and the structure of social relations can, through their impact on the degree of ascription or achievement in the society, impact on the ability of a country to base its eco-nomic wealth-creation on innovation rather than, say, mass production. Institu-tionalists therefore argue that the conditions of economic survival through specialization around national strengths tend to preserve nationally distinctive patterns of organization, even within a fully open and globalized competitive sys-tem.

Institutional analysis acknowledges the significance of culture, but it also allows for the possibility of cultural modification either through the influence of ideas contained in worldviews (such as Confucianism, the Protestant Work Ethic, or Marxism) or through changes in economic and political forces. The state is seen to play a particularly important role in establishing conditions for these last two factors. The institutional perspective therefore contextualizes culture, and in so doing considers both the influence of material forces and systems of ideas. I shall argue that this broad approach is extremely significant for a comparative cross-national understanding of organization and its evolution.

Whereas cultural theorists tend to regard culture as an immutable given, institutional theorists recognize that institutions and the norms they support do adapt to economic and technological forces, albeit often slowly and with some resistance. They have not, however, been able as yet to throw much light on how such adaptation takes place, and in particular the role that organizations and their leaders may play in this. This is not a trivial point, because the development of new organizational forms today in the light of economic pressures and technological possibilities may lead to their emulation more widely within the institutional system, including government, given the respect now accorded to the supposed efficiency of business methods. Indeed, large business organizations may today be in a position to exert influence over not just the structures but also the policies of institutions. Alarm is expressed at the power of big corporations to shape the regulatory and legal conditions of even highly institutionalized contexts, such as that of the United States (Mokhiber & Weissman, 1999).

There is in fact a problem in the weak theorization of how organizations are formed with reference to institutions as contextual analytical references (Loveridge, 1998). What students of national business systems have generally offered is an observation of congruence between forms of business organization and the nature of governmental, financial, technological, educational, and community bodies, so giving rise to national or regional taxonomies. They assume that the functions performed by such bodies and the regulations or other constraints they impose upon firms, substantially explain the ways that the firms are governed, the range of specialties they internalize, and their philosophies of management. This leaves unexplained the extent to which the key actors in firms can themselves determine the agendas of institutions through lobbying, co-optation, the threatened withdrawal of cooperation, and so forth. This potential for social action is clearly not a trivial issue for organizational theory, because it bears directly upon the question of how much strategic choice decision makers have for developing or maintaining their preferred organizational arrangements. It was actually a central focus of an older school of institutional analysis exemplified by Selznick's famous study of the TVA (Selznick, 1949).

TOWARD THEORETICAL SYNTHESIS

Given that the two sets of perspectives, low and high context, contribute in diverse ways toward the cross-national study of organization, it is relevant to ask whether attempts to reconcile them are likely to facilitate progress in this field of study. One view is that they are rooted in incommensurable paradigms and that sensible dialogue between them is therefore not possible. This is the present de facto position in the field of cross-national organizational studies, whether by intention or by default. The alternative is to seek a bridge between the two sets of perspectives that will lead at least to constructive discourse and perhaps to synthesis. This was, in fact, the key recommendation emerging from a commentary on the Special Research Forum appearing in the *Academy of Management Journal* in 1995 on "International and Intercultural Management Research":

> we suggest that the field integrate its working definitions of nation and culture and create an understanding based on various facets of nations and cultures, including economic, legal, cultural, and political systems. The key to conducting quality international or intercultural research is to understand the context in which firms and individuals functions and operate (Earley & Singh, 1995, pp. 337-338).

Low context perspectives refer primarily to the influences on, even imperatives for, organization seen as emanating from economic and technological development. These forces are mainly *material* in nature and take effect through socially structured activities such as markets and programs of technological innovation. By contrast, high context perspectives identify influences on organization that are mainly *ideational* in character. The values and norms to which they refer are, however, expressed and reproduced through the medium of social institutions, some of which like legal systems and religious bodies have their own highly structured forms. Indeed, material and ideational forces are institutionally linked. In most, if not all, societies, market transactions and technological property rights are subject to institutional regulation that expresses the normative priorities of those societies. So an institutional analysis would seem to offer an appropriate path toward synthesis.

A fruitful basis for reconciling these different perspectives, and one that is institutional in nature, has actually been on offer within social theory for many years. This is Max Weber's framework for the analysis of socioeconomic development (Schluchter, 1981; Mommsen, 1989). Weber focused on the material and ideational forces driving social change. He used this framework to account for the emergence of the Western capitalist system as well as bureaucracy as its characteristic organizational form (Gerth & Mills, 1946; Weber, 1964). While Weber's two forces are not identical to low and high context factors as I have described them, there is quite a close correspondence.[5]

First, according to Weber, there are dynamic material forces of an economic and technological nature that give rise to efficiency-oriented rules and codified knowledge. These forces thus encourage the development of what Weber called "formal rationality." Formal rationality concerns literally the form of social arrangements in terms of routines, structures, and so forth. As societies "modernize" their economies and technologies, so they adopt a more complex division of labor and institutional arrangements. This increases their requirement for formal rationality. It is expressed both in legally sanctioned organizational innovations such as the joint-stock company and in more autonomous developments such as hierarchical corporate forms. Although countries vary in their level and form of economic development at any one point in time, an implication of the materialist dynamic is that the organizational structures and processes characterizing industrializing nations will become increasingly similar (Kerr et al., 1960). Convergence is expected to accelerate as national economic systems become part of the same global economy and as cross-border transnational corporations (TNCs) account for increasing shares of activity in many sectors.

Second, there is the influence of substantive values and idealism, as expressed, for example, in Confucianism, the Protestant Ethic, or political ideologies. They shape "substantive rationality," which concerns the meaning that people give to social organization and to the processes that take place within it such as the exercise of authority. Substantive rationality is rather more far-reaching than "culture," at least in the sense accorded to the latter by organization theory. While it is expressed by cultures, it is also conveyed in ideologies and systems of knowledge that claim an ultimate validity. Various social institutions provide vehicles for the articulation and reproduction of substantive rationality: religions, governments, and business schools are among these.

Substantive rationality can impact importantly on the structural principles of organizations, as well as on how people behave and relate within them. An example is the legitimacy accorded to the stakeholder and communitarian principle of corporate governance in continental Europe resulting in measures such as the European Union's Fifth Directive on industrial participation. However, one would only expect cross-national convergence in organizational substantive rationality to come about if there were a convergence of dominant ideas and principles between the institutions that frame and propagate it. This is certainly happening within the European Union, and may be replicated in other regional blocs. The increasingly popular and largely American-inspired international management education movement, centred on the MBA, is another vehicle for convergence in substantive organizational rationality (Locke, 1989).

National integration within political and economic regional blocs and the rapid international growth of business education do not, however, proceed independently of materialistic forces. They are associated with economic and technological integration. In Weber's analysis, materialistic and ideational forces have the potential to impact on each other. On the one hand, the Protestant Ethic laid foundations for the spirit of Western capitalism, and the Confucian ethic shaped the spirit of Chinese capitalism (Redding, 1990). On the other hand, the capitalist economy itself has a significant international impact on people's values and expectations in areas such as personal achievement, lifestyle, and employment. As discussed later in this essay, the interdependence of the materialistic and the ideational is an insight of great importance for understanding the organizational impact of contemporary "globalization."[6]

Weber did not adopt a wholly deterministic view of social development. He allowed for the role of "social action," which is intentional action oriented toward others. The intention behind such action may be informed by calculation, values, emotion, or tradition (Weber, 1978). In other words, action may be motivated and guided by material interests, ideals, or a combination of both. It is not, however, necessarily a slave to the contextual forces that express materialism or idealism. There is always a possibility for initiative and innovation on the part of those who make or influence decisions on organization. The role of social action will assume particular importance when I apply the Weberian perspective to the evolution of organization within its international context.

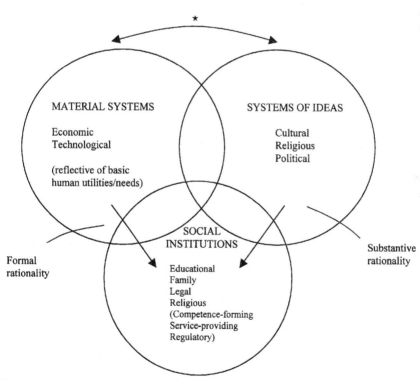

Notes: *Material and ideational systems can have a direct impact on each other. Thus economic and techno-logical rationales are themselves systems of ideas, while economic rationales have been defined by reli-gious precepts such as the Protestant Ethic.

Figure 1. A Weberian Interpretation of Organizational Context

Figure 1 offers a view of organizational context that is derived from the Weberian analytical framework. Following Weber, it identifies material and ideational systems as the two primary forces in the evolution of this context, and at the same time it recognizes their interdependence. These systems are seen to imbue a nation's social institutions with both formal and substantive rationalities. Such institutions comprise the third major component of organizational context. Some institutions, chiefly the educational system, help to form organizational competencies. Others, such as the banking and insurance system, provide intermediate services, and other support services such as health care. Yet others impose legal and regulatory constraints. Governmental bodies may be involved in each of these roles.

The integrative and comprehensive character of the Weberian framework offers two main advantages to the analysis of organizational context. It encourages a balanced appreciation of the contextual factors impacting upon organization, balanced in the sense that these are not viewed narrowly within the confines of a single theoretical lens, be this low or high context, idealist or materialist. I note shortly how this approach helps to unpack a major contemporary phenomenon for organization—globalization—that is often identified with the economic dimension but which actually alludes to a combination of material forces and powerful ideas. Second, the framework encourages us to take greater care in specifying the contextual location of any given organization with respect to the likely impact upon it of both material forces and the dissemination of ideas. This points to the virtue of framing propositions in future with more precise reference to the extent that an organization is affected by international material forces and value systems as opposed to local ones. An example would be the proposition that an organization will more strongly reflect the substantive rationality of its domestic national culture the more it is autonomous of both external materialist forces (such as international competition) and external values (such as those imported by a foreign partner).[7]

Arguably the most valuable contribution of this perspective lies in the way it encourages us to reframe questions for research. It does not assume a specific national or regional context either to be inconsequential outside its relation to the world economy or, at the other extreme, to be comprehensively self-accountable in terms of culture or national institutional system. Instead, the perspective draws attention to the way organizations are situated in regard to international versus local material and ideational systems. Mainstream cross-national organizational research has notably failed to address the issue of how global and local forces, together and in relation to each other, bear upon the nature of organization.

On the material side, the question becomes how organizations are situated vis-à-vis international systems, such as international auditing conventions or the systematic quality benchmarking organized by the ISO, which are in turn stimulated by the expectations of actors in financial and product markets. To what extent do Chinese enterprises, for example, engage in the international systems of trade, finance, and technology that impose common materialistic pressures, such as international competition? The general hypothesis is that the more they are incorporated into the global system, the less differentiated Chinese organization and management systems can remain from those of other similarly incorporated organizations in other parts of the world with which they are competing. In the case of China, the conditions attached to entry into the World Trade Organization (WTO) would further open the door to the impact of global economic forces (Lardy, 1999). It is therefore germane to ask how far the Chinese authorities are acting upon the premise that their country's long-term development needs oblige them to accept such conditions. The other side of the coin is to ask to what extent Chinese enterprises can maintain their currently preferred management and organizational practices under these circumstances, and whether some are better situated to do so than others.

Staying with the example of China, questions arise on the ideational side concerning the exposure that the members of Chinese organizations have to foreign values. If they engage in international business, does this tie them into a set of international institutional expectations and regulations on matters such as transparency of transactions and accounts? If Chinese enterprises have become affiliates or close business partners of TNCs, are their members likely to take on board foreign business norms and practices through the impact of strong corporate cultures and management systems? Do those local nationals who live in an urban environment with its increasingly Western lifestyles and media culture, and are connected to the Internet and other international communication media, absorb non-Chinese values to a greater extent than the members of Chinese organizations who are not so exposed? It may be hypothesized that the greater this international exposure, the more Chinese managers and other personnel will absorb foreign norms and apply them to their organizational behavior.

These questions imply that an organization's level of autonomy from external materialistic forces and values will vary even within a single country depending on its positioning within that country: its economic sector, the size and scope of its activities, whether it is in an urban or rural location, and so forth. This implication is profoundly significant for the design of comparative organizational research.

The Weberian perspective is also helpful for addressing the question of whether the impact of economic and technological forces for convergence is likely to differ according to the level of organization in question. A review of the then available literature led me to conclude that those organizational features of firms which linked closely to external institutions such as the capital market, or which were constrained by the economics of technology and scale, were more likely to show convergence (Child, 1981). These are the strategic and "macro-level" features of management and organizations, such as the structures of corporate governance and of executive management. By contrast, behavioral norms and styles of managing would be more likely to reflect cultural expectations and norms concerning how people should relate to each other and how the individual should relate to the collectivity. Interpersonal behaviors and styles are relatively insulated from the material forces in an organization's environment. International accounting criteria and performance norms are increasingly being applied to public companies, and investors, parent companies, and regulators scrutinize their policies. However, the behavioral processes through which these policies are implemented are likely to be left to local discretion, and this permits some adaptation to local cultural preferences. So while it is broadly true to say that material factors and cultural values both shape organization, it is important always to specify exactly which aspects of organization constitute the focus of one's inquiry.

There is, then, reason to expect variations and differential rates of change in organization even within a given society. To return to our example, one may note how this appears to be occurring within the field of Chinese organizations. Just at the time that some academics are taking up the thesis that, because of indigenous Chinese values, Chinese-led enterprises pursue a distinctive approach to management (Yang, 1998), more and more leading Chinese entrepreneurs and managers seem to be adopting what they call "modern management" based on Western practice! (Austria, 1998). This strongly suggests that it is not fruitful to attempt to predict Chinese organizational practice simply by reference to shared cultural values. Other forces are also in play.

The Weberian approach offers useful antidotes against the temptation to ascribe explanatory primacy to any one theoretical perspective. It qualifies the current dominance that economic universalism enjoys in policy discussions by stressing the need to allow room for the influence of ideas and values. Equally, it cautions against any tendency to ascribe overriding explanatory power to national culture. The example just given, and other evidence, suggests that cultural theorists have assumed too much homogeneity and too much cultural "stickiness" within national systems of management. As we all know, management philosophies and organizational practices can differ considerably within the ambit of a single national "culture." The question is sometimes asked in this respect whether Hewlett-Packard or General Motors is the typical U.S. company.

The dynamic interplay between ideas and institutional forces demonstrates the fallacy of regarding culture as immutable. Cultures can themselves change under the influence of both institutional and material developments. When institutions change, people may adapt their values quite rapidly. China under the impact of the economic reform again provides an instructive example. Ralston and his colleagues (1999) found large contrasts in value-orientations among different generations of managers in the PRC, with the younger generation tending to demonstrate greater acceptance of "Western" values such as individualism. The experience of East and West Germany has shown how work-related values and behavior can diverge substantially across two generations within the same nation due to the impact of different economic and political systems (Frese et al., 1996; Grabher, 1995). It also appears that people can accommodate culturally to organizational and work practices which derive from different sets of values, if these are accompanied by positive material benefits such as secure employment or good rewards. An example is the positive response of workers to Japanese practices in regions of the UK that had long-established local industrial traditions (Oliver & Wilkinson, 1992). Companies can also change their corporate cultures and organizational philosophies, as did many U.S. corporations in response to the "crisis" in American manufacturing of the 1970s and 1980s.

The broad historical sweep encompassed in the work of Weber and other fathers of sociology further suggests that the combination of materialistic and institutional features contained in the notion of "stage of development" have their own impact upon cultural development and so, in turn, upon organizational behavior. The virtues often lumped together as Confucian—hard work, respect for elders, strong family ties, passion for learning and knowledge—are traditional values that were probably as much a part of Victorian England as they are of Chinese communities today (Bendix, 1956). While great systems of thought undoubtedly have had an impact upon the way that people think and organize, this may have been to some extent because they were "right" for the material circumstances of the period in which they had most practical influence. Thus, in contemporary circumstances, "empowerment" may be a quintessentially Anglo-Saxon idea but its spread to other cultural regions may be primarily to do with the pressures arising from international competition to raise productivity, to be responsive to local customer demands, and to enhance employee contributions to incremental innovation.

These considerations suggest that we have to become quite subtle in our theorizing about the characteristics of organization in different countries, as well as about the organization of transnational value chains. We have to ask specific questions about the contexts that apply to the units whose organizational forms or behavior is the subject of study: such as the historical period, the economic sector, the nature of international economic involvement, the level of organization, and which occupational and generation groups are involved. My basic contention, however, is that much of this subtlety can be provided through reference to already available theoretical perspectives that provoke the necessary questions. The challenge is to bring these together within a single framework.

GLOBALIZATION: CONTEXTUAL ANALYSIS APPLYING THE WEBERIAN FRAMEWORK

There are two reasons for attending to globalization at this point. First, it is the major contextual development bearing upon cross-national organization, and its implications cannot be ignored. Second, the analysis of globalization is quite fragmented. While it has been primarily associated with a reduction in the national barriers to the operation of economic forces, it is also being linked to profound changes in values, attitudes, and personal identity (Giddens, 1998, 1999). It should therefore be amenable to the form of integrative analysis concerning material and ideational systems that I am recommending.

Globalization has been variously defined, reflecting in part different disciplinary assumptions (Parker, 1996). An interdisciplinary group of European scholars has recently offered a useful comprehensive definition. "'Globalization' comprises a host of facts and observations such as the accelerated growth of world trade and direct investment since the mid-80s, the global distribution of the value added chain of companies (which has been made possible through decreasing transport costs, widespread application of new information technologies and new management concepts) or the global integration of money and capital markets. Yet globalization is not only an economic phenomenon, but rather includes the contracting role of the nation-state, and the emergence of other social values and ways of life." (Steger, 1998, p. 1).

One may note how this definition refers both to material economic and technological forces on the one hand, and ideational ones on the other. These forces today operate primarily through the agency of transnational corporations, nation-states, and supra-national agencies (Dicken, 1998). The liberalization of trade and of capital movements, combined with the rapid increase in information diffusion through new communication technologies, is seen to decrease market imperfections and allow competitive market forces to gain strength. This trend is supported by the pressures exerted on nation-states by international institutions like the WTO toward the removal of international trade barriers and by the IMF toward transparency and economic rationality in financial transactions. Although these moves have clear material consequences, they are also legitimated by a dominant ideology that appeals to economic rationality and the validity of "global standards" in matters of financial accounting and disclosure of information. The power of these ideas plays an important role in promoting moves toward globalization. The velocity of circulation of ideas and information is increasing dramatically via the Internet and the internationalization of higher education, not least management education. As a result, ideas are becoming increasingly shared, and practices transferred, between different countries.

Dore (1999) notes, for example, that despite Japan's strong "post-Confucian" communitarian organizational ethos, many Japanese are advocating a fundamental change in the country's business system to take it toward the American "shareholder value" model which would favor shareholders rather than employees. This is being legitimated by reference to global standards of corporate governance. These global standards turn out on examination to reflect the ideology of Western business schools and the increasing influence of their graduates in Japanese industry. A shift from Japanese to American models could have profound interlocking effects on the governance structures of Japanese companies, on their internal decision processes, reward systems, and work organization.

There is a widespread assumption that globalization refers to a growing national "borderlessness" which is already well underway, and that this is leading to greater homogeniety and uniformity. It is here that a note of caution needs to be sounded, because globalization does not have a consistent social impact. Paradoxically, at the same time as transactional boundaries weaken, there is a increased awareness of cultural differences and a growing celebration of cultural diversity (Robertson, 1995). The same increasingly intensive international circulation of ideas through the Internet, telecommunications, and other media that promotes the dominant economic ideology seems to be strengthening cultural and subcultural identities at the same time. The technology enhances communication between the members of cultural groups and provides opportunities for their self-expression. It also appears that people's awareness of their own culture and identity is promoted by the provision of more information about other societies or communities, which enables comparisons that clarify cultural distinctiveness. The search for new business opportunities through catering for local preferences is another facet of this greater awareness and appreciation of cultural distinctiveness. Globalization may therefore be stimulating divergent as well as convergent developments in organization. On the one hand it facilitates a centralized standardization of organizational practices and products; on the other hand it promotes local identities which encourage decentralized organizational responses.

There is a tendency in popular discussion to assume that economic and technological forces provide the dynamic behind globalization. While they are undoubtedly of great significance, ideas also continue to play a role and we can make more sense of globalization as a phenomenon by taking account of how the ideas interface with its material aspects. Thus, the notion of "one world" is a powerful idea per se, which undoubtedly has considerable appeal in terms of humanistic values. Nevertheless, its credibility depends on the material changes that allow for globalization, namely the lowering of economic and transportation barriers and the spread of integrative communications technologies. Equally, the diffusion of ideas about management through the medium of business schools is facilitating the adoption of new organizational forms centered around models such as "heterarchy" (Hedlund, 1986), "hypertext" (Nonaka & Takeuchi, 1995), and "the transnational solution" (Bartlett & Ghoshal, 1989). These are among the more influential examples, and it is interesting to note that they emanate from three different cultural zones—Sweden, Japan, and the United States, respectively. Yet the claims made for the validity of these new models are that they are adapted to emerging worldwide material conditions. That is, they meet the economic requirements of managing global value chains and promoting innovation better than previous models.

Implications for Organization Cross-Nationally

It follows from the previous discussion that one cannot generalize about the nature and trend of organization around the world without locating the particular case in its context (Cheng, 1989, 1994). That context will be international or local to varying degrees. It will expose organizations differentially to the pressures of competition and technological change. The identity of the people living and working in the location may be strongly attached to, and defined by, local culture or it may be more multicultural in nature.

What one can do is to examine the features of organization that appear responsive to global material trends, those that appear to reflect a globalization of ideas, and those that are more susceptible to high context local influences. This exercise will clearly demonstrate the need for a multilevel and multidimensional approach to the subject.

There are a number of identifiable organizational responses among companies to global economic and technological forces (Steger, 1998; Ghoshal & Bartlett, 1998). Many companies are shifting their preferred mode of organization toward forms of horizontal coordination such as teams, networks, and partnerships. Under the pressure of competition and rapid technological advance, innovations are being introduced simultaneously rather than sequentially, so as to ensure a return on R&D given shortening product life cycles. This is encouraging the use of integrated cross-specialist teams within firms and the formation of technological partnerships between firms. In order to reduce costs and to source where economically most advantageous, companies are dis-aggregating their value chains in order to place supplies and production in the most favorable locations. They may retain the ownership and management of such activities, or they may out-source them. Similarly, in order to increase market penetration through cultivation of local markets, companies are increasingly entering into distribution arrangements with local partners, sometimes before making a commitment to production. The complexity of value chains is increased as firms expand their product and geographical scope, often through merger and acquisition. These moves are usually motivated by considerations of augmenting or defending market power under intense global competition, and are moving many industries toward oligopolistic global industry structures.

The effect of these changes is to soften both the internal and external boundaries of the firms concerned. The dis-aggregation of value chains moves companies toward a network mode of organization (Nohria & Eccles, 1992), and the use of advanced information and communication technologies permits the development of "virtual" organization (Hedberg et al., 1997). External boundaries are blurred with the increasing recourse to strategic alliances and strategic partnerships with suppliers. In industries such as automobiles, pharmaceuticals, and telecommunications, alliances have become the nodal points of extensive international networks. The softening of internal organizational boundaries, plus the increasing need to extend discretion and initiative to local units which are close to the situation and staffed by trained people, encourages a shift from relying on hierarchical control and direction toward "heterarchy" (Hedlund, 1986). This approach encourages local flexible modes of direct coordination and control through joint aims and targets agreed by the people concerned, rather than relying on directions from headquarters. There is also a corresponding shift from individual decision making to group decision processes. These trends do not, however, imply an abdication of top management direction but rather a move toward less direct and more strategic control via the deployment of capital, the making of key appointments, and the fostering of a trust-based corporate culture among the core group of managers.

At the same time, a globalization of organizational ideas and practices is under way. Calori and De Woot (1994, p. 53) note that some of the European company directors they interviewed perceived a narrowing of the gap between American, European, and Japanese management philosophies and practices, "especially in multinational corporations which are in direct contact with the three continents." A study of British firms acquired by companies with a range of home-base nationalities (American, British, French, German, and Japanese) found that certain changes were introduced by the acquirers in the belief that they represented good practice regardless of their nationality. These included more attention to strategy and company image, more training, moves toward performance-related reward systems, more open communication, team-based R&D, greater use of automation and IT, more cost control, a greater emphasis on quality, and more use of teams (Child et al., 2000). Lu and Björkman (1997) found among joint ventures between Chinese and TNC partners, that the latter endeavored to introduce standard international HRM practices into the local context, especially for selection, training, and rewards. Child and Yan (1998) found that the transnational status of foreign partners was a more consistent and powerful predictor of the strategies and practices adopted by their joint ventures in China than was the national origin of those partners. The transfer of organizational practices in these ways into new national settings reflects the power of TNC organizational cultures. Although the practices may originate in response to perceived exigencies of the international economic and technological context, once they become standardized, they are essentially artifacts of corporate cultures and ideational in nature.

There is evidence, then, to support the view that globalization, both of material forces and of ideas and practices, is shaping key parameters of organization across different countries. The principal agent of this process is the TNC. Not only are TNCs introducing organizational standardization across national borders, they are themselves innovating organizational forms in the search for ways to manage transnational operations effectively. The search for a "transnational solution" (Bartlett & Ghoshal, 1989) leads directly to the thesis of convergence among TNCs, namely that "leading corporations should gradually be losing their national characters and converging in their fundamental strategies and operations" (Pauly & Reich, 1997). The argument that transnational scope calls for similar novel organizational adjustments is based on the premise that "the same challenges faced all managers everywhere as the world's increasingly linked economies sped toward the twenty-first century" (Bartlett & Ghoshal, 1989, p. x). Or, as Ohmae has stated (1990, p. 94), "Country of origin does not matter. Location of headquarters does not matter. The products for which you are responsible and the company you serve have become denationalized."

The model for the "denationalized" TNC has increasingly become that purveyed in the large U.S. and international business schools from which these companies draw their career managers, and at which their senior executives attend programs on the latest thinking. An important component of the model is a long-term strategic orientation and, as indicated by Mintzberg's (1994) critique, one that has been predicated on strategic planning. Consistent with their size and with business school precepts, TNCs are expected to rely heavily on contractual arrangements and on a high level of internal formalization. Both contracts and formal systems are likely to be of a standardized nature, since TNCs seeking to benefit from global products or technologies, and having considerable ownership-specific advantages, are more likely to derive benefits from this policy than are non-TNCs.

Formalization and standardization of structures and systems are not, however, considered to be sufficient foundations by TNCs for effective cross-national management (Doz & Prahalad, 1993). They also seek to achieve consistency of behavior and process through the development of high-quality competencies among key personnel who are loyal to the corporate culture. TNCs therefore attach considerable importance to training, especially managerial training. Their support for business schools and investment in corporate "universities" stems largely from a belief that they must develop a core of highly professional executives, sharing a similar corporate culture and managerial approach, in order to maintain sufficient integration and control across their worldwide operations. These managers are likely to be deployed by TNCs into the key positions within affiliates and joint ventures in order to ensure integration with corporate policies and procedures (Edstrom & Galbraith, 1977).

While the process of internationalizing organizational practices on the part of TNCs is supported by their corporate cultures, it tends to suppress the influence of national cultures. Nevertheless, many researchers see national culture as continuing to be critically important in the selection of organizational structures and methods (cf. Hofstede, 1991; Hampden-Turner & Trompenaars, 1993). For example, Calori, Lubatkin, and Very (1994) conclude from their research that French companies prefer to exercise formal control of operations rather than informal control through teamwork in their UK acquisitions; the latter approach characterized American acquirers. Their view is that firms are liable to carry their home practices with them as they move into foreign markets. They are in this sense agents for the migration of culturally defined organizational practices. Others, like the contributors to Whitley (1992b), stress the importance of national or regional institutions and infrastructures in influencing the extent to which cross-border acquisitions actually become consolidated within the organizational systems of the foreign acquirers. The question therefore arises as to how and where, within an overall trend toward globalization, national cultures and institutions will continue to shape organizational forms and behavior.

National differences in *cultural* values are most likely to influence matters such as personal style, desired rewards, how people relate with others, and the degree of contextual structuring they seek. Contiguous organizational practices include decision making, reward systems, the conduct of meetings, communication, trust, and the structuring of jobs. These are the micro-level aspects of organization and organizational behavior: the level of individuals and their immediate working context. This is the organizational level where the impact of national cultures is most apparent and where there can be a practical managerial reaction to it.

The cultural values held even by individuals or small groups of people can, however, have a significant impact on a macro-organizational feature such as a company's organization, if those people happen to be chief executives or directors of boards. This validly points to the need to give due weight to cultural preferences in terms of the position power that people may have to put them into effect. It does not, however, gainsay the previous conclusion that companies facing global competition and innovation may today be experiencing strengthening pressures to adapt their modes of organization away from culturally preferred approaches. The result can be considerable tension between, for example, the traditional management of family entrepreneurs and that advocated by their successors eager for international expansion (Ng, 1996).

By contrast, national differences of an *institutional* nature can impact upon both micro and macro aspects of organization. A micro-level example is the way that national systems of education and training (competence formation) affect the degree of available organizational choice in the design of jobs and allocation of responsibilities, as Sorge and Warner (1986) noted from comparisons of Germany and the UK. An example at the macro level concerns the different national regulatory systems of company law and corporate reporting. These bear upon arrangements for corporate governance, including the structuring of stakeholder rights to participate in information and policy making (Hawley & Williams, 1996). In many developing countries, for example, government regulations mandate a sharing of corporate governance between foreign investing and local firms in the form of equity joint ventures.

Whitley's (1992a, 1992b) analyses of Asian and European business systems identify ways in which the sophistication of intermediary institutions in different countries has a bearing on the organization of firms in terms of their sources of financing (ownership), modes of control, and internal specialization. The nature of a country's intermediary institutions may call for modifications in organizational practice because they impact on the availability of resources, such as working capital and specialist support services. If these are absent or inadequately provided within a country's institutional framework, then a company will have to modify its organization to provide these internally or secure them elsewhere. Similarly, the skills of available managers, technicians, and employees will impinge on the internal structuring of work. These constraints may be quite significant for local firms, but rather less so for large TNCs. The latter are usually able to rectify resource or skill deficiencies themselves without any necessary disturbance to their preferred modes of internal organization. The quality of the institutional infrastructure in a particular country is thus likely to have a differential influence on organization, depending on the ability of a company to draw upon compensating resources from elsewhere.

Other institutions, however, possess a mandatory power over the organizations located within national or, as with the European Union, regional boundaries. Such institutions are usually governmental, or have the backing of law and, in some cases, organized public opinion. They may enforce certain organizational arrangements through the power of law, or via their articulation of strong social values. The latter is becoming increasingly the case with protection of the physical environment and the propagation of local community interests. These policies can come into conflict with those articulated by international companies in the name of globalization, and this typically pitches the TNC and agencies of the nation-state against each other. The solutions that are negotiated will ultimately depend on the bargaining power of the respective parties and there is hence an element of indeterminacy here. Insofar as the agencies prevail, they can bring national criteria to bear on the governance of organizations and the policies they can legitimately pursue.

Theorizing about organization cross-nationally therefore cannot avoid taking specific contexts into account.[8] Every organization is located differently with respect to global and local national forces, and their material or ideational foundations. An organization's global disposition, in terms of sector, scale, spread, and external networks establishes a set of contingencies that bear upon which structures and systems it can effectively adopt to assist the fundamental processes of decision-making control, coordination, reward, and learning. These contingencies derive primarily from competitive pressures that today increasingly impinge on public bodies such as government departments, hospitals, and universities in terms of comparative performance ratings, as well as on business companies. An organization's national location at the same time brings into play institutional contingencies, not all of which TNCs can offset through their bargaining weapon of foreign direct investment (Ferner & Quintanilla, 1998).

The cross-national context of organizations may be mapped in terms of the distinctions just made between (1) the global and local levels at which (2) material and ideational forces operate. Figure 2 does this with examples for each quadrant. While this is a static analysis, not accounting for organizational or contextual evolution, it does serve to clarify some of the key contextual configurations that impact on a given organization. In so doing, it also raises a number of pertinent questions. For example, do organizational decision makers regard global material and ideational forces with the same sense of urgency and/or as requiring the same kind of action vis-à-vis the external constituents who are involved? Is their

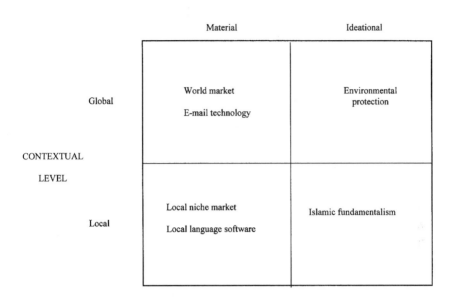

Figure 2.   Cross-National Organization Context

response therefore similar or different? When organizations are under different pressures from both global and local considerations, which set of forces will prevail and on what features of organization will they bear? Answers to questions such as these may contribute to theoretical advance because they direct our attention toward understanding how material and ideational systems at both global and local levels interact in their effect on organizations.[9]

The distinctions made in Figure 2 are essentially comparative between countries; they are consistent with the conventional cross-national approach. However, they are also relevant to research on cross-national organizational forms. Bartlett and Ghoshal (1989) identified four types of cross-border firm: the international, multinational (multi-domestic), global, and transnational. It may be hypothesized that when designing their organizations, global, and to a lesser extent international, companies will need to pay attention primarily to factors identified by low context theories since they are situated primarily in the global/material quadrant of Figure 2. By contrast, multi-domestic companies will find the high context approach, and research informing it, most relevant. For research to be relevant to transnational firms, it will need to combine low and high context approaches, so that all the quadrants of Figure 2 apply more or less equally to the transnational case. By encompassing low and high context perspectives, global and local levels,

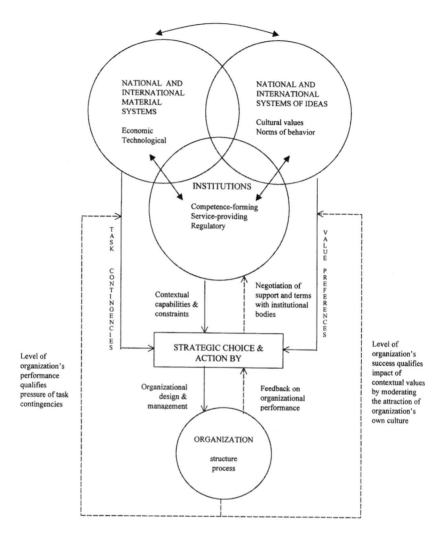

Figure 3.   An Evolutionary Framework for
Cross-National Organizational Analysis

material and ideational forces, this theoretical mapping advances our capability *both* to locate organizations in their cross-national context *and* to understand the conditions under which one form of cross-national organization may be preferred to another.

A Framework

Figure 3 brings together the material, ideational, and institutional components of organizational context with a representation of the ways, just discussed, that these have relevance for organization. There are multiple contextual domains with multiple channels of influence on organization. These reflect the theoretical insights provided by the perspectives considered earlier. In working through Figure 3, it is important to keep in mind that specific cases will vary in how they are situated with respect to the key components of the framework. These include the local and international context, and the nature of strategic choice exercised by organizational leaders.

Figure 3 depicts material and ideational systems as impacting on organization both directly as well as through the medium of institutions. Material systems have a direct impact through the economic and technological contingencies they present for the ways in which companies and other bodies can organize themselves to accomplish their tasks. They establish task contingencies for those designing and managing organization (Donaldson, 1996). Systems of ideas have a direct impact on organizations through the values and normative precepts they express.

However, the members of a company or other unit, especially those exercising its managerial functions, perform an interpretative role with respect to the organizational implications posed by these material and ideational inputs. The capabilities, services, and constraints arising from communal, national, and international institutions, provide the indirect route whereby material and ideational systems have a potential influence on organization. These inputs from institutions are also subject to interpretation by organizational members. Their interpretations, and the actions that organizational members consequently decide to take, inject an element of strategic choice into the model which is consistent with the role accorded to social action in Weberian analysis. In other words, organizational arrangements do not simply reflect the impact of external material or ideational forces, but are also the product of conscious, intentional action allows us to incorporate strategic choice into the analysis (Child, 1997). The framework permits us to take into account the possibility that both the contextual location of an organization and the intentionality and understanding of its actors will have a bearing on its structure, processes, and policies.

Strategic choice is also informed by the feedback of information on the performance of an organizational unit. Organizational performance is seen both as a trigger for managers to attempt to negotiate with institutional bodies, and as a factor that can moderate the direct influence of material and ideational systems. In the latter case, the level of performance achieved may qualify the pressures on organization coming from material and ideational systems respectively. If, say, a company is performing well, this should afford it some "slack" in terms of having to respond immediately and in a predetermined way to task contingencies deriving from competitive economic and technological conditions. Success may therefore enable it to preserve certain preferred national modes of organizing, even if there are strong international conventions. Similarly, if a company is performing well and reflects this in its terms of employment, it may thereby be able to develop a commitment among its members to its own culture that qualifies the impact of national cultural norms. I have seen this take place in Sino-foreign joint ventures, where the foreign partner is an TNC seeking to introduce its own corporate culture. The feeling that the joint venture offers them a good long-term future makes local staff much more willing to accept the foreign partner's organizational cultured practices.

Thus the framework in Figure 3 does not depict a simple contextual determinism. Those having a significant say on the framing of organizational structures and processes are not cast in a purely reactive role vis-à-vis the context. In the light of their own ideas and preferences on organization, and informed by information concerning the performance of the units they manage, such leaders may endeavour to negotiate with external institutional bodies over the terms under which they are regulated, the opportunities they are offered, and the support they are afforded. As Peng (2000) concludes from his comparative studies of transition economies, the dynamic interaction between institutions and firms allows for strategic choices to be made, some of them concerning organization and employment, and the quality of such choices has important implications for future performance. These strategic choices include possibilities for realigning a firm's external position in regard to, say, market power, such as forming alliances with foreign firms. Alliances can themselves act as channels for the introduction of new organizational practices.

Just as the Weberian analysis on which I have drawn was concerned to account for social development and evolution, so the contribution of the framework in Figure 3 is not confined to the comparative-static type of research that has formed the mainstay of cross-national organizational research. The multiple feedback loops and dynamic relations it depicts, both within context and between context and organization, in fact identify conditions for both organizational and contextual evolution. Redding notes in his commentary how, for example, the success of business organizations operating within democratic systems in delivering "societal purposes with wide legitimacy" has undoubtedly reinforced democratic capitalism as a set of ideals and the institutions supporting it. It is inevitable that institutions are judged and modified according to the social performance of the organizations they are intended to support and regulate; not just the other way round. In turn, the effectiveness of institutions impacts on the legitimacy of the values they express. Through the competencies educational systems develop and the regulatory frameworks set out by national and supranational legal systems, institutions also condition the application and impact of economic and technological forces.[10] The emergence of giant global firms and business groups, having the economic and technological clout to negotiate directly with national and regional institutions, has shortened and intensified these reciprocal linkages between global systems, national and supranational institutions, and the business firm.

QUESTIONS OF METHODOLOGY: RESEARCH DESIGNS AND OPERATIONAL EQUIVALENCE

Two important methodological questions for cross-national organizational research arise from the theoretical considerations raised in this essay. First, which research designs facilitate an application of the integrative and dynamic framework I have advocated? Second, can ways be found to underpin further the synthesis of different theories by increasing conceptual consistency between them?

Research Design

As Mohr (1982) points out, there is a broad choice between variance and process research designs. Variance designs are oriented toward the discovery and prediction of variance in phenomena of theoretical interest. Process designs are oriented toward the discovery of the configurations and processes that underlie patterns of association or change. This distinction can be applied to the study of organization cross-nationally, bearing in mind the need for contextual sensitivity and theoretical pluralism previously emphasized.

The tradition of comparing national similarities and differences in organization adopts a variance approach. This now needs to progress beyond two serious limitations. One is that the research conducted within this tradition has often examined organizational characteristics only indirectly. Although more economical for a given sample size, the use of either standardized closed-ended scales, or of databases constructed for other purposes, is not a substitute for on-the-spot investigation that is sensitive to both interpretative and objective definitions of the subject matter. A more comprehensive examination of organizational variables will be required to take into account the range of propositions deriving from the multiperspective theoretical approach that this essay has claimed is desirable.

Second, research designs will need to take a more comprehensive view of context in order to locate units of study more precisely in relation to the factors that potentially impact on their organization. Much previous variance research failed to take account of the configuration of contextual factors within each country, preferring instead to limit itself to selected economic, cultural, or institutional factors. Without an adequate theory of how these factors might themselves interrelate, it has been tempting to ascribe the organizational variance not predicted by the selected variables to "noise" ascribed in a nontheorized manner to other ill-defined variables. These were treated merely as theoretically mysterious residuals. Thus what economic and technological contingencies failed to predict was often conveniently ascribed to "culture" without any theoretical justification

(Child, 1981). Investigations informed by cultural theory have normally taken lit-tle or no account of the material environment as expressed, for example, in terms of indicators of economic development. There was little sense of the context being a system of phenomena that, while each impacting on organization, are at the same time themselves in dynamic interaction.

In light of these considerations, future variance research will need to employ quite elaborate research designs that fulfill several conditions. There should be a more comprehensive theorization of both independent and dependent variables than has hitherto been typical. The theorization should refer to both low and high context perspectives and be clearly articulated in advance through hypotheses or other means. Guided by such theorization, cases will have to be selected with careful attention to how they are situated vis-à-vis the local and global factors hypothesized to have a potential impact on their organization. Account has to be taken of within-nation as well as of between-nation variance in contextual fea-tures. This specificity in respect of context is also commended by Earley and Singh (1995) in terms of what they call "the hybrid approach, which combines a comprehensive overview of the systems in which firms operate with examinations of the specific inner working of the systems themselves" (p. 337). With large-scale databases, these contextual variables could be examined post-sam-pling through multivariate analyses. In practice, there are very few databases that have been constructed with cross-national comparisons in mind, the International Organization Observatory being an exception (Clark, 1996).

A process approach to research is oriented toward change and development (Bhagat & Kedia, 1996). As such, it is more consistent with the evolutionary framework set out in Figure 3. It is concerned with the potential dynamics over time between material and ideational forces, and low and high context factors, and how these relate to organizational structure and process. It would therefore call for longitudinal research designs or at least ones that permitted insight into the impact of different forces on ongoing developments such as the process and rationales of decision making about organization. Decisions made about the man-ner and mode of company internationalization would provide a very suitable focus for such research.

Situations in which organizational units transact and interact closely across organizational boundaries would also permit an examination of dynamics of cross-national accommodation with reference to a range of potential contextual influences. Cases of foreign direct investment by companies are potentially well-suited to meet this criterion: such as greenfield investment in a new national environment, and acquisitions, mergers, and alliances between companies of dif-ferent nationality. Strategic alliances in which partners of two different nationali-ties share investment and control perhaps provides the most interesting case, because in principle it establishes a situation in which their economic rationalities and cultural preferences can have equal play within the institutional setting(s) in question.

Conceptual Consistency and Operational Equivalence

Moves toward theoretical synthesis are handicapped by a lack of conceptual consistency. This takes two forms. The same concept, such as control, is defined in a variety of different ways. Second, different concepts are also employed to refer to empirically similar phenomena. A further methodological challenge encountered in studying organizations cross-nationally is therefore to find ways of underpinning the synthesis of different theories by increasing the consistency and operational equivalence of their basic concepts.

We rely upon assumptions of conceptual consistency in order to undertake research that is comparative across cases and time. However, some students of culture maintain that conceptual terminology is particularly sensitive to cultural norms and values, and that the standardized operational dimensions employed are therefore highly vulnerable to differential interpretation in the different countries between which comparisons are attempted (Fang, 1998). Taken to their logical conclusion, the interpretive challenges posed by the nuances of indigenous culture and linguistic meanings cast doubt on our ability to engage in cross-national organizational studies at all.

This presents a significant difficulty in the way of achieving conceptual and methodological equivalence across cultural and linguistic borders. Can concepts such as control and relationship that are basic to organizational studies be assumed to have an equivalent social interpretation in different countries? American managers may, for instance, tend to think of "control" in terms of cybernetic regulation, whereas in some other societies it may be more commonly understood as the ability to command obedience. If this is the case, can we make valid cross-national comparisons through employing the same concept of control? Can we get the cross-national study of organization beyond the starting block?

The subject of relationship should provide a useful test of whether we can find a constructive way out of this dilemma. It is both central to organization as the coordination of collective activity, and it is an inherent aspect of social life that is widely seen to be culturally sensitive. Cultural dimensions prominent in the literature, such as such as individualism-collectivism, power-distance, and universalism-particularism, all concern relationships between people. Organized activity is by definition built upon relationship, and this is one of the concepts that those who doubt the possibility of operational equivalence between different cultures and linguistic systems single out for attention (e.g., Yang, 1998.)

Key aspects of organizational relationships include authority, interpersonal ties, and trust. These can be examined to see whether the concepts available for the study of each aspect can admit of sufficient equivalence across national settings to provide a valid basis for cross-national comparison. The approach I shall recommend is to try to go beyond the inconsistency imposed by different formal definitions of the concepts and to look instead for their constituent categories or dimensions. The intention is to arrive at a multidimensional operationalization of

the concepts that not only takes into account those aspects supposed to be prominent within a given culture but also permits an exploration of the possible overlap
and similarities between dimensions emphasized by different cultures. The question is whether this procedure offers the prospect of a common operational basis
for making comparisons within the space denoted by each concept. If it does, even
within this culturally sensitive area of organizational research, we can probably be
confident that it is possible to improve the cross-national operational equivalence
of other organizationally relevant concepts.

Authority

A detailed study of the changes in managerial authority in China under the economic reform led to the conclusion that its analysis was helpfully informed by
existing Western-derived concepts (Child, 1994). Despite China's marked cultural and sociopolitical contrasts to most other countries, the historical development of its industrial governance could be mapped in large measure by Weber's
distinction between the charismatic, traditional, and legal-rational foundations for
authority (Weber, 1964). Weber's approach allows one to start unpacking the constituent components of authority systems and to compare them in terms of the
degree to which they exhibit each component. This involves moving from his
"ideal type" analysis to a dimensional scheme whereby authority systems can be
compared across cases and through time in terms of the empirical configuration of
the elements identified by the ideal types.

The same Weberian authority categories continue to be useful for distinguishing the patterns of leadership found among Chinese firms today. Examples of
charismatic leadership can be found even within state-owned enterprises, and
indeed they are becoming more common as initiative is increasingly devolved to
these firms (Nolan & Wang, 1997). The traditional model of authority is found
among most private Chinese firms. Larger Chinese companies have incorporated
elements of legal-rational authority, especially when they have become listed on
stock exchanges and thereby subject to international financial and trading codes.
The keen interest in corporate governance within China and the sharp criticisms
of "crony capitalism" in East Asian economies bear the promise of a shift in the
direction of greater legal-rational authority. Weber's concepts therefore appear to
have high equivalence and utility across different societies. Equally, Etzioni's
(1961) distinction between the normative and instrumental bases for compliance
with authority appears validly to identify and map the main parameters involved
in the large-scale shifts between moral and material-based motivational policies
in Chinese organizations after 1949 (Child, 1995).

It is true that the philosophical evaluation people attach to authority is unlikely
to be the same in, say, the United States and in China. In the United States authority tends to be seen as inimical to individual freedom and fulfillment, and is consequently more or less regarded as an unfortunate necessity for achieving socially

desired ends through organized activity. In China such has been the pervasive influence of Confucian thinking at least since the Song Dynasty, that many people have come to accept authority virtually as an end in itself—certainly as a social good. As a result of these differences in evaluation and interpretation, the process of exercising authority, and the quality of interpersonal relationships through which it flows, tends to be different between the two countries.

The issue, however, is whether we can find a common basis on which to compare the nature of authority of, say, American, Chinese organizations, or those of other nationalities. For it is such comparison that would inform our understanding of the role that might be played, vis-à-vis other potential influences, by the different philosophical views on authority prevailing in the countries' respective cultures. Our argument is that existing conceptual frameworks like those mentioned can provide the methodological basis on which we can distinguish the different types of authority that are present in particular organizations and the forms of legitimacy on which they rest. The key step is to uncover their constituent dimensions and then to treat these as indicators for the purpose of comparison.

Interpersonal Ties

A reliance on implicit and highly personalized relationships is often taken to be a quintessential attribute of Oriental organizational behavior and business transacting, in contrast to that found in "the West." Chinese communities have evolved their own term for such relationships and the norms of reciprocity that apply to them—*guanxi*. So, however, have other communities with comparable relational systems such as Brazil—with its *jeitinho* (Rodrigues, 1996), Hungary—with its *uram batyam* (Child & Markoczy, 1993), and Britain—with its *the old boy network*. There are a variety of concepts here, but are they really substantively different? Would it be meaningful to try to consolidate them?

Tsui and Farh (1997) argue that Western relational demography and Chinese *quanxi* are related but distinct concepts, each identifying a range of interpersonal commonalities or ties that may influence the attitudes and behavior of organizational members toward each other. They maintain that the study of relationship and its impact on organization would be enriched by integrating the ideas behind the concepts. These authors make a convincing case for potential operational equivalence between Chinese and Western concepts of interpersonal ties, and their concern is to demonstrate this by uncovering the dimensions that lie behind the concepts.

This argument can be taken a stage further. Many of the bases of *guanxi* thought to be distinctively Chinese have actually applied in Western countries as well, especially the European ones that like China have largely continuous social traditions deriving from status-oriented social systems. We have to bear in mind how Europe contrasts in this respect with the United States, which has been a more open society that was shaped *de novo* around notions of democratic rights and in which formalized legal-rational criteria play a major part in holding the society together (Moore, 1966). Kin, family class background, and the "old boy network" have, for example, been very significant in the UK in the allocation and purchase of favors and preferential appointments. While such practices were most evident among the upper reaches of society in respect of public appointments, family connections were also influential in recruitment to lower-level industrial jobs. Reforms had to be introduced in the mid-nineteenth century to curb the influence of these interpersonal ties in the public sector, because the abuses and inefficiencies they encouraged became increasingly inconsistent with the demands of governing and defending a modern industrial society (Derry, 1968; Chapman, 1980; David, 1997). That these interpersonal ties have today lost much of their former impact in the UK and other European countries suggests that the economic and technological conditions which industrializing Asian countries are now coming to experience may carry more consequences for the nature of organizational relationships than does culture. Indeed, Guthrie's (1998) careful study indicates that specific *guanxi* practices based on special favors are of declining significance in China, as that country undergoes economic transition toward a rational-legal market system. *Guanxi* in the more general sense of establishing good business relations continues to be a necessary part of effecting and managing transactions, much as in any market economy.[11]

Thus *guanxi* probably has a wider international conceptual applicability than some cultural theorists have admitted. The concept does not describe behaviors and their normative underpinnings that are culturally peculiar to China. Its constituent dimensions can usefully be combined with those deriving from Western relational demography to provide a stronger operationalization of the concept "relationship" for cross-national comparative purposes.

Trust

The level of trust is intrinsic to the quality of relationships. Again, there are many who would argue that the nature of trust varies significantly between different cultural regions of the world. However, it is far less certain that we require a different concept to capture trust in Asia and the West, or even that we require a different theory to explain it.

Despite the considerable impact of Fukuyama's book (1995), the study of trust in social science did not necessarily start with Asian thinking. Alan Fox back in 1974 published a path-breaking treatise on *Beyond Contract: Work, Power and Trust Relations* in which trust is "seen as a key factor in organizational wellbeing" (p. 13). Fox began to develop our understanding of how trust could have different foundations, of which he distinguished two. First, "personalized trust" which is based on individual personal characteristics. Second, "institutionalized trust" in which the roles, rules, and relations that people impose on others indicate whether or not the latter are trusted. Thus, if a person is given little autonomy in an organization, this indicates that he or she is not trusted.

The concept of trust in the Western literature seems to be settling around the stabilization of the expectations that people have of others under conditions of dependence (Lane & Backmann, 1998). This means that the basis for trust lies in the conditions for such stabilization. The following are among those that have been identified: (1) reciprocal obligation based on contracts, the offering of hostages, or social conventions; (2) knowledge of the other party giving rise to a sense of predictability about their intentions and conduct; and (3) personal identification or emotional bonding (Lewicki & Bunker, 1996). When it is unpacked in this way and moved closer to its operational dimensions, the concept of trust appears to be sufficiently comprehensive to be applied validly to non-Western relationships and to capture much of the meaning behind them. The bases for trust contained within the concept can be related to the various forms of institutional or social (e.g., *guanxi*-like) support for it.

With considerations such as these in mind, I have previously concluded that that the main challenge to existing, Western, organizational theory posed by the unique situation of China, the major non-Western nation, is not one of further conceptual development (Child, 1994). It lies, rather, in the need to configure into relevant social gestalts the features of different national situations that can be captured by our existing concepts. This requires the development of operational measures that can combine key elements from those concepts and/or include items that reflect how the concepts apply in different societies. In effect, this was how the Aston Program proceeded in the 1960s toward a comprehensive basis for comparing organizational structures. Members of the Aston team drew comparative dimensions from previous conceptualizations by writers such as Weber, Fayol, Blau, and Thompson. The operationalization of these dimensions into a single comprehensive inventory enabled a range of distinct organizational configurations to be identified, and also permitted a more precise exploration of the relationships between organizational variables and their predictors (Pugh et al., 1969). In ways such as this, the unpacking of concepts to uncover a wider range of comparative dimensions amenable to operational measurement provides a necessary complement to the more integrated theoretical approach and more comprehensive research designs that this essay has advocated.

Some cross-cultural psychologists have also suggested a similar path of operational development. Cheung and colleagues (1996) in noting various methods that have been used to adapt psychological tests to other cultural milieux, comment that for comparative purposes "the construction of an inventory that includes the major culture-specific personality domains in addition to the culture-comparable (etic) personality constructs may be called for" (p. 182). This is recommending the identification of both emic and etic dimensions and their reconfiguration into a new inventory. Redding in his commentary on this essay cites Smith and colleagues (1989) as another example of an attempt to reconfigure and reintegrate operational measures along the lines advocated here; in this case measures of leadership style. The authors' intention was to be able to distinguish more adequately between the global characteristics of leadership style and the specific behaviors which are consistent with the cultural norms of different national settings, using items of greater precision and scope than those previously employed in comparative leadership research.

* * *

This essay has focused on fundamental questions that the study of organization cross-nationally must address if it is to progress. One is whether we can find an analytical framework that constructively synthesizes the present partial and sometimes narrow perspectives on the subject. A framework has been advanced that can incorporate the insights offered by the different perspectives, and that directs attention toward potential interaction between them. The framework avoids an uncritical acceptance of the primacy of any one perspective, together with its methodological or paradigmatic limitations. It carries a number of implications for the design of future research in this field of study.

Another question has been whether we can complement this theoretical synthesis through achieving greater conceptual consistency across theoretical boundaries via moving toward operational equivalence. I have suggested that this is possible and that it lies in the deconstruction of distinct, yet overlapping, concepts into their underlying dimensions. This battery of dimensions when applied to a range of different cross-national cases should then permit conceptual reconfiguration on an internally consistent basis. This procedure is not only a methodological complement to greater theoretical synthesis, but it is actually a necessary condition for effective comparative work to be undertaken at all.

ACKNOWLEDGMENT

The author is grateful for comments made on a previous draft of this paper by Nicole Biggart, Andrew Brown, Joseph Cheng, Leanne Chung, Roberto Duarte, Yuan Lu, Sek Hong Ng, Suzana Rodrigues, and Yanni Yan.

NOTES

1. International corporations were conventionally defined as those involved in business in two or more countries, but normally retaining a strong home-nation identity (Daniels & Radebaugh, 1992). The label "transnational corporation" (TNC), however, denotes a weakening of national corporate identity, since it refers to companies that locate significant parts of their value chains in at least two countries and often many more, rather than simply doing business internationally (cf. Dicken, 1998, Ghoshal & Bartlett, 1998).

2. This vivid terminology was proposed by Edward T. Hall (1976) as a way of distinguishing different cultural orientations. It was also employed by the Halls (1990) for distinguishing linguistic and other cultural differences that bear upon the nature of communication. For Hall, high context cul-

tures are those in which people are deeply involved with and sensitive to each other, sharing many meanings at a tacit and nonverbal level. I am employing the terminology in a broader, though somewhat comparable, sense to distinguish theoretical perspectives such that high context perspectives are those that are sensitive to national contexts including specificities of language and meaning.

3.   To quote Sorge (1982, p. 131): "there is no 'culture-free' context of organization, because even if organizational solutions or contexts are similar, they are always culturally constructed and very imperfectly interpreted as the reaction to a given constraint."

4.   More recently, Boisot (1995) has added a third dimension: the extent to which information is concrete and situation specific rather than abstract and situation general. This third dimension is highly relevant for the transfer of organizational knowledge and practice across nations, where it is often not the specific concrete practices that can be successfully transferred but rather the more abstract principles informing them. These principles then require recontextualization, that is, applied as new specific concrete practices that suit the new social context.

5.   Weber was himself not entirely consistent in his analysis of the two forces, particularly with respect to their relative influence on the development of modern capitalism and its organizational forms. For present purposes, I am adopting a general rather than a nuanced interpretation of Weber's analysis. While it does not do justice to the subtlety of his work, it is hopefully adequate enough to suggest a progressive direction for the cross-national study of organization.

6.   Schluchter (1981, p. 25) quotes the following passage of Weber's that "in the eyes of many interpreters has become a key to his work: 'Interests (material and ideal) not ideas directly determine man's action. But the world views, which were created by ideas, have very often acted as the switches that channeled the dynamics of the interests'."

7.   Biggart (1997, p. 5) recommends the "Weberian institutional perspective" for the comparative study of Western and non-Western economic organization because it is comprehensive, has no inherent Western bias, and therefore provides a potentially integrative theoretical platform: "[Weberian] institutional theory...accounts well for both ideal and material factors, may be used to explain both micro- and macro-level patterns of organization, may allow for the agency of actors, readily allows comparison, and has no inherent Western bias."

8.   Cheng (1989) identifies six potential advances that may arise from the application of a contextual approach: (1) it aims at explanation and prediction rather than just comparative description; (2) it focuses on an organizational phenomenon as the dependent variable, (3) by focusing on the organization rather than the nation or culture as the primary object of investigation, the contextual approach helps to shift attention from the independent to the dependent variable; (4) in substituting variables for country names, the contextual approach contributes to analytical clarity; (5) through this deconstruction of vague concepts like "nation" or "country," it also permits the cultural perspective to be broadened by taking institutional and economic factors into account; (6) it should contribute to the incorporation of societal context into organizational models. Cheng's argument is highly consistent with that advanced in the present essay.

9.   The author is grateful to Joseph Cheng for suggesting the use of the 2x2 matrix in Figure 2 and the questions that stem from it. The distinction between global and local levels is, of course, a gross oversimplification which is used here only for the purpose of making analytical distinctions. The term "local" is, for instance, insufficiently precise and fails to distinguish between region and nation-state. The region may be a more significant entity for organizations in some parts of the world than the nation-state, the phenomenon of Islamic fundamentalism being an example.

10.   The insertion of return arrows from institutions to material systems and systems of ideas in Figure 3 is intended to convey this reciprocal process.

11.   This case further demonstrates that the changing role of personal relationships in the history of both public and private organizations cannot be adequately understood by reference to national culture alone. Rather, it is necessary to take account of interactions between the material forces of industrial development and national cultures, along the lines suggested by Weberian theory.

REFERENCES

Adams, J. S. (1965). Injustice in social exchange. In L. Berkowitz (Ed.), *Advances in experimental social psychology*. New York: Academic Press.

Amable, B., Barré, R., & Boyer, R. (1997). *Les systemes d'innovation a l'ere de la globalisation*. Paris: Economica.

Applegate, L. M. (1995). *Designing and managing the information age organization*. Boston, MA: Harvard Business School Note # 9-196-003.

Austria, C. (1998). Management theory: Chinese practice. *Chief Executive Asia*, www.chief-exec.asiansources.com/ASIA/ISSUES/A97MYII1.HTM.

Bartlett, C. A., & Ghoshal, S. (1989). *Managing across borders: The transnational solution*. Boston: Harvard Business School Press.

Bendix, R. (1956). *Work and authority in industry*. Berkeley, CA: University of California Press.

Bhagat, R. S., & Kedia, B. L. (1996). Reassessing the elephant: Directions for future research. In B. J. Punnett & O. Shenkar (Eds.), *Handbook for international management research*. Cambridge, MA: Blackwell.

Biggart, N. W. (1997). Explaining Asian economic organization: Toward a Weberian institutional perspective. In M. Orru, N. W. Biggart, & G. G. Hamilton (Eds.), *The economic organization of East Asian capitalism* (pp. 3-32). Thousand Oaks, CA: Sage.

Biggart, N. W., & Guillén, M. F. (1999). Developing difference: social organization and the rise of the auto industries of South Korea, Taiwan, Spain and Argentina. *American Sociological Review, 64*, 722-747.

Biggart, N. W., & Hamilton, G. G. (1992). On the limits of a firm-based theory to explain business networks: The western bias of neoclassical economics. In N. Nohria & R. G. Eccles (Eds.), *Networks and organizations* (pp. 471-490). Boston, MA: Harvard Business School Press.

Blauner, R. (1964). *Alienation and freedom*. Chicago: University of Chicago Press.

Boisot, M. (1986). Markets and hierarchies in cultural perspective. *Organization Studies, 7*, 135-158.

Boisot, M. (1995). *Information space: A framework for learning in organizations, institutions and culture*. London: Routledge.

Boisot, M., & Child, J. (1988). The iron law of fiefs: bureaucratic failure and the problem of governance in the Chinese system reforms. *Administrative Science Quarterly, 33*, 507-527.

Boisot. M., & Child, J. (1996). From fiefs to clans: explaining China's emerging economic order. *Administrative Science Quarterly, 41*, 600-628.

Bond, M. H., & Smith, P. B. (1996). Cross-cultural social and organizational psychology. *Annual Review of Psychology, 47*, 205-235.

Buckley, P. J., & Casson, M. (1976). *The future of the multinational enterprise*. London: Macmillan.

Calori, R., & De Woot, P. (1994). *A European management model*. Hemel Hempstead: Prentice-Hall.

Calori, R., Lubatkin, M., & Very P. (1994). Cross-border acquisitions: An international comparison. *Organization Studies, 15*, 361-399.

Chandler, A. D., Jr. (1977). *The visible hand: The managerial revolution in American business*. Cambridge, MA: Harvard University Press.

Chapman, R. A. (1980). *The dynamics of administrative reform*. London: Croom Helm.

Cheng, J. L. C. (1989). Toward a contextual approach to cross-national organization research. *Advances in International Comparative Management, 4*, 3-18.

Cheng, J. L. C. (1994). On the concept of universal knowledge in organizational science: Implications for cross-national research. *Management Science, 40*, 162-168.

Cheung, F. M., Leung, K., Fan, R. M., Song Weizheng, Zhang Jianxin, & Zhang Jianping. (1996). Development of the Chinese personality assessment inventory. *Journal of Cross-Cultural Psychology, 27*, 181-199.

Child, J. (1981). Culture, contingency, and capitalism in the cross-national study of organizations. In B. Staw & L. L. Cummings (Eds.), *Research in organizational behavior* (Vol. 3, pp. 303-356). Greenwich, CT: JAI Press.

Child, J. (1994). *Management in China during the age of reform*. Cambridge: Cambridge University Press.

Child, J. (1995). Changes in the structure and prediction of earnings in Chinese state enterprises during the reform. *International Journal of Human Resource Management, 6*, 1-30.

Child, J. (1997). Strategic choice in the analysis of action, structure, organizations and environment: retrospect and prospect. *Organization Studies, 18*, 43-76.

Child, J., Faulkner, D., & Pitkethly, R. (2000). Foreign direct investment in the UK 1985-1994: The impact on domestic management practice. *Journal of Management Studies, 37*, 141-166.

Child, J., & Loveridge, R. (1990). *Information technology in European services*. Oxford: Blackwell.

Child, J., & Markóczy, L. (1993). Host-country managerial behavior and learning in Chinese and Hungarian joint ventures. *Journal of Management Studies, 30*, 611-631.

Child, J., & Yan, Y. (1998). National and transnational effects in international business: Indications from Sino-foreign joint ventures. *Working Paper no. 1998-006-01*, Chinese Management Centre, University of Hong Kong, December.

Clark, T. (1996). *European human resource management*. Oxford: Blackwell.

Daniels, J. D., & Radebaugh, L. H. (1992). *International business* (6th ed.). Reading, MA: Addison-Wesley.

David, S. (1997). *The homicidal earl: The life of Lord Cardigan*. London: Little, Brown.

Derry, J. W. (1968). *Parliamentary reform*. London: Macmillan.

Dicken, P. (1998). *Global shift: transforming the world economy* (3rd ed.). London: Paul Chapman Publishing.

Donaldson, L. (1996). The normal science of structural contingency theory. In S. R. Clegg, C. Hardy, & W. R. Nord (Eds.), *Handbook of organization studies* (pp. 57-76). London: Sage.

Dore, R. (1999). *Corporate governance and Asian values: The Japanese debate*. T.T. Tsui Annual Lecture in Asia Pacific Business, Hong Kong University, March 3.

Doz, Y., & Prahalad, C. K. (1993). Managing DMNCs: A search for a new paradigm. In S. Ghoshal & E. D. Westney (Eds.), *Organization theory and the multinational corporation* (pp. 24-50). New York: St. Martin's Press.

Drummond, A., Jr. (1997). *Enabling conditions for organizational learning: A study in international business ventures*. Unpublished PhD thesis, University of Cambridge, February.

Earley, P. C., & Singh, H. (1995). International and intercultural management research: What's next? *Academy of Management Journal, 38*, 327-340.

Edstrom, A., & Galbraith, J. R. (1977). Transfer of managers as a coordination and control strategy in multinational organizations. *Administrative Science Quarterly, 22*, 248-263.

Estanislao, J. P. (1999). Keynote address. In I. Yamazawa (Ed.), *Strengthening cooperation among Asian economies in crisis* (pp. 1-7). Tokyo: Institute of Developing Economies and Japan External Trade Organization.

Etzioni, A. (1961). *A comparative analysis of complex organizations*. New York: Free Press.

Fang, T. (1998). *Reflection on Hofstede's 5th dimension: A critique of "Confucian Dynamism."* Paper presented at the Annual Meeting of the Academy of Management, San Diego, August.

Ferner, A., & Quintanilla, J. (1998). Multinationals, national business systems and HRM: The enduring influence of national identity or a process of "Anglo-Saxonization." *International Journal of Human Resource Management, 9*, 710-731.

Fox, A. (1974). *Beyond contract: Work, power and trust relations*. London: Faber and Faber.

Freeman, C. (1988). Introduction. In G. Dosi, C. Freeman, R. Nelson, G. Silverberg, & L. Soete (Eds.), *Technical change and economic theory*. London: Francis Pinter.

Frese, M., Kring, W., Soose, A., & Zempel, J. (1996). Personal initiative at work: Differences between East and West Germany. *Academy of Management Journal, 39*, 37-63.

Fukuyama, F. (1995). *Trust: Social virtues and the creation of prosperity*. New York: Free Press.

Fulk, J., & DeSanctis, G. (1995). Electronic communication and changing organizational forms. *Organization Science, 6,* 337-349.

Gannon, M. J. (1994). *Understanding global cultures: Metaphorical journeys through 17 countries*. Thousand Oaks, CA: Sage.

Gerth, H. H., & Mills, C. W. (Eds.) (1946). *From Max Weber: essays in sociology*. New York: Oxford University Press.

Ghoshal, S., & Bartlett, C. A. (1998). *Managing across borders: The transnational solution* (2nd ed.). Boston: Harvard Business School Press.

Ghoshal, S., & Westney, E. D. (Eds.) (1993). *Organization theory and the multinational corporation*. New York: St. Martin's Press

Giddens, A. (1998). *The third way: The renewal of social democracy*. Oxford: Polity Press.

Giddens, A. (1999). *The runaway world*. The Reith Lectures. London: British Broadcasting Corporation (http://news.bbc.co.uk/hi/english/s...events/reith_99)

Grabher, G. (1995). The elegance of incoherence: institutional legacies in the economic transformation in East Germany and Hungary. In E. Dittrich, G. Schmidt, & R. Whitley (Eds.), *Industrial transformation in Europe: Process and contexts* (pp. 33-53). London: Sage.

Guthrie, D. (1998). The declining significance of *guanxi* in China's economic transition. *The China Quarterly, 154,* 254-282.

Hall, E. T. (1976). *Beyond culture*. Garden City, NY: Anchor Press.

Hall, E. T., & Hall, M.R. (1990). *Understanding cultural differences*. Yarmouth, ME: Intercultural Press.

Hampden-Turner, C., & F. Trompenaars. (1993). *The seven cultures of capitalism*. New York: Doubleday.

Hawley, J. P., & Williams, A. T. (1996). *Corporate governance in the US: The rise of fiduciary capitalism—a review of the literature*. Report to OECD, January.

Hedberg, B., Dahlgren, G., Hansson, J., & Olve, N-G. (1997). *Virtual Organizations and Beyond*. Chichester: Wiley.

Hedlund, G. (1986). The hypermodern MNC - A heterarchy? *Human Resource Management, 25,* 9-25.

Heider, F. (1958). *The psychology of interpersonal relations*. New York: Wiley.

Herzberg, F., Mausner, B., & Snyderman, B. B. (1959). *The motivation to work*. New York: Wiley.

Hickson, D. J., Hinings, C. R., McMillan, C. J., & Schwitter, J. P. (1974). The culture-free context of organization structure: a trinational comparison. *Sociology, 8,* 59-80.

Hickson, D. J., & McMillan, C. J. (Eds.). (1981). *Organization and nation: The Aston Programme IV*. Aldershot: Gower.

Hickson, D. J., & Pugh, D. S. (1995). *Management worldwide: The impact of social culture on organizations around the globe*. London: Penguin.

Hofstede, G. (1980a). *Culture's consequences: International differences in work-related values*. London: Sage.

Hofstede, G. (1980b). Motivation, leadership and organization: Do American theories apply abroad? *Organization Dynamics, 8,* 42-63.

Hofstede, G. (1991). *Cultures and organizations: Software of the mind*. Maidenhead: McGraw-Hill.

Hofstede, G., & Bond, M. H. (1988). The Confucius connection: From cultural roots to economic growth. *Organizational Dynamics, 16,* 4-21.

Johanson, J., & Vahlne, J-E. (1977). The internationalization process of the firm: A model of knowledge development and increasing foreign market commitments. *Journal of International Business Studies, 8,* 23-32.

Johnson, B. T., Holmes, K. R., & Kirkpatrick, M. (1998, December). Freedom is the surest path to growth. *The Asian Wall Street Journal, 1,* 14.

Kerr, C., Dunlop, J. T., Harbison, F., & Myers, C. A. (1960). *Industrialism and industrial man*. Cambridge, MA: Harvard University Press.

Kluckhohn, C. et al. (1951). Values and value-orientations in the theory of action. In T. Parsons & E. A. Shils (Eds.), *Toward a general theory of action*. Cambridge, MA: Harvard University Press.

Knights, D., & Murray, F. (1994). *Managers divided: Organisation politics and information technology management*. Chichester: Wiley.

Kogut, B. (1988). Joint ventures: Theoretical and empirical perspectives. *Strategic Management Journal, 9*, 319-332.

Kruglanski, A. W., & Freund, T. (1983). The freezing and un-freezing of lay inferences: Effects on impressional primacy, ethnic stereotyping and numeric anchoring. *Journal of Experimental Social Psychology, 19*, 448-468.

Lammers, C. J., & Hickson, D. J. (Eds.). (1979). *Organizations alike and unlike*. London: Routledge & Kegan Paul.

Lane, C., & Backmann, R. (Eds.). (1998). *Trust within and between organizations*. Oxford: Oxford University Press.

Lardy, N. (1999, April 19). China's breathtaking WTO offer. *Asian Wall Street Journal*, p. 10.

Lewicki, R. J., & Bunker, B. B. (1996). Developing and maintaining trust in work relationships. In R. M. Kramer & T. R. Tyler (Eds.), *Trust in organizations: Frontiers of theory and research* (pp. 114-139). Thousand Oaks, CA: Sage.

Liu, I-M. (1986). Chinese cognition. In M. H. Bond (Ed.), *The psychology of the Chinese people* (pp. 73-105). Hong Kong: Oxford University Press.

Locke, E. (1968). Towards a theory of task motivation and incentives. *Organizational Behavior and Human Performance, 3*, 157-89.

Locke, R. R. (1989). *Management and Higher Education since 1940: The Influence of America and Japan on West Germany, Great Britain and France*. Cambridge: Cambridge University Press.

Loveridge, R. (1998). Review of "The Changing European Firm –Limits to Convergence." *Organization Studies, 19*, 1049-1053.

Lu, Y., & Björkman, I. (1997). HRM Practices in China-western joint ventures: MNC standardization versus localization. *International Journal of Human Resource Management, 8*, 614-628.

McClelland, D. C. (1988). *Human motivation*. Cambridge: Cambridge University Press.

Maslow, A. H. (1943). A theory of human motivation. *Psychological Review, 50*, 370-96.

Mintzberg, H. (1994). *The rise and fall of strategic planning*. New York: Prentice-Hall.

Mohr, L. B. (1982). *Explaining organizational behavior*. San Francisco: Jossey-Bass.

Mokhiber, R., & Weissman, R. (1999). *Corporate predators: The hunt for megaprofits and the attack on democracy*. Monroe, ME: Common Courage Press.

Mommsen, W. J. (1989). The two dimensions of social change in Max Weber's sociological theory. In W. J. Mommsen (Ed.), *The political and social theory of Max Weber: Collected essays* (pp. 145-190). Oxford: Polity Press.

Moore, B. (1966). *Social origins of dictatorship and democracy*. Boston: Beacon Press.

Neuberg, S. L., & Newsom, J. T. (1993). Personal need for structure: Individual differences in the desire for simple structure. *Journal of Personality and Social Structure, 65*, 113-131.

Ng, D. W. N. (1996). Succession in the "Bamboo Network." *Financial Times: Mastering Enterprise*. No. 6, December 20, pp. 6-7.

Noble, D. F. (1977). *America by design: Science, technology, and the rise of corporate capitalism*. New York: Knopf.

Nohria, N., & Eccles, R. G. (Eds.) (1992). *Networks and organizations*, Boston, MA: Harvard Business School Press.

Nolan P., & Wang Xiaoqiang (1997). *The Yuchai diesel case*. Judge Institute of Management Studies, University of Cambridge, October.

Nonaka, I., & Takeuchi, H. (1995). *The knowledge creating company*. New York: Oxford University Press.

Ohmae, K. (1990). *The borderless world: power and strategy in the interlinked economy*. New York: Free Press.

Oliver, N., & Wilkinson, B. (1992). *The Japanization of British industry*. Oxford: Blackwell.

Orru, M., Biggart, N. W., & Hamilton, G. G. (Eds.) (1997). *The economic organization of East Asian capitalism*. Thousand Oaks, CA: Sage.

Parker, B. (1996). Evolution and revolution: From international business to globalization. In S. R. Clegg, C. Hardy, & W. R. Nord (Eds.), *Handbook of organization studies* (pp. 484-506). London: Sage.

Pauly, L. W., & S. Reich. (1997). National structures and multinational corporate behavior: Enduring differences in the age of globalization. *International Organization, 51*, 1-30.

Peng, M. (2000). *Business strategies in transition economies*. Thousand Oaks, CA: Sage.

Poortinga, Y. (1992). Towards a conceptualization of culture for psychology. In S. Iwawaki, Y. Kashima, & K. Leung (Eds.), *Innovations in cross-cultural psychology*. Amsterdam: Swets & Zeitlinger.

Porter, L. W., & Lawler, E. E. (1968). *Managerial Attitudes and Performance*. Homewood, IL: Irwin.

Pugh, D. S., Hickson, D. J., & Hinings, C. R. (1969). An empirical taxonomy of structures of work organization. *Administrative Science Quarterly, 14*, 115-126.

Qin Xiao (1999). A conceptual framework for the strategic restructuring of state-owned enterprises in China. *Chinese Management Centre Working Paper*, CMC1999-001-01, University of Hong Kong.

Ralston, D. A., Egri, C. P., Stewart, S., Terpstra, R. H., & Yu Kaicheng (1999). Doing business in the 21[St] century with the new generation of Chinese managers: A study of generational shifts in work values in China. *Journal of International Business Studies, 30*, 415-427.

Redding, S. G. (1990). *The spirit of Chinese capitalism*. Berlin: De Gruyter.

Redding, S. G. (1994). Comparative management theory: Jungle, zoo or fossil bed? *Organization Studies, 15*, 323-359.

Reed, M. (1996). Organizational theorizing: A historical contested terrain. In S. R. Clegg, C. Hardy, & W. R. Nord (Eds.), *Handbook of organization studies* (pp. 31-56). London: Sage.

Roberts, K. H. (1970). On looking at an elephant: An evaluation of cross-cultural research related to organizations. *Psychological Bulletin, 74*, 327-350.

Robertson, R. (1995). Glocalization: time-space and homogeneity-heterogeneity. In M. Featherstone, S. Lash, & R. Robertson (Eds.), *Global modernities* (pp. 25-44). London: Sage.

Rodrigues, S. B. (1996). Management in Brazil. In M. Warner (Ed.), *International encyclopedia of business & management* (pp. 2673-2682). London: International Thompson Business Press.

Scarbrough, H. (1996). Strategic change in financial services: The social construction of strategic IS. In W. J. Orlikowski, G. Walsham, M. R. Jones, & J. I. DeGross (Eds.), *Information technology and changes in organizational work* (pp. 197-212). London: Chapman & Hall.

Schluchter, W. (1981). *The rise of western rationalism: Max Weber's developmental history*. Berkeley: University of California Press.

Schumpeter, J. (1943). *Capitalism, socialism and democracy*. London: Allen & Unwin.

Selznick, P. (1949). *The TVA and the grass roots*. New York: Harper & Row.

Shleifer, A., & Vishny, R. W. (1997). A survey of corporate governance. *Journal of Finance, 52*, 737-783.

Smith, P. B., Misumi, J., Tayeb, M., Peterson, M., & Bond, M. (1989). On the generality of leadership style measures across cultures. *Journal of Occupational Psychology, 62*, 97-109.

Sorge, A. (1982). Cultured organization. *International Studies of Management and Organization, XII*, 106-135.

Sorge, A., & Warner, M. (1986). *Comparative factory organization: an Anglo-German comparison of manufacturing, management and manpower*. Aldershot: Gower.

Sorrentino, R. M., & Hewitt, E. C. (1984). The uncertainty-reducing properties of achievement tasks revisited. *Journal of Personality and Social Psychology, 47*, 884-899.

Steger, U. (Ed.) (1998). *Discovering the new pattern of globalization.* Ladenburg: Gottlieb Daimler-und-Karl Benz-Stiftung.

Streufert, S., & Swezey, R. W. (1986). *Complexity, Managers, and Organizations.* Orlando, FA: Academic Press.

The Economist (1992). China goes for broke. July 25, pp. 57-58.

Tjosvold, D. (1991). *Team organization: An enduring competitive advantage.* Chichester: Wiley.

Toffler, A. (1971). *Future shock.* London: Pan Books.

Tolbert, P. S., & Zucker, L. G. (1996). The institutionalization of institutional theory. In S. R. Clegg, C. Hardy, & W. R. Nord (Eds.), *Handbook of organization studies* (pp. 175-190). London: Sage.

Trompenaars, F. (1993). *Riding the waves of culture.* London: Economist Books.

Tsui, A. S., & Farh, J. L. (1997). Where guanxi matters: relational demography and guanxi in the Chinese context. *Work and Occupations, 24,* 56-79.

Weber, M. (1964). *The theory of social and economic organization.* Trans. by A.M. Henderson and T. Parsons. New York: Free Press.

Weber, M. (1978). *Economy and society* (G.Roth & C. Wittich, Eds., Trans.). Berkeley: University of California Press.

Whitley, R. D. (1992a). *Business systems in East Asia.* London: Sage.

Whitley, R.D. (Ed.) (1992b). *European business systems: Firms and markets in their national contexts.* London: Sage.

Williamson, O.E. (1970). *Corporate control and business behavior: An enquiry into the effects of organizational form on enterprise behavior.* Englewood Cliffs, NJ: Prentice-Hall.

Williamson, O.E. (1985). *The economic institutions of capitalism: Firms, markets, relational contracting.* New York: Free Press.

Wong, Y. C. R. (1998, November). Lessons of the Asian financial crisis. *HKCER Letters, 53,* 1-4.

Woodward, J. (1965). *Industrial organization: Theory and practice.* London: Oxford University Press.

Yang, C-F. (1998). *Indigenous cultural values and management practices.* Address given at the Inauguration of the Chinese Management Centre, University of Hong Kong, December 4.

Yang, K. S. (1994). *Indigenous psychological research in Chinese societies.* Taiwan: Kuew Guan.

Zuboff, S. (1988). *In the age of the smart machine.* New York: Basic Books.

CHILD'S THEORIZING ABOUT ORGANIZATION CROSS-NATIONALLY

VALIANT, BUT UNDER-ECONOMIZED

Peter Buckley

Whatever other criticisms are legitimately made of economics, no one has ever accused the subject of lacking an analytical cutting edge. Economic approaches, of course, figure in Child's "low context" perspectives. It is precisely the lowness of context that gives economistic approaches to organization, cross-nationally and otherwise, their power. The approach of economics (based on modeling [Buckley & Casson, 1998a]) seeks to focus on the central relationships by removing extraneous influences (e.g., through the *ceteris paribus* assumption). Analytical clarity comes at a price. The removal of context is a major part of the price. Many other social scientists (sociologists, political scientists, anthropologists) cannot stomach this laser beam focus and prefer "high context" perspectives (Granovetter, 1985). Often, this is because economists do not use their own techniques to maximum effect and, ironically, unduly narrow their field of vision by the choice of variables included in their models (Buckley & Casson, 1993). The solution to this, however, is not to take the approach of many in "international management" and to add on a box labeled "culture" with arrows from, and to, economic variables. Indeed, it is

Advances in International Comparative Management, Volume 13, pages 77-83.
Copyright © 2000 by JAI Press Inc.
All rights of reproduction in any form reserved.
ISBN: 0-7623-0589-4

arguable that many economistic approaches to transnational phenomenon have been *more* sympathetic to cultural differences than those who ring-fence culture in a separate domain, influenced and influencing other "variables" such as "economy": "political system," "social system" as if these were discrete entities.

It goes without saying that it is the duty of any analyst to make their assumptions about culture clear. But this is an inadequate response to the pervasiveness of cultural issues. Culture should be built into the model. It should be endogenous, not exogenous. The difficulties economists have faced in cross-national (read cross-cultural) work is that their assumptions are implicit, often unthinking. Hence the view that multinational firms are the same beast regardless of nationality of ownership, locational characteristics, and so on.

Much of economics represents a good first approximation. Where strong observed differences in these approximations is observed, there is clearly one (or more) unobserved variables at work. Here is primary evidence that (high) context matters. The branch of applied economics known as international business has been good at identifying these previously ignored intervening variables. Evidence for the veracity of this statement can be found in examination of the multinational enterprise in less developed countries, in the analysis of joint ventures and alliances, and in the literature which Child references as "models for the organization of international business."

THE MULTINATIONAL ENTERPRISE

Many theorists, following Buckley and Casson (1976), see the multinational enterprise (MNE) as simply a firm which owns and controls value-adding resources across national boundaries (or as a firm which has internalized one or more markets in intermediate goods across national frontiers). Thus, the MNE is the norm, uni-national firms are a special case. The analysis of the firm, and its strategy, is perforce a cross-national and cross-cultural exercise. Cultural differences are encompassed in transaction costs and in information costs. That these costs differ by spatial location, by nation, by region, and by cultural boundary (linguistic, religious, ethnic) should be as routine to theorizing as are differences in production costs or distribution cost.

The difficulty is that these costs are not discrete or co-terminous. Thus, normal accounting processes do not separate out these costs (Buckley & Frecknall-Hughes, 1998). This does not mean that they are unimportant. Indeed, I would want to argue that transaction and information costs exceed "physical" production and distribution costs in many industries and are increasing as a proportion of total costs.

If we were to decompose costs into transaction costs, information costs, and other costs, this might radically alter modeling and conceptions of strategy within firms.

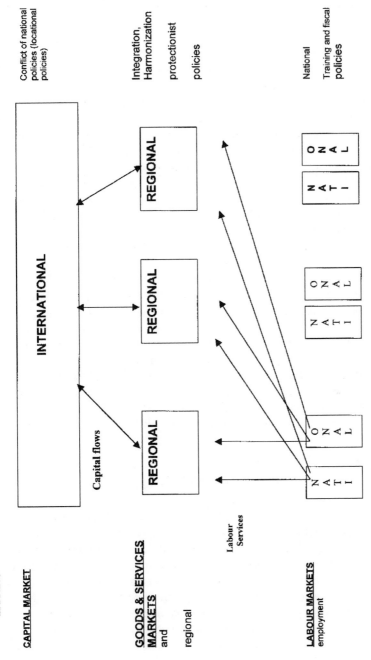

MARKETS

CAPITAL MARKET

GOODS & SERVICES MARKETS and

regional

LABOUR MARKETS employment

MANAGEMENT

Conflict of national policies (locational policies)

Integration, Harmonization

protectionist

policies

National

Training and fiscal policies

Capital flows

Labour Services

INTERNATIONAL

REGIONAL   REGIONAL   REGIONAL

Figure 1. Internationalization of Firms—Conflict of Markets

79

GLOBALIZATION, LOCALIZATION, AND REGIONALIZATION

Figure 3 of Child's paper bifurcates the contextual level into local and global. Unfortunately, this misses the most important level in the dynamics of international business strategy which is the region. Figure 1 suggests that "globalization" can be understood by considering the differential rates of progress to the global integration of markets in finance, goods and services, and labor (Buckley, 1996).

Child's approach largely abstracts from markets (unlike Weber's) and a short review here is appropriate (Swedberg, 1998). While global financial markets are largely integrated (such that independent national interest rate and/or exchange rate policies are difficult), regional markets are largely integrated at the regional level (EU, NAFTA, etc). Labor markets remain largely separate at the national level, even within economic and political blocs such as the European Union. The major beneficiaries of these differential speeds toward globalization are multinational enterprises who have access to cheap capital because of global competition in capital markets, gain economies of scale from regional integration (Buckley, Clegg, Forsans, & Reilly, 1999) and can pursue segmented strategies in labor markets to access (skilled) labor at the lowest possible costs.

Within this differentiated drive to globalization, the most important level is the regional one (Rugman, 1999). Within the most successful economic and political blocs—the EU followed by NAFTA, there is clear evidence that multinationals are moving from a multidomestic strategy, where each "national" economy was treated as a separate market, to an integrated regional one (Buckley, Clegg, & Forsans, 1999). Distinct strategies are emerging based on "hub and spoke" operations and new ownership strategies, relying on alliances and joint ventures, rather than wholly owned subsidiaries (Buckley & Casson, 1998b). These strategies have profound implications for the cross-national organization of multinational enterprises.

SOCIAL ANTHROPOLOGY

I have long since given up searching for a quotation which I once found, and then lost, to the effect that the only two successful social sciences were economics and social anthropology. While I would not wish to argue this claim, I would maintain that the two named social sciences have a great deal to offer each other, particularly in the creation of a better framework to understand cross-national organization (Buckley & Chapman, 1996b). Having worked with a social anthropologist (Malcolm Chapman) on an investigation of cooperative strategies, the creative tensions between the subjects are a fruitful avenue for development. Of particular importance is the rate of managerial perception in the analysis of transaction costs (Buckley & Chapman, 1997) also the reconstruction of history which underlies much of business "strategy" (Buckley & Chapman, 1996a).

The importance of anthropological approaches to culture is that they can be used to inform economic models. Mark Casson and I attempted this in the analysis of multinationals in less developed countries (Buckley & Casson, 1991). This encounter, between the modern "systems and scientific thinking" culture and the traditional culture, provides a polar extreme test case of the importance of cultural variables in economic models.

In addition, it is important not to forget geography. This point was emphasized above with regard to the "missing" regional dimension in Child's analysis, but it is important not to attribute social, political, or cultural elements to costs which are purely spatial. Physical costs and psychic costs must be kept conceptually distinct. But geography does interact with cultural and economic elements as factors in the long-run economic success of both firms and nations. The analysis of Buckley and Casson (1991), for instance, emphasizes the geographical determinants of entrepôt potential in development and the inhibiting role of geography where transportation costs prevent extension of the division of labor and specialization). Monocausal explanations are likely to be unsuccessful in explaining or predicting in these complex cases.

ORGANIZATION AND INDIVIDUAL ACTION

In theorizing about organizations, it is inevitable that we must consider the relationship between individuals and organizations. Issues arise such as the dissonance between the goals of the organization *in toto* and the individuals which comprise it. Again, the economic system-builders have colonized these issues. The principal agent model (note the word) addresses the issues (Jensen & Meckling, 1976) and Hirshman's "Exit, Voice and Loyalty" (1970) tackles the role of an individual's alternative strategy with regard to the organization (Buckley, 1999).

It is arguable that both of these basic models are culture-free (or culture-blind). The point is, however, that they are capable of extension to undertake the tasks which Child envisages. With a set of plausible supporting hypotheses invoking the role of culture differences (e.g., some cultures invoke, provoke, or sustain loyalty rather than others, agency costs are likely to be lower in more homogenous societies, language similarities will discourage exit and encourage voice, etc.), we can progress.

Similar arguments apply to the essentially game-theoretic models of interpersonal behavior which have shed light on the notion of trust (Buckley & Casson, 1988). It is entirely feasible to increase the highness of context in these models. Again, simple economics-based notions help. Trust can be an input or an output. It can be treated as a stock or a flow. It can be gained or lost at a cost. Building such "unconventional" elements into economic models is a hard task, but a worthwhile one.

In addition, the link between culture and entrepreneurial activity has often been noted but has not yet been fully developed, largely because entrepreneurship is difficult to model.

CONCLUSION: ECONOMIC UNIVERSALISM IN METHOD, NOT IN APPLICATION

It is a mistake to equate economic universalism with a given, fixed set of principles. The universalism of economics derives from method not from doctrine. Economists may have been unduly rigid in their choice of models and applications. My comment has attempted to show that this assumption needs to be relaxed. The inclusion of cultural variables in economic models of international organizations is proceeding apace—an example is Buckley and Cassons's analysis of joint ventures (1998b). Specifically, Chinese special assumptions need to be justified if they are alleged to influence organizational behavior in China. If they can be so justified, then there is no insuperable boundary to a "Chinese context" theory of organization. But we need to invoke Ockham's razor. Only when genuine extra degrees of explanation are gained are high-context variables justified. The task is to delineate where the extra-explanatory power arises and from whence it derives to price of admission. Then, a new generation of models can begin.

REFERENCES

Buckley, P. J. (1996). Strategic foreign direct investment. In G. Boyd & A. M. Rugman (Eds.), *Euro-Pacific investment and trade*. Cheltenham: Edward Elgar.

Buckley, P. J. (1998a). *International business: Economic and anthropology, theory and method*. London: Macmillan.

Buckley, P. J. (1998b). *International strategic management and government policy*. London: Macmillan.

Buckley, P. J. (1999). Alternatives to decline, threat of scarcity: Exit, voice, loyalty and institutional response. *Management International Review, 39*(1) (Special Issue), 45-53.

Buckley, P. J., & Casson, M. (1976). *The future of the multinational enterprise*. London: Macmillan.

Buckley, P. J., & Casson, M. (1988). A theory of cooperation in international business. In F. Contractor & P. Lorange (Eds.), *Cooperative strategies in international business*. Lexington, MA: Lexington Books.

Buckley, P. J., & Casson, M. (1991). The multinational enterprise in less developed countries: Cultural and economic interaction. In P. J. Buckley & J. Clegg (Eds.), *Multinational enterprises in less developed countries*. London: Macmillan.

Buckley, P. J., & Casson, M. (1993). Economics as an imperialist social science. *Human Relations, 46*(9), 1035-1052.

Buckley, P. J., & Casson, M. (1998a). Models of the multinational enterprise. *Journal of International Business Studies, 29*(1), 21-44.

Buckley, P. J., & Casson, M. (1998b). Analysing foreign market entry strategies: Extending the internalization approach. *Journal of International Business Studies, 29*(3), 503-20.

Buckley, P. J., & Chapman, M. (1996a). Wise before the event: The creation of corporate fulfilment. *Management International Review, 36*(1), 95-110.

Buckley, P. J., & Chapman, M. (1996b). Economics and social anthropology—reconciling differences. *Human Relations, 49*(9), 1123-1150.

Buckley, P. J., & Chapman, M. (1997). The perception and measurement of transaction cost. *Cambridge Journal of Economics, 21*(2), 127-145.

Buckley, P. J., Clegg, J., & Forsans, N. (1999). Foreign direct investment and free trade areas: The NAFTA case. *Canadian Journal of Regional Science* (forthcoming).

Buckley, P. J., Clegg, J., Forsans, N., & Reilly, K. T. (1999). *Evaluation of foreign direct investment in the united states in the context of trade liberalisation and regionalisation*. University of Leeds. Mimeo.

Buckley, P. J., & Frecknall-Hughes, J. (1998). Transfer pricing and economic functions analysis: The Japanese paradigm. *Applied Economics, 30*(5), 621-629.

Granovetter, M. (1985). Economic action and social structure: The problem of embeddedness. *The American Journal of Sociology, 91*.

Hirshman, A. O. (1970). *Exit, voice and loyalty*. Cambridge, MA: Harvard University Press.

Jensen, M. C., & Meckling, W. H. (1976). Theory of the firm: Management behavior, agency costs and ownership structure. *Journal of Financial Economics, 3*, 305-66.

Rugman, A. M. (1999). *Multinational enterprises and the end of global strategy*. Seventh International Conference at the Sorbonne, June 17-18.

Swedberg, R. (1998). *Max Weber and the idea of economic sociology*. Princeton, NJ: Princeton University Press.

REFLECTIONS ON ORGANIZING IN THE TWENTY-FIRST CENTURY

John R. Kimberly

John Child is a scholar. Furthermore, John Child is a management scholar, a status that is all too rare in the contemporary business school rush to marry theory and practice, to demonstrate relevance, and to create partnerships between the worlds of academic research and business. The occasional spectacular success of efforts to commercialize the results of management research and the entry of the consulting giants into the arena have created confusion about how intellectual value is created. It is *not* by telling clients what they want to hear or by selling the latest "buzz." That may create commercial value, but it does not create intellectual value. Intellectual value is created through the application of the capacity for thought and critical reflection to the articulation (and, occasionally, the solution) of puzzles. Intellectual value does not always translate directly into commercial value. Yet it is the bedrock upon which sustained commercial value is built.

John Child is not confused about how intellectual value is created. His classic article on strategic choice (Child, 1972), for example, opened an important new vista for organization theorists of the era by suggesting the significance of decisions made at the top of the organizational hierarchy for organizational structure and performance. Although this suggestion may, with the passage of more than a

Advances in International Comparative Management, Volume 13, pages 85-93.
ISBN: 0-7623-0589-4

quarter of a century, appear "obvious" to some, the impact of the "dominant coalition" and/or of "leadership" on organizational performance is still hotly debated.
The intellectual value of the article lies in the way in which it framed the question;
it was not written with a splash in *Business Week* or *The Financial Times* in mind,
but with the goal of helping to clarify some contemporary questions about the
relationship between organizational structure and performance. And its legacy
endures.

His essay on "theorizing about organization cross-nationally" is just the latest
demonstration of his commitment to scholarship. The essay is broad in its sweep,
informed yet not unnecessarily encumbered by the writing of others, and original
in the perspective it develops. Perhaps most significant, it is the result of an intellectual journey stimulated by personal experience. Although the essay is about
theorizing, it is not based on theorizing from the armchair. John's commitment to
understanding organization cross-nationally is long-standing and deep. He has
lived in China, he has taught there, and he has done research there. His effort to
synthesize the implications of his own cross-national experience for management
research more generally deserves a careful read for this reason alone. To be asked
to reflect on it and react to it is at once a challenge and a pleasure.

ON THE ELEPHANT AND ITS PARTS

The overall goal of Child's essay is laudable. He sees a "field" which is fragmented and theoretical perspectives that are, at least on the surface, incompatible
at best and occasionally contradictory. The solution he advocates is the development of a perspective which, rather than going down yet another distinctive path
and risking further fragmentation, seeks to bridge existing perspectives. He seeks
integration where others have tended to differentiate. He calls for conciliation
where others have pursued proliferation. He argues for a holistic approach where
others have proceeded on a piecemeal basis.

It is difficult to take issue with the objective he sets for himself. His argument
in this respect has an almost folksy quality to it. In the abstract, who would argue
against an approach based on integration, reconciliation, and holism and firmly
anchored in Weber's distinction between the material and the ideational? Not I.

I would, however, like to raise a number of questions that emerged as I reflected
on how the argument is constructed. And I leave it to you to determine the extent
to which these questions compromise Child's fundamental argument in any
meaningful way.

What Crisis?

In the first paragraph of his essay, Child alludes to a "sense of frustration and
crisis" with regard to theory and research on cross-national aspects of organiza-

tion, and later he speaks of "confusion and paralysis" in approaches to the subject matter. We ought, perhaps, to excuse a modicum of scholarly histrionics, recognizing that their purpose is to justify the path he has chosen. However, I do not sense anything approaching crisis. What I sense instead is a remarkable opportunity born of changing material and ideational circumstances of the sort he describes eloquently later in the essay. The explosion of cross-national organizing activity spawned by new technology and changing conceptions of product/market junctions has created the need for fresh theorizing and research driven by new perspectives. This is hardly a crisis.

What is "the Elephant"?

From the opening paragraphs and throughout the essay, Child refers to "the field" as though there were a widely shared understanding of what the field is. I am not certain that there is this understanding. The ambiguity he notes about whether the field should be defined as the cross-national study of organization or the study of cross-national organization begs the question, because it is not obvious to me that either of those constitutes a "field." An area of inquiry at most, but not a field. For me, the fundamental question is whether one can speak meaningfully of an elephant, that is, whether there is an underlying structure and coherence to questions and approaches despite the variety in what is visible externally. My sense is that the answer is "no," and that the only common thread which joins these questions and approaches is some interest in how and why various phenomena manifest themselves as they do across national borders.

On this issue, we may have a potentially serious difference of views. Child believes that "subtle theorizing" about the characteristics of organization in different countries is required and that much of the subtlety is at least nascent in available theoretical perspectives. This belief leads him to advocate the creation of a single framework, and this is the challenge he sets himself in the paper.

I do not disagree about the need for subtle theorizing. I do wonder, however, about the feasibility—even the desirability—of creating a single framework. Such a venture assumes that there *is* an elephant out there and that its trunk, tail, legs and ears are all part of the same beast. But suppose we use a different metaphor? Suppose we move from the animal kingdom to the world of geopolitics and ask whether creating a single framework to join the different available theoretical perspectives to which Child refers is not a bit like creating the USSR to join the various separate republics. An overarching structure superimposed on highly divergent constituent entities may result in a sense of order for a period of time, but also masks real and substantial differences. John may be correct in his assumption that the differences among available theoretical perspectives are not so deep as to lead ultimately to fatal disharmony were a single framework to be created. I am less certain than he.

Organization or Organizations?

The essay is beautifully nuanced in a number of places, the mark of a seasoned pro in the sport of scholarly research and writing. One place where the nuance was missing and where articulation would have been helpful, however, is in the connection between the title of the essay and the text. The title states that the essay concerns theorizing about *organization* cross-nationally, yet the text deals more with theorizing about *organizations* cross-nationally. Which one is it, John, or is it both?

The question is important because of what I take to be potentially significant differences in theoretical orientation associated with the two words. If the focus is truly on theorizing about organization, the perspective is a good deal broader than if the focus is on theorizing about organizations. The latter has a certain ontological status that links it closely to organization theory whereas the former evokes more generic processes and is not as clearly linked to a particular body of theory. The link to organization theory is non-trivial, for OT is based largely on Western conceptions and thus brings to the analysis of the cross-national a strong bias regarding the object(s) of analysis. It would be ironic in my view if, in an essay designed to build bridges and confront the impact of context directly, the perspective were itself implicitly firmly rooted in a view having a strong context-based view of the phenomenon. Perhaps the focus ought, as Karl Weick has argued, to be on organiz*ing* rather than on organiz*ation* or organiz*ations*.

How Long is Longitudinal?

Child is absolutely correct in his criticism of cross-sectional research and his call for longitudinal perspectives and research designs. He joins many others in this call. One cannot possibly understand processes of change without observing change.

Calls for longitudinal research alone, however, will not ensure that that kind of research will be undertaken. Barriers to longitudinal research are well known and need not be rehearsed yet another time here. There is a more important question, however, a substantive question, that needs to be raised. How long is longitudinal? Simply to assert that cross-sectional research is severely limited and that the antidote is longitudinal research begs this important theoretical question. What is actually needed is a theory of change which itself contains the answer to the question of appropriate time frame. In other words, we need to know enough about the phenomenon we are studying to be able to specify how long longitudinal should be. Should the time frame be weeks, months, years, decades, or centuries? We may be walking a fine line between social science and history here, but the important point is that in addition to more longitudinal research, we need more sophisticated theorizing about change to enable more sophisticated (and appropriate) longitudinal designs to be developed. This, of course, is a point that goes way beyond Child's essay and applies to research on change in general. But his criticism of cross-sectional work provides yet another opportunity to reiterate it.

The Globalization of Business Education

There is no question that Western business schools have been a major force in driving certain principles of and approaches to business around the globe, and an increasing number of researchers are both recognizing and attempting to document their impact. My own sense is that although the model Child presents in Figure 2 anticipates and allows for b-school influence on organizational practice in non-Western contexts, the text underemphasizes this impact. At this point, then, this remains an empirical question. But I would be willing to wager that the impact of an M.B.A. education on organization cross-nationally is high and getting higher. One has to look no further than the number of North American and European business schools that are establishing a presence in Asia and Latin America through a combination of greenfield bricks and mortar investments (e.g., INSEAD in Singapore), strategic alliances, and/or joint ventures to witness the extensiveness of the impact. Beyond these initiatives is the burgeoning number of "distance learning" experiments (e.g., Duke) that are taking M.B.A. education global in a different sense. Considering the present and likely future impact of this activity, one is led to the inescapable conclusion that Child should pay more attention to it in his assessment of organization cross-nationally.

What Constitutes "Equivalence" in Cross-National Research?

Equivalence is an issue that confronts any effort to do cross-national research. Because all scientific research involves comparison, one needs to be certain that comparisons are made among observations that are equivalent in some desired way. When equivalence is problematic, the validity of comparisons is compromised and we encounter the issue of what is referred to colloquially as "comparing apples and oranges."

Child recognizes this issue in his essay, and raises it directly in the section on Research Design and Operational Equivalence. He also refers to it less directly in his discussion of the influence of national context—or institutional variables—on organization. I would like to sharpen the issue further.

As my colleagues Hamid Bouchikhi and Phil Rosenzweig and I have argued (Kimberly et al., 1998), pursuing equivalence self-consciously is essential whether research is conducted in a laboratory setting or in the field, or whether in a single country or multiple countries. However, because cross-national research involves many differences—including, for example, languages, cultures, social institutions, and legal systems—it confronts a higher level of complexity, thus heightening the challenge of achieving equivalence.

The majority of management research is unconcerned with this issue, as it is undertaken in a single country and thus effectively controls for national context. Adler (1983) has called this "parochial" research. We prefer the less pejorative term *single country research*. However, as Child points out, there is a small but rapidly growing body of research that seeks explicitly to determine the degree of generalizability across national borders by taking a study developed in one country and replicating it in another or others. *Replicative research*, or what Adler (1983) has called "ethnocentric" research, however, also has limitations. Because the questions that motivate the research, the variables identified for study, the theorized relationships among these variables, and the way they are operationalized tend to emanate from a single national context, the extent to which they may be valid in another is problematic. Simply back-translating questionnaires does not address these fundamental issues.

This problem, too, has been widely recognized, and Child addresses it convincingly in his essay. Gaining an understanding that is anchored at least partially in context demands that we refrain from imposing the theories or assumptions of one country onto another and instead seek areas of equivalence. Adler has called research of this sort "comparative." I prefer calling it *cross-nationally equivalent* research, as all research is, at some level, comparative.

Cross-nationally equivalent research can be achieved by ensuring equivalence at several points in the research process, as Adler (1983), Cheng (1994), and Rosenzweig (1994), among others, have suggested. In seeking to conduct this type of research, however, another problem is encountered, the tradeoff between specificity and generality. The more a model, or a set of findings, is specific to a given subject—be it an industry, an individual, or a country—the less it can be generalized across subjects; and, conversely, efforts to maximize generalizability across subjects come at the expense of depth in understanding any single subject. Thus, if equivalence is assured at each stage of the research process, the price may be depth of understanding about any particular country. We call this outcome *surface equivalence*.

Adler and her colleagues (1989) experienced the limitations of *surface equivalence* in their cross-national study involving China. While seeking to ensure equivalence in their variables and their methodology, they found that a valid interpretation of responses by Chinese managers to a questionnaire developed in the West was impossible because of the different conceptions of the term "truth"— what was meant by the Western researchers evoked something altogether different in the Chinese respondents. The data they gathered—although equivalent on the surface—did not produce meaningful conclusions because they had overlooked the need to understand the Chinese context in depth. Thus we see the downside to *surface equivalence*, as it comes at the expense of depth and relevance. More generally, if one studies only those things that are exactly the same across countries, restricting inquiry to include terms that are identical across languages, variables that are related identically in each context, and methods that exhibit neither observer nor respondent bias, we may limit ourselves to a narrow subset of issues, a subset that may not even include the most interesting questions for study. Indeed, one might question whether in the extreme such an approach to research is feasible as a practical matter.

As this problem has been recognized, some have advocated field-based, idiographic research as a solution. Boyacigillar and Adler, for example, recommend the study of management systems "on their own terms," and advocate the pursuit of "thick descriptions of organizational phenomena and the contexts in which they are embedded" (1991, p. 279). Idiographic research that seeks to understand phenomena "on their own terms"—what Child might refer to as "high context" research—brings us to the other extreme—specificity at the cost of generalizability. And it brings us full circle, returning to what are, in effect, single-country studies.

Cross-national research thus faces a basic and difficult problem, which Ronen (1986, p. 48) has stated succinctly: "The fundamental problem is our ability to describe behavior in terms that are meaningful to members of a given culture while retaining the ability to compare behavior in that culture with that in others." *Single-country studies* (whether "thick" or "thin") and *replicative studies* may produce a thorough understanding of one country but have doubtful generalizability, whereas an emphasis on *surface equivalence* yields generalizability of dubious substantive significance.

How might a balance between these two be struck? We advocate the pursuit of *deep equivalence*, seeking depth and equivalence simultaneously. The need for a new approach was signaled to me by the results of a study of hospital innovation in the United States and France I carried out with a French colleague (Kervasdoue & Kimberly, 1979). The study was designed as a replication of the U.S. research in France. The fundamental question examined was the relationship between hospital structure and rates of innovation adoption, the notion being that certain structural characteristics would likely be associated with higher rates of adoption than others. The research strategy pursued was replication: the concepts and variables used in the U.S. study were also used in France. Great care was taken to ensure that field protocols were translated accurately from English into French and that variables were measured in identical fashion in the two countries.

The "results," however, were surprising in at least two respects. First, during the data collection process, the respondents in French hospitals had difficulty answering some questions and provided unexpected answers to others. The questions that were difficult for them to answer had to do with decision-making authority in the hospital; the questions that yielded unexpected answers had to do with hospital financial support for research, physicians' travel to professional meetings, and use of outside speakers in the hospital. Second, the regressions showed the model being tested having much stronger support empirically in the United States than in France.

One conclusion we drew from this research was that we had mis-framed the problem. By not taking explicit account of the institutional differences between the two countries and their health care systems, important influences on how innovations diffused to hospitals were overlooked. In Child's terms, we framed the research in "low context" terms and focused on the material at the expense of the ideational. Not only were the organizational arrangements in hospitals in the two countries different, but so were the institutional contexts in which these arrangements were embedded. The diffusion of innovation to hospitals could not be understood by using a single "culture-free" model. And it could not be understood without reference to contextual factors operative in each country.

Had the field researchers not reported trouble with some of the questions in French hospitals and had the actual empirical results not been so different for French and American hospitals, the fundamental question of the appropriateness of the replication strategy would undoubtedly not have been raised. But once raised, this question led to a much deeper concern for the conditions under which cross-national research is typically undertaken, the kinds of assumptions about equivalence that are typically made, and the validity of conclusions that are drawn on the basis of the research. It led to the conclusion that cross-national research must embrace differences in national context while retaining an ability to make valid comparisons—and hence to advocate the pursuit of *deep equivalence* in this sort of research. In this respect, Child's bridging argument makes sense. Research and theorizing about organization cross-nationally must allow for the simultaneous achievement of both specificity and generalizability.

CONCLUSION

John Child has presented the reader with a carefully crafted, wide-ranging essay on theorizing about organization cross-nationally. My objective in commenting on his essay has been not only to applaud the effort but also, as someone who has lived outside the United States on four different occasions and who has wrestled with many issues similar to the ones he articulates, to raise a number of questions that my experience and his essay together provoked.

One certainty emerges from this reflection on organizing in the twenty-first century, and that is that profound changes in both the material and ideational are underway and they are altering and will continue to alter the organization landscape significantly. Issues of structure, authority, commitment, and identity will of necessity play out very differently in the world that is becoming than they have in the world that has been. We need to have both the foresight and the intellectual plasticity to encompass these changes in our theorizing and our research. John Child's essay, although clearly not providing all the answers, just as clearly provides much grist for the intellectual mill. Thanks, John.

REFERENCES

Adler, N. J. (1983). A typology of management studies involving culture. *Journal of International Business Studies, 14*, 29-47.

Adler, N. J., Campbell, N., & Laurent, A. (1989). In search of appropriate methodology: From outside the People's Republic of China looking in. *Journal of International Business Studies, 20*(1), 61-74.

Boyacigillar, N., & Adler, N. J. (1991). The parochial dinosaur: Organization science in a global context. *Academy of Management Review, 16*, 262-290.

Cheng, J. L. C. (1994). On the concept of universal knowledge in organization science: Implications for cross-national research. *Management Science, 40*, 162-168.

Child, J. (1972). Organizational structure, environment and performance—the role of strategic choice. *Sociology, 6*, 1-22.

Kervasdoue, J., & Kimberly, J. R. (1979). Are organization structures culture free? In G. England et al. (Eds.), *Organizational functioning in cross cultural perspective*. Kent, OH: Kent State University Press.

Kimberly, J. R., Bouchikhi, H., & Rosenzweig, P. M. (1998). *In pursuit of "deep equivalence": Notes on a strategy for cross-national management research."* Paper presented at the Academy of Management Annual Meeting, San Diego.

Ronen, S. (1986). *Comparative and multinational management*. New York:John Wiley & Sons.

Rosenzweig, P. M. (1994). When can management science research be generalized internationally? *Management Science, 40*, 28-39.

ORDER, INTEGRATION, AND COLLABORATION
PROGRESS IN COMPARATIVE MANAGEMENT

Gordon Redding

The main obstacle to progress in the field of comparative management theory is the massive complexity of the explanatory challenge, given the inability to make the universals of some other discipline's such as economics or psychology, apply convincingly in different geographies. The disciplines great weakness is the tendency toward monocausalism: thus proposals that it is all a matter, or even mainly a matter, of culture, or of certain institutions or values, or universal rationalities.

It is intellectually dishonest to explain organizations entirely in terms of particular determinants, and it is intellectually very confusing to explain them in terms of seemingly endless lists of causal factors, all of which have a claim to attention. Caught between these two barriers the subject has tended to go around in circles and has done so for nearly 40 years, as a stream of reviews has reminded us (Roberts, 1970; Barrett & Bass, 1976; Child, 1981; Adler, Doktor, & Redding, 1986, Beaty & Mendenhall, 1990; Boyacigiller & Adler, 1991; Triandis, 1992; Redding, 1994). What John Child now offers is a way out of this circularity, a possible escape from the commonly referred to jungle. It is an important proposal and its

Advances in International Comparative Management, Volume 13, pages 95-106.
ISBN: 0-7623-0589-4

merits should see it taken seriously as a framework for research planning by individuals and by institutions widely.

It would be a platform for multidisciplinary work and interdisciplinary cooperation and it fits well in a context where the middle terrain between economics and sociology is being respectably settled by new disciplines: socioeconomics; new institutionalism; business systems theory, and so on, all of which are integrative and overarching, though they tend to fit uneasily into standard academic subdivisions.

The agenda is of course not new and the history of attempts to deal with it contains some daunting lessons about wrestling with such complexity. Major integrating theorists such as Marshall or Weber have tended to be followed by more diffracted studies until new major theorists again attempt an integration across disciplines. The sociology of university research structures results in fierce protection of disciplines and often aggression toward others and this is imimical to multidisciplinary work. Recent integrators such as Amitai Etzioni in sponsoring socioeconomics, Mark Granovetter with economic sociology, Peter Berger with economic culture, Richard Whitley with business systems, and now John Child with the cross-national study of organizations, are rare in their ability to transcend the mind-set and paradigm of a core discipline. As such their work deserves the most serious attention.

The essential questions return persistently, like grass growing through concrete. Culture is influential, but to what extent, and by what means? In his major review of the lessons of history for the understanding of societal progress toward material wealth, Landes proposed a clear set of design principles around which policies for action could be formulated, but concluded that in generating action "If we learn anything from the history of economic development, it is that culture makes all the difference" (Landes, 1998, p. 516). He is not a monocausalist but advocates an important inclusion in the account. So too Fukuyama (1995) has connected "the social virtues" with the creation of prosperity and sees those virtues varying by culture. Similarily Huntington (1996) has outlined world politics as a clash of civilizations and thus of value systems. The historical heart of the question is put by Eisenstadt at the end of his recent major comparative study of Japanese civilization when he says that only the future will tell us

> whether we are indeed witnessing the "end of history," the ultimate convergence of industrial societies and the development of one worldwide, modern civilization, or instead the development of multiple, continually interacting, fluid yet distinctive modern civilizations (Eisenstadt, 1996, p. 445).

The notion of civilizations being appropriate envelopes in which to analyze economic activity, and by extension the assumption that world development patterns are likely to remain multiple, has been treated by Hamilton (1994) who makes an important epistemological point in examining the role of civilization in patterning economic activity. He notes that few theorists have treated the question "because to do so one needs to construct a conceptual framework that allows for a *continuity of causation*—for a production and reproduction of similar forms—across time and space" (p. 185). In essence the literature on the question has instead been concerned to argue the case usually for either the state or the market to have engendered "modernity." It tends to have expressed itself in a contest between different institutional spheres for primary causation of a specific end condition. Such accounts have had "a pernicious effect on our understanding of civilizational phenomena…because our understanding of how societies and economies are organized becomes trapped in Eurocentric explanations for historical change" (p. 190).

To escape from this universalist type of explanation, and at the same time to come to terms with explaining how patterns of organizing economic behavior produce and reproduce themselves through time and space, requires acceptance of a unit of analysis and if not that then at least a framework of analysis, which is disturbingly rare in the field of management theory.

As Cheng has pointed out, "the organizational science profession has so far focused almost exclusively on 'context-excluded' relationships in the search for universal knowledge…evidenced…in the lack of theoretical models that integrate the societal context into the analysis of organizations" (Cheng, 1994, p. 164). The profession needs to accustom itself to a new unit of analysis.

That unit is the functioning societal system incorporating and focusing on the organization but going beyond organizational boundaries, and studied as a whole system *per se*. Comparison is of systems, not of parts. The issue is not whether one element is more basic than others. Instead, the search is to understand the "configurational resonance among all the elements" (Hamilton, 1994, p. 190). As Ragin (1987) has pointed out in arguing for the comparison of social systems and learning from how Whitley (1992) has operationalized such advice, the issue in comparative social science is how to move on from the sterile—because decontextualized—comparison of deracinated elements. Until now comparative management theory has not got very far as it circles around the comparison of leadership style or organizational structure, or work attitudes, in country A versus country B.

Whitley's (1992, 1999) work on business systems has been a rare and important advance in the field because of the virtue it displays of presenting complete analyses of functioning business systems. As did Weber, he works within a cultural boundary, takes institutions as central to the explanatory framework, and also sees the institutional structure as reflecting older and deeper structures which he prefers to label institutional when others might label them cultural. He also uses ideal types as a means of making the complex interactions tractable. The end product is a typology of coherent business contexts but with their derivation and their current functioning made comprehensible. Firms in their societies become understandable comparatively.

Flowing from these considerations are two core questions. Does the framework proposed by Child offer an equally rich basis for analysis? And does it do so with a different emphasis? At a more practical level it should perhaps also be seen in terms of implementation, and two further criteria: does it form an inspiring basis for intellectual cooperation between disciplines: and is it likely to foster research programs by stimulating new processes of conceptualizing and operationalizing its key components. If the answer is yes on all fronts then an important advance has been made. To consider these questions I shall later take the not entirely hypothetical case of a research center dedicated to comparative management and considering the adoption of the model in question as its main conceptual platform for the foreseeable research future.

CHILD'S EVOLUTIONARY FRAMEWORK AS A BASIS FOR ANALYSIS

The first point to note about the proposed framework is that it is designed to explain evolutionary processes and thus it meets the challenge identified by Hamilton of avoiding the mechanical cause and effect predictions of, for example, "what produced the Asian miracle" or "what is needed for modernization." This is a dynamic process model and it is concerned with understanding as much as with demonstrated connections. It is concerned to handle the incorporation of both systemic change, as for instance in the evolving economy of China, and also interaction between components as different in nature as the material and the ideational, as organization structure and organization process. The phrase "cross-national" implies acceptance of the nation-state as the primary envelope and although obviously one presumes flexibility in this, it serves to emphasize that the role of government, and the national institutional structure would be strongly involved in the account.

It is unclear as to whether the dynamics of the process being studied demand more or less free actors and this becomes an important consideration. The centrally planned economy of a totalitarian state could be mapped onto this model in terms of the categories themselves. They would in some instances be vestigial as for instance in matters of performance feedback or strategic choice. But can the inner workings of the patterns of determinacy be assumed to be similar across comparisons? Would we see a variety of species emerging by some universal evolutionary process, or do we have a variety of evolutionary trajectories? At what level might it be possible to generalize? This question is of course posed from an economics type of perspective, where market forces are deemed to standardize the context and to allow enquiry into more specific connections. But it is nevertheless an issue as to whether or not the model stretches to include contexts where behavior might be irrational from the standpoint of most economics and most psychology and yet might account for much activity in, say, China, Vietnam, and other places in varying degrees. On this point, Whitley has been scrupulous in restricting his various analyses to conditions where market forces are at work, but this may be due to his interest in comparing varieties of oranges and not tomatoes and oranges.

The Whitley framework, as with that of Weber, concentrates heavily on the determining role of institutions and also sees them at two levels. First, the proximate influences in which firms are embedded, and then the further, older, or deeper influences in which the proximate are in turn embedded. Whitley does not specifically address as a category the material systems of economic and technological rationality, but he does not filter them out of his analytical accounts either. Having them specifically addressed as in Child's proposed model, will perhaps see them handled more clearly and accessibly. The point is to foster their inclusion systematically without handing over primacy in the final account, a move which will doubtless provoke controversy, but by providing a wider explanation in which debate can be constructively engaged, there may result some valuable tempering of the universalism which so characterizes their use.

A similar kind of logic applies to the treatment of systems of ideas, including culture, as a separate analytical category but intertwined with the material. Such interlocking should do much to add impetus to the directional trend where "cross-cultural" is replaced by "cross-national" and the explanandum made more complex and more challenging in the interest of some eventual breakthroughs in understanding.

The real dilemma has always been to explain *how* culture works, in other words to trace the connections between national or international systems of ideas into patterns of social values, and then into the crystallizing out of stable institutions. How are the values and the institutions causally connected? How might one operationalize Eisenstadt's (1968) notion of the "transformative capacity" of the ideas.

I would propose here, as an alternative perspective on how environments are shaped that the mechanisms of this process connecting culture and institutions be seen in three aspects. First, the vertical ordering of society and second, the horizontal ordering of society connect closely with the two dominant aspects of culture identified in a long research tradition empirically and labeled most evidently by Hofstede (1980) as power distance and collectivism-individualism. These two dimensions of societal order can be traced in the evolution of institutions as at least significant if not sole determinants. The third main influence is that of rationality, an obviously complex and subtle field still very little understood. The dominant presentation of it is via the Cartesian rationality of economic man in perfect markets, but as well as being ungrounded this avoids recognition of two other features of the general question of rationality: first, there are alternative rationalities to the Western scientific one, in other words, alternative mental frameworks via which to interpret reality (Maruyama, 1974); second the capacity to organize a state efficiently to pursue stated aims, the substantive rationality to get done what needs to be done, appears to be largely culturally conditioned, and highly significant in either stimulating or inhibiting "activism" and coordination in the economic arena.

As Gellner has pointed out "the sphere of culture remained more immune than some others to the spread of rationality.... In a way, the irrationalization of culture is the obverse of the pervasive rationalization of cognition" (Gellner, 1992, p. 150).

In this regard, Child's reminder on the workings of rationality is timely and significant. In differentiating between formal (and material) rationality and substantive (and ideational) rationality, but seeing both converge as influences on the formation and workings of societal institutions, he provides an important sense of direction for formulating research questions. Especially so, as he points out, when the interplay of these forces is so central to the workings out of globalization in practice. The work of Boisot (1995) in describing the cultural conditioning of "information space" is revelatory of the kind of new understanding which can be released when such analysis is pursued. Thus the cultural preconditioning of vertical order, horizontal order, and rationality may well be the most fruitful avenues for exploring the linkages to institutions.

A related but minor question here is that of reciprocal determinacy, as it is possible to argue that institutions foster ideas in return. Ideas of participation and consensus in Japan today are likely to owe much to the longstanding institutions of local government set in place centuries ago. It is a two-way arrow. It would, for instance, be hard to deny that national systems of ideas and of institutions are themselves influenced by organizational outcomes just as much as they influenced organizations. The emergence of democratic capitalism as a set of ideals, and the elaboration of the fabric of institutions supporting it have doubtless been reinforced by the success of organizations in such systems in delivering on societal purposes with wide legitimacy. It is not at all clear in the diagram proposed by Child in his Figure 2 how this feedback loop works, unless it is intended that the "task contingencies" and "value preferences" go both ways, in other words, back into the realm of ideas as well as forward into strategic choice. This would be crucial to the evolutionary theme in the explanation as without feedback there would be no learning.

Another field of determinacy where understanding remains very limited is that between institutions and organizations and in this regard Child identifies three functions of institutions: forming competence; providing service; regulation. These are useful indicators of research direction, but could well be added to and strengthened by a close consideration of the functions of facilitation and transformation which they serve. As Child might say, the process needs to be unpacked and its components laid out.

To help unpack the influences flowing between institutions and organizations it may be useful to consider what is made available for use by managers as the essence of an explanation. What institutions do is to amplify or suppress the availability of certain facilitating elements. The most obvious example is the availability of finance through a well-developed banking system with all its attendant institutional components such as joint stock companies, exchanges, an accounting profession, and so on.

In the total facilitating process the essentials are arguably three: finance to build and equip what is needed; human talent to make use of what the investment buys; and a framework of adequate trust relations to foster exchange based on the achievement of credible commitment. In other words, the availability of financial capital, human capital, and social capital. But availability is too simple a notion for the explanatory task here. What needs to be understood are the channels of "delivery" of these facilitating features and the way such alternative structures influence the typical, or perhaps stereotypical organization. If in the Anglo-Saxon case a businessman goes to the stockmarket for capital, in the Japanese case to sister companies, in the Korean case to the government, or in the Chinese case to a group of friends, then this will establish quite different patterns of stakeholder behavior, of investment priorities, of strategic planning horizons, and of decision structures. So too with the creation and allocation of human skill and talent, as it will vary not just in amount, but in specificity of application, in the organizing of its availability, and in the structures of it augmentation.

Social capital, manifest, for example, in the institutional fabric of civil society as a supplement to interpersonal trust, will, by its availability and by its particular structures, have a determining influence on the patterns of economic exchange, cooperation, and coordination, all of which become visible at the organizational level of analysis. There is much ground here for the exploration of how social capital and its availability to an organization via its members, can result in adaptive efficiency in ways not explained by theories of markets or in several conventional approaches to organization theory such as transaction costs, population ecology, or resource-based analysis (Moran, 1999). Because such capital is social, it is then inevitably connected into society, and into particular societal understandings about trust.

A major difference which appears between the Whitley model and the proposed Child model is that in the former there is a unifying thread running through the description of the business system. This lies in a theme of coordination and control and is reminiscent of Mintzberg's (1979) use of the same concept at the organizational level of analysis. What Whitley proposes is a set of coordinative control structures and processes which help to frame the description of something inherently very complex. The business system is seen as three coordinative arrangements: one in the field of ownership and the putting together and controlling of the organization as a functioning mechanism; a second in the field of wider coordination between organizations across an economy; the third the coordination of organizational members other than owners into a state of cooperation with the organization. Consciously oversimplifying it is possible to argue that Mintzberg's breakthrough in classifying organizational types was to identify five coordinating/ control mechanisms as "the most basic elements of structure, the glue that holds organisations together. From these all else follows" (Mintzberg, 1979, p. 3). Whitley's breakthrough may prove to be the derivation of a typology of societal economic structures based on coordination and control at a different level of analysis from that of internal organizational structure. The latter explanation is arguably more complex because of a quantum leap in the number of variables in the account, but the focus on coordination as the core of a typology has proved fertile once and may well do so again.

Having implied that there are evidently rich rewards from the business systems model in terms of its explanatory power, it is essential to acknowledge that the challenge of comparison as such was only half of Child's agenda in proposing his new framework. The other half is to facilitate the study of cross-national organizations, proliferating as they are at inordinate speed. This agenda is inevitably also comparative, but not centrally so. It is much more concerned with the organizational embracing of variety, and it brings into focus an issue so far largely ignored: that of how global and local forces, together and in relation to each other, bear upon the nature of organization. Its use would additionally bring into the account questions of strategic choice, and of the degrees of organizational independence from both the material and ideational sets of influences. This is a set of questions which the business systems model is able to answer only indirectly. It will in fact answer them very well in terms of explaining how the components of cross-national firms (from individual employees to indigenous divisions) are likely to behave and why. It will be very informative about the constituent parts of alliances, joint ventures, and other hybrids, but its core agenda is the configurational resonance among the elements, system by system, rather than the mixing of such systems.

USING THE FRAMEWORK IN RESEARCH

For a researcher, or an institution, considering new work in the field of comparative management, the stimulus provided in Child's paper comes in two forms. First, the framework itself forces new and necessary perspectives, fields of enquiry, and arenas for interaction among influences onto the research design agenda. It is a reminder of how much needs to be included in any final account, no matter how refined a single enquiry may be.

Second, in the creation of it, a number of specific areas of new enquiry have been identified, and they bring up to date the advice given in earlier reviews, such updating being now essential in light of the speed of globalization.

It is worthwhile now noting this advice, in summary form, in the interests of stimulating its adoption, and assessing its viability.

In essence, and in consort with the earlier critical discourse in the field, Child proposes six endeavors to be embarked upon and makes three observations about methodology. The specific new fields of enquiry, identified now as a possible set of research agendas are as follows. They are presented here as separate fields but could be also linked.

New Forms of Operationalizing Key Concepts

The challenge being met here is that of conceptual equivalence across cultures so that a concept such as "control" can be used in ways which are protected against unseen differences in meaning which might affect researching it comparatively. It will be necessary to disaggregate the notion into its underlying constituents and then subsequently to reconfigure and re-integrate it so that it becomes a better-tuned and doubtless more complex instrument for comparative work. An example of work of this nature is that of Smith (1989) in the study of leadership.

Indigenous Behavioral Theory

The influence of the ideational appears to flow into the micro processes of organization so that organizational behavior becomes heavily dependent on societal context, arguably much more so than in the case of structure, governance, and strategy, where more universal and material factors are in the ascendant. This requires the construction of more situational organizational behavior theory, grounded in different societies, and sufficient to generate implications for organizational design.

Definitions of Nations and Culture

Integration of definitions is needed to foster the understanding of the role of culture in the wider societal frame of reference, and to place it in a way which takes account also of the parallel forces of economic logics, legal constraint, and political influence. It may then be possible to get inside the workings of rationality, both its formal and material version, and its substantive and ideational versions.

Institutional Evolution and Influence

There are large gaps in knowledge about the interface between institutions and organizations. Specific research needs here are (a) the processes whereby institutions are formed and have an impact on organizations, (b) how do institutions and their attendant norms adapt to the material forces of an economic and technical nature, and to the ideational forces which may be running in parallel, (c) what is the interplay between the institutional and organizational worlds in the light of strategic choice.

Mechanisms and Processes of Globalization

To see globalization in terms of the interplay between formal and substantive rationality in conditions of strategic choice, can then lead to questions about the level of autonomy of firms from external influence and standardization. Two significant questions emerge: which organizations are likely to be influenced; and which aspects of organizing will be driven toward convergence?

Systemic and Inter-systemic Change

Historically there is a shifting sequence of coincidences where important sets of determinants flow together for periods and then flow apart. The nineteenth-century availability of Victorian values coincided as it were happily with other features in the Anglo-Saxon context. So too Confucian ideals during the resurgence of the regional ethnic Chinese in Asia after 1950. Ideals of empowerment are also seemingly influential in emerging Western organizational responses.

What is the nature of change brought into play here ideationally? What features of organization respond to different pressures for change? What changes due to material trends, what to global ideas, and what to the high context local influences? Answers to such questions require multilevel and multidimensional research of challenging complexity.

Research Methodology

In addition to considering the above new research themes, any researchers would also benefit from the proffered advice on research method. The lessons here are:

a. The need for a more comprehensive examination of organizational variables, preferably by direct enquiry rather than via surrogate measures alone, in order to handle the new multiple perspective,

b. a more comprehensive inclusion of contextual features and the avoidance of resort to residuals,

c. more elaborate research designs, including: more comprehensive theorization about variables; the inclusion of high and low context perspectives; illustration of both local and global influences at work; acknowledgement of within-nation variance as well as between-nation,

d. use of both comprehensive views of systems and at the same time specific inner workings,

e. the development of large databases (seen as very rare so far) with which to track the features noted above,

f. studies of the dynamics through time of the interactions among aspects such as the material, the ideational, low context, high context, structure, and process. A longitudinal study of processes of internationalization in a firm could, for example, embrace such interactions and be very revealing of the underlying theoretical issues.

The adoption of all or part of such a research agenda, and the willingness to take seriously the methodological advice on offer in Child's paper, would undoubtedly foster long-overdue progress in comparative management theory. One might also express the hope that stimulus to multidisciplinary work would be provided by the vision of what might be achievable, and how it might be achieved. The cooperation between institutions necessary, if the appropriate data banks are to be constructed, is worthy of strong advocacy.

REFERENCES

Adler, N. J. (1983). Cross-cultural Management Research: The Ostrich and the Trend. *Academy of Management Review, 8*(3), 226-232.

Adler, N. J., Doktor, R., & Redding, S. G. (1986). From the Atlantic to the Pacific century: Cross-cultural management reviewed. *Yearly Review of Management of the Journal of Management, 12*(2), 295-318.

Barrett, G. V., & Bass, B. M. (1976). "Cross-cultural issues in industrial and organizational psychology. In M.D. Dunnette (Ed), *Handbook of industrial and organizational psychology* (pp. 1639-1686). Chicago: Rand-McNally.

Beaty, D. T., & Mendenhall, M. (1990). *Theory building in international management: an archival review and recommendations for future research.* Academy of Management Annual Meeting, San Francisco.

Boisot, M. (1995).*Information Space*. London: Routledge.

Boyacigiller, N., & Adler, N. J. (1991). The parochial dinosaur: Organizational science in a global context. *Academy of Management Review, 16*(2), 262-290.

Cheng, J .L. C. (1994). On the concept of universal knowledge in organizational science: Implications for cross-national research. *Management Science, 40*(1), 162-168.

Child, J. (1981). Culture, contingency and capitalism in the cross-national study of organizations. In L.L. Cummings & B.M. Staw (Eds.), *Research in organizational behavior* (Vol 13, pp. 303-356). Greenwich CT, JAI Press.

Eisenstadt, S. P. (1996). *Japanese civilization: A comparative view*. Chicago: University of Chicago Press.

Eisenstadt, S. N. (1968). *The protestant ethic and modernization: A comparative view*. New York: Basic Books.

Fukuyama, F. (1995). *Trust: The social virtues and the creation of prosperity*. New York: Free Press.

Gellner, E. (1992). *Reason and culture*. Oxford: Blackwell.

Hamilton, G. G. (1994). Civilizations and the organization of economies. In N.J. Smelser & R. Swedberg (Eds.), *The handbook of economic sociology*. Princeton, NJ: Princeton University Press.

Hofstede, G. (1980). *Culture's consequences*. London: Sage.

Huntington, S. P. (1996). *The clash of civilizations and the remaking of world order*. New York: Simon and Schuster.

Landes, D. S. (1998). *The wealth and poverty of nations*, New York: Norton.

Maruyama, M. (1974). Paradigmatology and its application to cross-disciplinary, cross-professional, and cross-cultural communication. *Dialectica, 28*(3-4), 135-196.

Mintzberg, H. (1979). *The structuring of organizations*. Englewood Cliffs, NJ: Prentice-Hall

Moran, P. F. (1999). *Value creation and social capital.* Unpublished doctoral dissertation, INSEAD.

Ragin, C. C. (1987). *The comparative method.* Berkeley: University of California Press.

Redding, S. G. (1994). Comparative management theory: jungle, zoo or fossil-bed? *Organization Studies, 15*(3), 323-360.

Roberts, K. H. (1970). On looking at an elephant: An evaluation of cross-cultural research related to organizations. *Psychological Bulletin, 74*(5), 327-350.

Smith, P. B. et al. (1989). On the generality of leadership style measures across cultures. *Journal of Occupational Psychology, 62,* 97-109.

Triandis, H. C. (1992). Cross-cultural industrial and organizational psychology. In M.D. Dunnette (Ed.), *Handbook of industrial and organizational psychology* (Vol 4, pp. 103-172). Palo-Alto, CA: Consulting Psychologists Press.

Whitley, R. (1992). *Business systems in East Asia.* London: Sage.

Whitley, R. (1999). *Divergent capitalism.* Oxford: Oxford University Press.

ON THE INTEGRATION OF COMPARATIVE AND INTERNATIONAL MANAGEMENT
COMMENTS ON CHILD'S ESSAY

Oded Shenkar

John Child should be commended for taking on a difficult task. In an essay tracking previous efforts packaged as special issues or research forums of such journals as *Management Science* and *The Academy of Management Journal*, he takes stock of "cross-national organization and management" and revisits classical topics such as the universality of management thought and convergence versus divergence. Child goes a step further, however. In addition to reviewing the field and its theoretical underpinnings, he proposes an integrative approach leading to a unifying theoretical framework as a way of advancing the current state of knowledge.

Periodic assessments and soul searching are essential parts of the scientific process, and Child takes up the challenge quite well. In my opinion, however, his contribution lies neither in revisiting established concepts on theoretical diversity, universality, and convergence, nor in providing an integrative framework that is by and large in line with extant theories on modernization. His main contribution,

Advances in International Comparative Management, Volume 13, pages 107-112.
Copyright © 2000 by JAI Press Inc.
All rights of reproduction in any form reserved.
ISBN: 0-7623-0589-4

somewhat hidden in this essay, has to do with pinpointing the current disconnection between comparative and international management. This seemingly simple suggestion is of major theoretical and practical significance.

In this very brief comment, I review Child's propositions on the state of the field as well as his proposed framework. I state my concerns that the "tidy garden" Child sees does not come at a price of sacrificing the theoretical pluralism and diversity that are the essence of the scientific process. Finally, I delineate some ideas for mid-range theory development (Merton, 1956) that builds on the modernization literature while seeking to close the gap between comparative and international management.

A WORD ON TERMINOLOGY

The adjective Child chooses to label the field, "cross-national," clearly seeks to avoid the pitfalls of the more commonly used term of "cross-cultural management" and its embedded bias toward cultural explanations. While suffering from other limitations (see Ronen, 1986, for a review), "cross-national management" is more comprehensive and neutral in connotation. Disagreements on terminology are often seen as indicative of a low level of paradigm development (Lodahl & Gordon, 1972). In a field as broad and integrative as management, the disagreement may simply reflect the variety of lenses the field offers with which to view the world. Those lenses are derivatives of the plural theoretical frameworks that are embedded in core disciplines and which make up its comprehensive if disjointed knowledge base.

The distinction between "comparative" and "international" management is an old one. Comparative management is, well, comparative. It refers to such questions as how and why the management styles of Japanese and U.S. executives are similar in some respects but different in others. International management, in contrast, refers to the actual *crossing* of national boundaries, for example, the mode of entry used by the MNE when investing in a foreign market. This field is also often called "multinational management," a term which implicitly assumes that international management is the rightful domain of the large MNE, something that the empirical evidence does not bear in an era where small firms engage in international activities without becoming "transnational" or "global." "Multinational" has become however a unifying term for a camp arguing that the MNE is the core of international business scholarship.

WHERE WE ARE: THE STATE OF THE FIELD

Child's point of departure is what he sees as the deplorable state of the field of cross-national management. He senses a crisis and laments the lack of direction and the absence of visible progress over 30 years of research. This conclusion, based on a review written by Gordon Redding, is debatable. In my opinion, the advance in both comparative and international management has been quite remarkable, if uneven. The knowledge that we have today is far superior in theory, method, and empirical scope. A wider range of theories, whether home grown or imported from core disciplines such as economics and sociology, is now in use, with new theoretical frameworks emerging (e.g., option theory in international strategic management). Greater methodological sophistication, whether in instrument adaptation or nonparametric analysis, is evident, and with it, a greater diversity of research methods. Empirical research, aided by international networks and a growth in institutional sources, has advanced in both scope and rigor.

In the past, we have made it a habit to lament the difficulty of doing comparative and international research, so much so that we would start the typical article with a "disclaimer" explaining how difficult and expensive it was. In international trade terms, we wanted to be treated as an "infant industry," protected from the theoretical and methodological rigor demanded in our disciplinary foundations. That we no longer seek such protection and have our work admitted into the disciplinary outlets, is a measure of how far we have gone. This obviously does not mean that no further progress is needed, but it does put things in perspective and has a bearing on how we should proceed.

If I take issue with Child's view of the state of cross-national management, I am in complete agreement with him that where we are seriously lacking is in the knowledge flow across the two fields. I believe that the relationship between the two is more important and useful than the distinction between "low context" and "high context" theories. While comparative management has been often associated with "high context" perspectives versus the "low context" perspective of international management, there is no one-to-one correlation between the two. Nor is it a static or homogeneous picture. Some proponents of universal need theories such as McClelland actually recognized that needs varied across societies (e.g., McClelland, 1963). Universal motivation and leadership theories have gradually been replaced with process theories better suited to accommodate national variations. The point is that comparative as well as international management rely on a diverse theoretical base encompassing both convergence and divergence forces, albeit in different configurations.

As bodies of knowledge, comparative and international management remain mostly separate, with little or no communication, minimal cross-over, and no systematic mechanisms for cooperation with the possible exception of overlapping membership in professional associations. This disjunction represents a serious problem to two fields that are in fact complementary. To comparative management, the exclusion of an international management perspective has meant a steady decline in relevance. In an age of globalization, interest in mere differences has become, well, academic. At the same time, the neglect of comparative management has robbed international management of what could have been its most important theoretical and methodological base.

IN DEFENSE OF THEORETICAL PLURALISM

Theoretical pluralism, in and of itself, is a healthy phenomenon. It broadens the scope of research questions, analysis, and interpretation as well as expands the repertoire of methodological strategies. Where Child sees confusion and paralysis, I see diversity and opportunity. Proponents of "cultural theory" will surely attribute this to my non-British upbringing, but I somehow don't view the "tidy garden" as an ideal. The garden may be orderly yet boring, neat but uninspiring. The garden offers a respite from the real world, but it is neither the real world nor its most effective representation. While I share Child's views on the importance of integration, I am concerned that such integration does not sacrifice theoretical pluralism. What I would like to see, and I believe Child too, is an integration effort that is based on and retains theoretical diversity.

Child's comprehensive review of some of the relevant theories influencing management thought shows the value of theoretical pluralism. Each of the theories (and one could argue with the choice) offers a different perspective, a unique lens from which to look at and analyze managerial phenomena based on different underlying assumptions and using a different methodological strategy. Some, such as institutional theory, already combine multiple theoretical insights. Others, such as theories of economic universals, do not, but they do bring a perspective on the world that has the potential to cross-fertilize other theories even if by way of conflict.

It is the meeting of comparative and international management that makes the juxtaposition of theoretical perspectives possible. What's a better way to examine the role of culture than to subject it to the test of international encounter between firms and individuals? Likewise, how is it possible to examine claims for economic universals in the absence of an in-depth comparison of national economic and business systems? This worthwhile effort of integration will be counterproductive, however, if it ends up suppressing theoretical diversity and development by offering a single model that predicts the obvious but fails to explain the most interesting and important outlying cases. What comes to mind is the lament of frustrated economists upon discovering that Japan was not behaving quite as expected in its reaction to exchange rate alignment, for example, not increasing its import goods consumption to the tune of the yen appreciation. The explanation that "Japan does not fit the model" was obviously an admission of both theoretical and applied failure. This is one trap we should avoid.

IN SEARCH OF AN INTEGRATIVE FRAMEWORK

To students of development and modernization, the ongoing debate in the management literature on convergence and divergence is a classical case of déjà vu. Convergence forces existed before, albeit not at the same level and magnitude of the Internet age. Then as now, proponents of convergence judged all societies by how far they were off the Western benchmark, extrapolating how quickly they were going to be Westernized. It did not happen then and I doubt that will happen now, but this remains a legitimate debate to the extent that we are not limited to one particular model which we may have to reject once a new Japan comes along.

The idea to look at Max Weber for inspiration is excellent if not original. A result of premature closure, many students of organization know of Weber only from the terse and mostly erroneous descriptions found in management textbooks, mostly in relation to his frequently abused model of bureaucracy. That Weber's framework of research and analysis was closely related to his own national and social background (e.g., Pye, 1968; Shenkar, 1984; Weber, 1964), does not make it less useful. Weber offers many promising cues on combining an economic and a sociological perspective on organizations, while simultaneously tying them with technological and national developments. In his treaty, *The Religion of China*, Weber (1951) is explicit in his portrayal of the interplay between forces which in modern management thought have become compartmentalized.

Most important, Weber shows how diverse forces combine to create organizational phenomena in a way no single explanation could, offering a promising platform for theory development (e.g., Bendix, 1974; McNeil, 1978; Collins, 1980). Weber's much abused model of bureaucracy is a good example. Touted in current texts as an example of a closed-system analysis, it is anything but. A part of his broader theory of social and economic organization, Weber shows organizational structure and processes to be a product of authority relations and economic development, among others, and how they were shaped by both internal and external forces over the years. It is this comparative and longitudinal perspective that we should follow.

The crucial portion of literature missing from Child's essay is that on modernization, in particular the post-Weberian tradition of analysis exemplified by the work of S.N. Eisenstadt (e.g., 1963, 1973). Scholars of modernization engaged in a direct effort to integrate comparative and international management. They not only asked such questions as how did the Chinese system of government differ from the Japanese one, but also what happened when China was faced with foreign influences. Scholars of modernization offered a comprehensive framework covering not only cultural values but also social institutions, long before there was an institutional school in economics or management. They studied the social and political groups who were the "carriers" of those values and researched the implications for organizational processes (e.g., Eisenstdadt, 1968).

It is beyond the space of this brief comment to present a thorough review of the literature on modernization and its related realms, but I will use an example or two to show its relevance to Child's framework. One example is Etzioni's compliance classification. This framework has already been used to explain the interplay of ideology and efficiency and its impact on Chinese organizations (Skinner & Winckler, 1969). Another indicative example is Child's attribution of organizational variation in convergence patterns to the relative impact of international institutions. The sociological and modernization literature would offer an alternative, in fact complementary explanation. From this perspective, variable convergence is the result of organizations being variably situated along cultural center and periphery (Shils, 1962 and elsewhere) and having different "pattern maintenance" functions (Parsons, 1956; see Shenkar, 1984, 1996, for an application to China). It is this variety of thought that we must retain and that it is well within the Weberian tradition.

REFERENCES

Bendix, R. (1974). *Work and authority in industry: Ideologies and management in the course of industrialization.* Berkeley: University of California Press.

Collins, R. (1980). Weber's last theory of capitalism: a systematization. *American Sociological Review, 45*, 925-942.

Eisenstadt, S. N. (1963). *The political systems of empires.* New York: The Free Press.

Eisenstadt, S. N. (1968). Some reflections on the variability of development and organizational structures. *Administrative Science Quarterly, 13*, 491-497.

Eisenstadt, S. N. (1973). *Tradition, change and modernity.* New York: Wiley.

Lodahl, J. B., & Gordon, G. (1972). The structure of scientific fields and the functioning of university graduate departments. *American Sociological Review, 37*, 57-72.

McClelland, D. (1963). Motivational patterns in Southeast Asia with special reference to the Chinese case. *Social Issues, 19*, 6-19.

McNeil, K. (1978). Understanding organizational power: Building on the Weberian legacy. *Administrative Science Quarterly, 23*, 65-89.

Merton, R. K. (1956). *Social theory and social structure.* New York: Free Press.

Parsons, T. (1956). Suggestions for a sociological approach to the theory of organizations. *Administrative Science Quarterly, 1*, 63-85.

Pye, L. W. (1968). *The spirit of Chinese politics: a psycho-cultural study of the authority crisis in political development.* Cambridge, MA: MIT Press.

Ronen, S. (1986). *Comparative and multinational management.* New York: Wiley.

Shenkar, O. 1984. Is bureaucracy inevitable? The Chinese experience. *Organization Studies, 5* (4), 289-306.

Shenkar, O. (1996). The firm as a total institution: Reflections on the Chinese state enterprise. *Organization Studies, 17* (6), 885-907.

Shils, E. (1962). *Political development in the new states.* The Hague: Mouton.

Skinner, G. W., & Winckler, E. A. (1969). Compliance succession in rural Communist China: A cyclical theory. In A. Etzioni (Ed.), *A sociological reader of complex organizations.* New York: Holt, Rinehart & Winston, 410-438.

Weber, M. (1964). *The theory of social and economic organization* (trans. Henderson & Parsons). New York: The Free Press.

Weber, M. (1951). *The religion of China* (trans. Hans H. Gerth). New York: The Free Press.

A COMMENT ON THE COMMENTARIES

John Child

The four commentaries on my paper by Buckley, Kimberley, Redding, and Shenkar advance discussion of the subject in a number of ways. This short comment addresses certain of the key points they make.

The first issue concerns the correctness of my assertion that we face a problem in studying organization cross-nationally. Kimberly and Shenkar both question whether there should be "a sense of frustration and crisis" in regard to theory and research in this area. They maintain that considerable advances have been made in the theory, method, and scope of research. Given the explosive rate of progress in organized cross-national activity, and the new communications technologies that facilitate this, it is not surprising that scholars have to work hard to keep up with, and make sense of, what is going on. This, however, lends the subject its importance and excitement, and it constitutes a challenge rather than grounds for pessimism.

I would not wish to dispute the progress that has been made. Nevertheless, the subject continues to suffer from an ambiguity about its primary focus and from the lack of a unifying theoretical framework. Shenkar instances the disjunction between comparative and international management. These two bodies of knowledge are complementary, yet have so largely gone their own mutually exclusive

Advances in International Comparative Management, Volume 13, pages 113-116.
Copyright © 2000 by JAI Press Inc.
All rights of reproduction in any form reserved.
ISBN: 0-7623-0589-4

ways. As a consequence, there have been missed opportunities. In Shenkar's words:

> To comparative management, the exclusion of an international management perspective has meant a steady decline in relevance. In an age of globalization, interest in mere differences has become, well, academic. At the same time, the neglect of comparative management has robbed international management of what could have been its most important theoretical and methodological base.

My argument is that we cannot fully capitalize on the richness of diverse theoretical perspectives unless we make some progress toward building bridges between them. This is not to criticize theoretical pluralism, but rather to say that we need to find a way of building upon it. It seems to me that the disjunction between theoretical perspectives constitutes a major challenge, assuming that each has potentially something valid to offer to our understanding of cross-national organization. That was the point of departure for my essay.

As Kimberley notes and questions, there is an underlying assumption here that we can talk about a "field" of inquiry when addressing organization cross-nationally. Otherwise, the disjunctions between comparative and international management, or low and high context perspectives, would not necessarily give rise to significant missed opportunities. If this is not a coherent area of inquiry, there would not be much point in seeking an integrative framework. I borrowed the well-worn metaphor of the elephant to express my view that there is an identifiable field of cross-national organization, albeit one of large scope and complexity. The metaphor, of course, points to a phenomenon that is of itself sufficiently large and diversified to be open to quite different interpretations if viewed from different perspectives. It does not exclude the possibility that such "animals" come in various colors, shapes, and sizes due to their history of evolution within particular contexts. In other words, my assumption is that the phenomenon of organization, defined as purposeful managed collective activity, centers on a number of common dimensions that are present, albeit in varying degrees and forms, whatever the national context. For this reason, it constitutes a coherent area of study.

The intended focus of the essay is on organization rather than organizations. It is concerned with the organizing of collective activity rather than with specific units having their own legal or social identity. Perhaps, as Kimberly argues, it would be better to employ Weick's term "organizing," except this could imply the total privileging of process over structure which I have sought to avoid. Internationalization is bringing about major changes that render it hazardous to theorize about "organizations" in terms of their previously familiar appearance. The concept of organizations with clearly defined and stable boundaries is becoming increasingly redundant with the growth of alliances, networks, virtual organization, self-employed contracting, and e-commerce, which is proceeding apace cross-nationally. These new arrangements are all modes of organization or organizing, but ones that are not necessarily, or even typically, centered on the fixed clusters of transactions that we have traditionally called organizations.

How we organize cross-nationally is coming to matter more and more. This is why Shenkar is correct in emphasizing the urgency of a meeting between comparative and international management. He sees this as enabling the juxtaposition of their theoretical perspectives, as advocated in my essay. I would maintain, however, that it is equally the juxtaposing of perspectives that offers the way forward to effecting a meeting between these two approaches.

Redding's previous review of comparative management theory, and his research into East Asian capitalism, have been sources of inspiration for my essay. He has consistently emphasized that in order to understand the nature of organization we have to appreciate how it is socially embedded. Business organization, in his view, has to be analyzed in the context of the business systems in which it is located. These systems differ according to the cultures and institutions that have molded them, so that there are many national and regional variants of capitalism. The *Spirit of Chinese Capitalism* (the title of Redding's path-breaking study) is thus distinct from that of American and even Japanese capitalism. In his commentary, Redding elaborates how a study of functioning social systems incorporating and focusing on the organization is required, and how our understanding of organization cross-nationally would benefit from this perspective. Redding is at one with Weber in regarding economics as a cultural science, and he has employed an essentially Weberian analysis to delineate the limits to the Western legal-rational forms of organization in whose historical emergence Weber was particularly interested. Redding quotes Landes approvingly, that in economic development "culture makes all the difference."

It is instructive to contrast Redding with Buckley, as advocates respectively of the high and low context approaches. Buckley seems to doubt whether the incorporation of cultural variables will add much to explanation. In any case, he maintains, cultural variables are encompassed in transaction costs and information costs. It is the focus on material factors rather than on social context that gives economic approaches their power. He does, however, draw a distinction between markets that are "integrated" at national, regional, and international levels, suggesting that the contrasts in scope between these levels are giving rise to new strategies by multinational corporations. Buckley's recognition that markets are integrated reminds us how they, like other institutions, are socially organized and regulated along a number of dimensions that can make for national and regional differences, such as formal legal regulation and the less formal controls exercised by interest groups. The efficiency of markets may be the touchstone for economic analysis, but it would seem to be perilous to abstract from the social forces that can impinge upon that efficiency.

The debate between Buckley and Redding is germane to the key question of whether a constructive synthesis of different theoretical perspectives is possible. Their standpoints are opposed, but this does not necessarily mean they are irreconcilable. I believe that the main link between them lies in the concept of "value." Economic explanations depend on prices being attached to the positive social benefits offered by goods and services as well as to social costs. Different cultures and social systems place different values on these items, and this is where economics and culture come together. The extent to which national settings affect prices depends on whether they coincide with market boundaries and on the extent to which there is institutional intervention in those markets. In some cases there are global markets which set global prices with little or no effective institutional influence. In other cases, prices are strongly impacted by cultural preferences and institutional intervention. This suggests that in exploring the relevance of different markets for the cross-national organization of multinationals, which Buckley advocates, it is not sensible to divorce economics from social context. It supports the thesis that there is potential synergy between economic and sociocultural theories in accounting for the forces that shape the nature of organization and organizational actions in the world today.

Last but not least, I am indebted to Redding for the service he has provided in clarifying the research agendas and methodological implications contained in my essay. This has added appreciably to whatever contribution it otherwise makes.

PART II

ARTICLES

_____

INSTITUTIONAL INFLUENCES ON ORGANIZATIONAL CONTROL
A COMPARATIVE EXAMINATION OF AGENCY THEORY IN SINO-JAPANESE AND SINO-AMERICAN JOINT VENTURES

James A. Robins and Zhiang Lin

ABSTRACT

This paper reports empirical research on the applicability of agency theory in international joint ventures in the People's Republic of China. The research suggests that significant differences exist between Sino-Japanese and Sino-American joint ventures and that these differences reflect institutional effects associated with the nationality of foreign partner firms. The findings have important implications for the scope of organizational theories based on traditional utilitarian principles and for many of the prevailing approaches to comparative research on organizations. The paper argues that neither a narrow focus on the effects of local culture nor the search for universal theories of organization is suitable for the real complexity of contemporary international organizations.

Advances in International Comparative Management, Volume 13, pages 119-148.
Copyright © 2000 by JAI Press Inc.
All rights of reproduction in any form reserved.
ISBN: 0-7623-0589-4

The universality of theories of social and economic organization is one of the old-est and most basic concerns of the social sciences, and it has shaped work in orga-nization studies throughout the history of the field. For more than a century social scientists have been deeply divided over the significance of society and culture in economic organization and the degree to which general theories can be used to understand organizations in different sociocultural settings. These issues continue to play a major part in organization studies, both in comparative research on man-agement and in recent efforts to build new organizational theories on microeco-nomic foundations (Boyacigiller & Adler, 1991; Earley & Singh, 1995; Lammers & Hickson, 1979; Moe, 1984; Nilakant & Rao, 1994).

The issues examined in these different fields have been similar, but the work on international and comparative management has had little influence on discussion of topics in organizational economics such as the scope of agency theory. Although agency theory has become the dominant paradigm in a number of disci-plines (Bricker & Chandar, 1998; Hunt & Hogler, 1990; Kaplan, 1983; Nilakant & Rao, 1994), discussion of the applicability of the theory has been couched largely in terms of acceptance or rejection of axioms about individual rationality (Donaldson, 1990; Hirsch, Friedman, & Koza, 1990). The possibility that those axioms might be more suitable for certain social contexts than others has received only limited attention, despite the existence of a substantial body of comparative research on the sociocultural bases of organizational behavior.

There also has been a good deal of empirical research on the question of whether administrative structures and control systems actually resemble models drawn from agency theory (e.g., Davis & Thompson, 1994; Eisenhardt, 1985; Sapienza & Gupta, 1994; Tosi & Gomez-Mejia, 1989), though much less work has been done on the scope of agency theory or the conditions that might affect the applicability of the theory in different social settings (Bird & Wiersema, 1996). With a few exceptions (e.g., Bird & Wiersema, 1996; Chia, 1995), research on agency relations has been confined to a relatively narrow range of topics studied within North America and Western Europe (Wellbourne, Balkin, & Gomez-Mejia, 1995).

This has left two major questions about the scope of organizational economic theories such as agency theory largely unexplored: whether the theories are pecu-liar to the North American and European settings in which they have been devel-oped and tested, and whether the applicability of the theories varies for individuals in different institutional contexts within any given national society. This paper responds to both questions. It looks at agency theory in a setting out-side North America or Europe, and it examines the influence of institutional fac-tors other than local culture on the applicability of the theory. Local society or culture is one of the important factors that may influence individual views of eco-nomic behavior, but individuals within a given society also may exhibit system-atic differences due to other types of institutional effects (Kaplinski & Posthuma, 1994; Lincoln & Kalleberg, 1990).

This is not a conventional cross-cultural study. The research examines the applicability of agency theory among Chinese managers working in joint ventures in the People's Republic of China (PRC). It is closest to the type of research that Earley and Singh (1995) have described as "reduced form," as a primary objective of this study is to assess the degree to which a major theoretical approach developed within the United States may be useful for analyzing similar organizational issues in different social settings (Boyacigiller & Adler, 1991). This paper avoids the extreme positions that either view ideas as purely culture-bound or strive for a universal science of economic organization. The position adopted here is that economic organization is embedded within complex social and institutional frameworks that can be investigated in a systematic fashion (Cheng, 1994; Granovetter, 1985; Lin & Hui, 1999).

The paper is divided into two major sections. The first part of the paper provides a brief review of some basic principles of agency theory, attempts to place the theory in a broader context, and looks at institutional factors that may affect the applicability of theories of this type. The discussion of agency theory in this part of the paper is not intended to be a comprehensive treatment of the approach. Eisenhardt (1989), Levinthal (1988), Moe (1984), Nilakant and Rao (1994), and others have published extensive discussions of agency theory elsewhere. The purpose of this review is to provide an overview of the implications of agency theory for the nature of jobs and incentives in different types of organizations.

Institutional theory provides a basis for expectations about differences between Sino-Japanese and Sino-American joint ventures. Most research on international organizations such as joint ventures has focused on the effects of local cultures of host countries; however, institutional theory offers grounds for anticipating isomorphism with foreign parent firms as well. Foreign parent firms of ventures in emerging or transitional economies often play major roles in management training and organizational design, and foreign regulatory regimes may constrain control systems in joint ventures as well. Many practices differ substantially between Japanese and U.S. firms (Brown et al., 1997; Kagono et al., 1984) and the analysis of agency relations in Sino-Japanese and Sino-American joint ventures offers a good opportunity to explore the influences of parent firms.

The second part of the paper presents empirical findings that address the issues raised in the first section. The analysis described in this section is based on a survey of managers in several Sino-Japanese and Sino-American joint ventures in Shanghai, PRC. Eighty-one Chinese managers were interviewed using a detailed questionnaire covering a variety of issues related to the nature of their work, the form of performance evaluation, reward systems, and their views of a number of general elements of exchange and economic behavior. All managers were employed in joint ventures with major multinational corporations, and all of the joint ventures were in manufacturing industries.

The paper concludes with a brief discussion of some of the implications of the research. The study provides evidence that certain features of agency theory may be applicable to Chinese managers, but the applicability of the theory also varies across different types of joint ventures. There is an important indication that the concepts and attitudes held by Chinese managers in joint ventures vary with the nationality of foreign partner firms, and that these institutional effects may have significant implications for the generality of agency theory and other similar liberal, utilitarian theories as tools for understanding organization and control. The existence of these institutional effects also highlights the need for broader approaches to international research on organizations.

AGENCY RELATIONS AND INSTITUTIONAL EFFECTS IN INTERNATIONAL JOINT VENTURES: THEORETICAL CONSIDERATIONS

Agency Theory

The central tenets of agency theory are relatively simple. As Perrow (1986) has pointed out, the approach developed by Jensen (1983) and others posits three basic axioms about economic behavior: individuals engage in self-interested (optimizing) behavior, social relations can be decomposed into contracts "governed by competitive self-interest," and contracts are likely to be violated because they are costly to monitor and enforce (Perrow, 1986, p. 12). Exchange relationships of all types—ranging from market transactions to employment—are treated as contracts between "self-interested" individuals. These contracts establish incentives for individual economic behavior under specific assumptions about the definition of "self-interest." Analysis of the incentive properties of contracts provides a basis for expectations about the behavior of individuals who are party to specific types of contracts (Eisenhardt, 1989; Jensen, 1983).

The three axioms of agency theory identified by Perrow (1986) reflect a view of social relations that is deeply rooted in specific European traditions. The idea that society can be treated as a set of contractual arrangements among individuals with conflicting self-interests represents English utilitarianism in almost pure form. The central premises of agency theory have been passed down to contemporary economists from utilitarian and liberal social theorists such as Hobbes, Locke, and Mill (Robins, 1993). These concepts have come to play an important role in the prevailing ideologies of many Western nations, but their relevance to societies that do not share these traditions is far less certain (Bird & Wiersema, 1996).

The degree to which social and organizational theories developed in Western societies may be useful in settings other than North America and Western Europe has been widely questioned (e.g., Bird & Wiersema, 1996; Boyacigiller & Adler, 1991; Hofstede, 1983; Shenkar & von Glinow, 1994), and some of the strongest challenges to the universality of theories based on European traditions have come from researchers studying Asian societies (e.g., Adler et al., 1986; Bond, 1986; Lytle et al., 1995; Triandis, 1989). Shenkar and von Glinow (1994), for example, have argued that a wide variety of Western theories may be unsuitable for the study of organizations in China, while Bird and Wiersema (1995) have posed important questions about the validity of agency theory for analysis of organizations in Japan. The objections that have been raised to the use of Western organizational theories within Asian societies generally have emphasized the influence of national cultures on organizational behavior, with researchers arguing that prevailing attitudes and practices in non-Western societies may be fundamentally different from those of North America (Adler et al., 1986; Boyacigiller & Adler, 1991; Shenkar & von Glinow, 1994).

Institutional Effects on Joint Ventures

These questions about the influence of national culture on organizations are important but incomplete. As Scott (1991) has pointed out, national culture represents only one of the major sources of institutional effects on social relations. Organizations such as international joint ventures are likely to be subject to a variety of other institutional influences, including strong pressures for isomorphism with foreign parent firms (Abo, 1994; Kaplinski & Posthuma, 1994).

The study of Chinese managers in international joint ventures offers an excellent opportunity for an analysis of these issues. The managers surveyed in this study are Chinese nationals whose education and training prior to joining joint ventures took place within the PRC. Many of the respondents have had previous experience in Chinese state-owned enterprises, and some have spent periods in training at parent companies in Japan or the United States since joining the joint ventures. In many regards, the managers examined in this study epitomize a new class of people whose lives bridge the worlds of agrarian and industrial society, socialism and capitalism, and the Chinese past and future. These types of dualities—which play important roles in the lives of many managers in newly industrializing societies—also increase the likelihood that individuals will vary in the manner in which they view economic behavior and the ideological tenets of capitalism.

The fact that the organizations in which respondents work are joint ventures also is important. Joint ventures are neither truly local nor genuinely foreign organizations. They combine managers and management practices from foreign and domestic parent organizations, and they commonly devote substantial resources to training personnel in new techniques and styles of management. Efforts to transplant foreign management styles into joint ventures vary considerably, and the nationality of the foreign parent firm may have important bearing on those practices (Kaplinskyi & Posthuma, 1994).

Joint ventures provide exceptional opportunities for the study of theories of control such as agency theory. The resolution of problems of control is central to the successful management of joint ventures, and controls are one of the few areas of organization that may be explicitly negotiated in forming joint ventures. Standards and practices for control systems are among the most strongly institutionalized features of the societies in which parent firms operate, and isomorphism between joint ventures and parent companies in this domain is likely. International joint ventures provide a natural setting for examining whether institutions in the societies of parent firms serve as sources of institutional differences among joint ventures.

Finally, international joint ventures also have great practical importance. International organizations such as joint ventures probably represent the fastest growing type of private firms in the world. The majority of world economic activities in the next century may well take place in currently emerging economies, and the expansion of economic activities in those nations is being achieved largely through the creation of international cooperative ventures. Research on institutional, cultural, and social factors that shape organizations of this type is vital to organizational studies.

Organizational Isomorphism

There are a number of reasons why international joint ventures are particularly likely to be influenced by the norms and practices of their foreign parent companies. DiMaggio and Powell (1983) have described the sources of isomorphism between organizations in terms of *coercive*, *mimetic*, and *normative* influences. All of these forms of isomorphism can be expected to have an important impact on international joint ventures. This is especially true of joint ventures operating in emerging economies, where legal standards and business practices may be less sharply defined and enforced than in the societies of parent companies.

Coercive isomorphism may be very important for international joint ventures in developing countries such as China. Parent companies in developed industrial societies typically are subject to a variety of regulatory and reporting requirements that affect both overseas and domestic operations. Publicly traded firms are accountable to investors for uses of capital abroad as well as at home, and the financial reporting required by domestic markets of parent companies may necessitate controls in overseas ventures that far exceed requirements of the societies in which the ventures operate. Parent companies also may be subject to a variety of other legal requirements—such as restrictions on bribery or environmental hazards—that create liability in home countries for the activities of overseas joint ventures. Because standards for business practice vary among industrial nations, these forms of coercive isomorphism are likely to result in differences among joint ventures that reflect underlying differences among the societies of foreign parent firms.

Mimetic isomorphism can be expected to have similar effects, particularly for joint ventures operating in societies where large-scale private enterprises still are somewhat novel. Foreign parent companies typically serve as models for systems and practices designed to reduce uncertainties associated with these new types of economic organization. Companies in developing countries that seek joint ventures in order to gain management skills or knowledge often are effectively establishing programs of mimetic isomorphism in the process.

The normative influences that come with professionalization of management typically play a role in joint ventures as well. Companies operating in emerging economies characteristically face major shortages of managers, and in-house training programs run by expatriates are common. Local managers also may be sent abroad for training in the home facilities of foreign parent companies. In both cases, the development of professional skills involves learning concepts and attitudes about management prevalent in the societies of parent companies. Management development within joint ventures in emerging economies largely is built on the principle of normative isomorphism; the success of training is likely to be measured by the degree to which local managers understand and accept practices of the foreign parent firm.

All of these factors combine to make it probable that significant institutional differences will develop among joint ventures operating in the emerging economies of countries such as China. In certain important ways, the success of an international joint venture relies upon the creation of institutional effects of this type. If the norms and practices of a joint venture deviate too far from the acceptable standards of parent firms, the venture risks being defined as a failure and terminated. This is especially true for organizational controls, where pressures to conform to standards set by parent firms are likely to be severe.[1] These institutional effects suggest a very general proposition about the applicability of agency theory across joint ventures with parent firms of different nationalities:

Proposition 1. Emerging economy joint ventures are likely to employ incentive and control systems that vary with the nationality of parent firms.

Joint ventures may experience pressures of this sort from both parent organizations, and these pressures may sometimes threaten the stability of ventures (Contractor & Lorange, 1988; Kogut, 1988). However, companies in emerging economies often seek foreign partners in order to gain access to sophisticated management and technology, and the local parent actually may exert pressure to increase these potentially isomorphic transfers (Schaan & Beamish, 1988; Tallman, Fladmoe-Lindquist, & Robins, 1997). This coincidence of interest between parent firms in creating isomorphic change underscores the likelihood of foreign parent influence in successful ventures (Geringer & Hebert, 1989; Kaplinski & Posthuma, 1994). Alignment of interests between parent companies may be more fragile where financial controls are concerned, but this also is the area where foreign parents are likely to be most bound by fiduciary responsibilities and least able to accept strong local influence.

Institutional effects of this type can be seen not only in the adoption of formal procedures or controls but also in concepts and attitudes held by individuals within organizations. Zucker (1991[1977], p. 83) describes the way institutions shape individual ideas and motivations succinctly:

> Each individual is motivated to comply because otherwise his actions and those of others in the system cannot be understood...the fundamental process is one in which the moral becomes factual.

The ability to produce these effects among individuals within organizations is critical to the success of economic institutions in creating what Jepperson (1991, p. 149) has called "...socially constructed, routine-reproduced programs or rule systems" that can facilitate highly complex forms of economic coordination (Scott, 1991).

Institutional effects of this type on Sino-American and Sino-Japanese joint ventures are likely to influence the applicability of agency theory. As indicated above, agency theory is rooted in Western utilitarian and liberal traditions that have not had major importance in Japanese society (Bird & Wiersema, 1995). Management practices and norms that are commonplace in the United States would be alien in many Japanese enterprises, and the relevance of Western theories to Japanese firms has been challenged on a variety of grounds (see Dunphy, 1987 for a review). The influence of parent firms suggests that controls may differ in Sino-Japanese and Sino-American joint ventures (Brown et al., 1997), and managers within the companies may have different attitudes toward control systems (Azumi et al., 1984; Kaplinski & Posthuma, 1994). These differences may take the form of direct similarities to foreign parent firms, or joint ventures may be influenced by norms within foreign firms that define the relationship between parent companies and joint ventures. This suggests another very general proposition about institutional effects on joint ventures due to the nationality of parent firms:

Proposition 2.   Attitudes of local managers toward incentive and control systems in emerging economy joint ventures are likely to vary with the nationality of parent firms.

Institutional Influences on Agency Relations in Joint Ventures

Some of the most basic premises of agency theory are likely to be sensitive to institutional differences of this type. The analysis of contracting in agency theory treats the employment relationship as an asymmetrical bond between principal and agent in which the principal attempts to exert control over the behavior of agents through the adoption of specific forms of contract that have identifiable incentive properties (Jensen, 1983; Perrow, 1986; White, 1985). The choice of incentives, in turn, is based on assumptions about the preferences and calculus of utility of individuals (Levinthal, 1988).

Programmability and Control

As Eisenhardt (1989) has pointed out, this view of the relationship between principals and agents gives rise to the idea of a tradeoff between control based on the monitoring of employee activities and the use of incentives tied to the outcomes of economic activity. The most fundamental principle of agency theory probably is that rewards based on behavior and rewards based on the outcomes of behavior are alternative mechanisms for achieving the same end—mitigating the effects of goal conflicts between the owners and managers of firms (Eisenhardt, 1989). The form of the tradeoff between these two types of control ultimately is determined by the utility attached to different rewards by principals and agents and the difficulties of monitoring behavior. When monitoring of managerial behavior can be accomplished relatively easily, fixed rewards such as salaries and standard bonuses generally assume greater importance in systems for control (Jensen & Meckling, 1976).

Monitoring of behavior typically will be cost efficient in situations where tasks can be readily analyzed and comprehensively described. Under those circumstances it is easy to formalize and codify job requirements, and ex ante specification of appropriate levels of compensation is not problematic. Eisenhardt (1989) has referred to this issue in terms of the "programmability" of tasks. The relationship between activities and rewards posited by agency theory leads to the expectation that programmability of jobs will be linked to the use of fixed forms of compensation. This relationship between programmability and rewards is one of the most fundamental empirical implications of agency theory for control systems.

The relationship between programmability and fixed forms of compensation can be expected to be more important for Sino-American joint ventures than Sino-Japanese joint ventures for two reasons: the influence of Western liberalism in the United States, and the fact that neither Japanese nor Chinese societies have been strongly influenced by the same utilitarian and liberal traditions (Maruyama, 1984). Isomorphism with U.S. parent firms is likely to result in Sino-American joint ventures incorporating control systems and norms that embody liberal principles. Although isomorphism with Japanese parent firms might be equally important for Sino-Japanese joint ventures, it would be less likely to result in the adoption of practices that conform to the principles of agency theory. On the contrary, evidence exists that preferences for monitoring of work activities may be independent of task structure in Japanese enterprises (Lincoln & Kalleberg, 1990). This suggests two more specific implications of Proposition 1, above:

Proposition 1a.   Programmability of jobs will be positively associated with fixed forms of compensation in Sino-American joint ventures.

Proposition 1b.   Programmability of jobs will have no relationship to the use of fixed forms of compensation in Sino-Japanese joint ventures.

If the premises of agency theory hold true only in Sino-American joint ventures, it would suggest important institutional influences from U.S. parent organizations. However, the failure to find comparable agency relations in Sino-Japanese joint ventures would be more ambiguous; it might indicate the influence of Japanese parent firms, the influence of Chinese culture and institutions, or both. The important point is that differences between joint venture types in the degree to which agency relations are significant would indicate institutional effects that equal or exceed the influence of local culture.

Agency Relations and Institutional Effects on Individuals

The arguments about control systems outlined above follow one of the characteristic assumptions of agency theory: the idea that observed systems for control are efficient. Agency theory, like other microeconomic theories, operates from the premise that the pressure of competition will result in more efficient social arrangements supplanting less efficient ones. In the case of agency theory, competition focuses on the organizational form, and the outcome of competition is an allocation of effort and rewards that jointly maximizes utility for principals and agents (Jensen, 1983). Observed control systems are assumed to be efficient solutions to problems of organization, under constraints imposed by social and technical conditions.

These assumptions have drawn some of the most severe criticisms of agency theory. Perrow (1986), Tinker (1988), and others have argued that the assumption of joint utility maximization ignores basic relationships of power and authority within organizations. Perrow (1986) has characterized these elements of agency theory as part of a broader ideology aimed at rationalizing inequalities, while Tinker (1988) has described the assumption that efficient control systems will prevail as "Panglossian" in its willful naiveté.

Although the responses of critics such as Perrow (1986) and Tinker (1988) may be extreme, they highlight an important problem. The assumption that observed control systems will be relatively efficient serves as an important analytical convenience in agency models, but it is a weak approximation of reality. Control systems are blunt instruments, and the degree to which any specific system of controls maximizes utility for a given individual or set of individuals within an organization may be quite variable.

Recognition of this indeterminacy has helped to spawn a new stream of research on the question of whether agency theory can help to explain individual preferences for incentive and control systems. Questions about preferences among contracting arrangements (Conlon & Parks, 1992; Parks & Conlon, 1995) or the impact of control systems on job satisfaction (Chia, 1995) recently have been explored in experimental and survey research. In this work, agency theory provides hypotheses about the types of organizational arrangements that can be expected to be satisfactory to individuals.

In this research the link between control systems and individual satisfaction provides a means of examining whether individuals appear to have utility functions that correspond to the assumptions of agency theory. If individual utilities match the assumptions of the theory, then theoretically efficient control systems also will be utility maximizing. Departures from the arrangements dictated by agency theory would result in lower individual utility and less satisfaction. Support for a relationship between controls that follow the precepts of agency theory and individual satisfaction has been taken as evidence for the applicability of the underlying axioms of the theory to a given group or population (Chia, 1995; Conlon & Parks, 1994).

Agency theory has relatively straightforward implications for the impact of job characteristics and control systems on individuals when the assumption of social efficiency is suspended and the analysis shifted to this individual level. The tradeoff described above between monitoring and risk-sharing offers a basis for forming expectations about the responses of managers to control systems. As Eisenhardt (1989) observes, agents generally can be expected to prefer reward systems that involve less risk-sharing, all other things held equal. When jobs are highly programmable and rewards might be calibrated to the efforts of employees, evaluation systems that focus on other types of criteria can be expected to be less satisfactory for managers. The effort to monitor jobs with little programmability creates a similar agency problem: individuals are held accountable for processes they cannot control.

When agency theory is used in this way—to form expectations about individual responses to control systems—the underlying assumptions of the theory take on new importance. The capacity of agency theory to predict individual responses to control systems can be expected to vary with the degree to which individuals embrace the underlying principles of "economic rationality" that lie behind the theory. As suggested above, supporters and detractors of agency theory generally have treated this question as a purely axiomatic issue. *Homo economicus* either has been taken as a reasonable representation of the human race (e.g., Jensen, 1983) or a grotesque fabrication (e.g., Perrow, 1986; Tinker, 1988).

Real human beings probably fall somewhere between these extremes, and utilitarian ideas about social relations may not be equally appropriate for Sino-Japanese and Sino-American organizations. As Zucker (1991[1977]) has pointed out, institutionalization ultimately rests on the fact that individuals come to see certain types of normative social relations as factual. The institutionalization of norms of utilitarianism in the United States, for example, is vividly illustrated by the manner in which Jensen (1983) and his followers treat ideas such as self-interest and opportunism as simple facts of social life. If agency relations that resemble Western models are institutionalized within Sino-American joint ventures, they will have a noticeable effect on the way managers view control systems. As suggested above, the link between agency theoretic controls and satisfaction has been used to examine whether individuals appear to have personal attitudes that conform to the utilitarian axioms of agency theory. If foreign partner firms exert institutional influences on ventures independent of local culture, managers in U.S. ventures are more likely to have incorporated some of these utilitarian views. At the same time, liberal ideologies are not typical of Japanese industrial culture (Lincoln & Kalleberg, 1990) or Chinese organizations (Shenkar & von Glinow, 1994), and neither influences from Japanese parent firms nor Chinese parent companies would be likely to inculcate attitudes associated with utilitarianism (Maruyama, 1984). Managers in Sino-American joint ventures therefore might be expected to react unfavorably to controls that deviate from the form suggested by agency theory, while managers in Sino-Japanese joint ventures might not have similar attitudes. This leads to a specific interpretation of Proposition 2:

Proposition 2a. Managers in Sino-American joint ventures will be less satisfied with control systems when they deviate from the patterns of programmability and monitoring suggested by agency theory.

Proposition 2b. The attitudes of managers in Sino-Japanese joint ventures toward control systems will be unaffected by the programmability and monitoring of their jobs.

It is important to look at both the influence of foreign parent firms on control systems within joint ventures and the attitudes of managers toward those controls. Both issues are vital to understanding the degree to which agency relations may be shaped by institutional influences. Organizational control cannot rely entirely upon coercive relationships—the concepts and attitudes of managers must be, to some degree, consonant with the structure and controls of organizations (Parsons, 1956). The essence of institutionalization lies in the creation of that type of symmetry between the views held by individuals and the practices of organizations.

AGENCY RELATIONS AND INSTITUTIONAL EFFECTS IN INTERNATIONAL JOINT VENTURES: EMPIRICAL EVIDENCE

The simple set of propositions outlined above provide a means of examining key questions about institutional effects on joint ventures in China. They touch on issues that are central to the examination of institutionalization: organizational systems of control and the responses of individuals to those controls. These questions were examined empirically using survey research carried out in the PRC. Eighty-one Chinese managers employed in four Sino-Japanese and two Sino-American joint ventures in Shanghai were surveyed in the summer and fall of 1995. Following initial field interviews with senior managers in the joint ventures, a systematic survey was administered to managers at several levels in the companies. The survey was designed to provide information on both the relationship between job characteristics and controls and the views of managers toward control systems. All of the joint venture companies were manufacturing enterprises affiliated with multinational corporations.

The instrument initially was written in English by the investigators, after field interviewing—carried out in Chinese, Japanese and English—with senior corporate staff in joint ventures. The English instrument was translated into Chinese by faculty at Fudan University in Shanghai, then back-translated into English at the investigators' home institution. Translations and back-translations were checked for accuracy by native speakers of English and Chinese. The final Chinese version of the instrument was cross-checked by speakers of local Shanghai and other regional Chinese dialects to ensure standard usage of language.

The survey was administered by faculty and graduate students from Fudan University in Shanghai. Personal delivery of the instrument to managers helped to minimize response error, and more than 85 percent of all Chinese managers currently employed in the six joint ventures completed the questionnaire. The completed surveys were processed at the investigators' home institution.

The survey instrument collected data on a variety of subjects including personal demographics, characteristics of jobs and control systems, perceptions of the firm and work relations within the firm, and individual views of a number of aspects of economic life not directly related to the work life of respondents. Demographic data and some descriptive items were collected using open-ended questions, but most items were structured as closed-ended questions using seven-point Likert scales. Responses to all open-ended questions were translated from Chinese to English and checked for accuracy in translation.

The majority of variables examined in this analysis were indices formed from multiple survey items. All items used in the indices were scored on seven-point Likert scales. The control variable measuring tenure of managers in parent organizations was the only item used in the analysis that was not scaled; it was a direct report of the number of months respondents had worked in the Chinese parent organization prior to joining the joint venture. Details (in English translation) of specific questions used in the indices are reported in Appendix A.

Operationalization of Concepts

Sets of survey items that covered similar issues were first examined using principal components analysis. This exploratory analysis helped to identify groups of variables that were closely interrelated and potentially measured common phenomena. Combinations of items identified in the exploratory analysis were scrutinized for content validity prior to index construction, and items that did not have strong face validity were rejected. Factor loadings of variables that were combined in indices ranged from slightly over .50 to greater than .80, with the majority of items above .70. All factors had eigenvalues greater than unity and strong factor separation. The indices were averages of standardized scores for the underlying survey items.

Rewards Based on Inputs

Input-based rewards—that is, controls that link rewards to inputs rather than the economic performance of outputs—were operationalized in terms of fixed forms of compensation such as salary and annual bonuses. An index was created with two components: respondent ratings of the importance of fixed salary in overall compensation and ratings of the importance of standard bonuses (annual or holiday) in compensation. The two items combined in a single factor with loadings of .79 and .66 respectively. Higher scores on the index (FIXCOMP) indicated greater importance of rewards of this type.

This strategy of measuring the importance of fixed forms of compensation by means of respondent ratings was chosen for a number of reasons. Although respondent reports of compensation practices cannot be assumed to be as reliable as archival data, the use of personnel data from the companies would have been deeply problematic. Data from company records on the actual compensation of individuals could not have been used without violation of subject confidentiality. Respondents completed questionnaires anonymously, and identification of subjects for the purposes of associating archival data with individual responses would have destroyed that anonymity.

Field interviews also indicated sensitivity to self-reporting of the compensation received by individuals, and serious resistance to participation in the study was anticipated if respondents were asked to report figures for personal income. The items used in the survey did not evoke similar sensitivities, and anonymous self-reports of the relative importance of different types of compensation have reasonably good face validity. The use of common scaled items for this type of measure also improved the reliability of data pooled among organizations and used for comparative analysis across different types of organizations.

Performance Evaluation

Managers' views about the accuracy of performance evaluation were operationalized in an index composed of four survey items. The items emphasized two issues: the degree to which compensation reflects performance, and the accuracy of criteria used for evaluation of performance (see Appendix A for details). All items had factor loadings greater than .70, and the Cronbach alpha for the index was .8021. Higher scores on the index (EVALUATE) indicated that respondents felt that control systems did a good job of rewarding performance.

Monitoring

The significance of monitoring was operationalized in terms of the importance of evaluation by supervisors. Respondents were asked to rate the importance of supervisors' evaluations in determining rewards, including pay and promotions. Three types of supervisory evaluation were examined in separate survey items: evaluation of individuals by supervisors, evaluation of work groups by supervisors, and evaluation of business units by supervisors. The three items combined in a single factor with loadings greater than .70, and the factor showed strong separation from indicators of performance-based evaluation. The items were used to create an index (MONITOR), with higher scores indicating greater importance of monitoring by supervisors. The Cronbach alpha for the index was .7940.

Programmability

Programmability was operationalized in an index based on three general features of jobs: difficulty of explaining a job to others, difficulty of defining an objective measure of performance, and difficulty describing the effects of work on the cost or quality of products. Each of these items reflects one of the necessary conditions for programmability. The ex ante specification of tasks that is the essence of programmability requires activities that can be codified, measured objectively, and that have a well-defined linkage to important features of outputs (Eisenhardt, 1989). In the exploratory analysis, these three survey items formed a single factor with loadings ranging from .75 to .82. They were combined in an index (PROGRAM) that was scaled so that higher scores indicate greater programmability of jobs. The alpha for the index was .7702.

Tenure in Chinese Parent Organization

Analysis of the relationship between programmability of jobs and fixed forms of compensation was controlled for the tenure of managers in the Chinese parent companies prior to joining the joint ventures. The discussion of institutional effects in the first section of this paper emphasized the impact of foreign partners on joint ventures—in part as a corrective to the tendency to treat international joint ventures as purely local organizations. However, both foreign and domestic partners can be expected to exert important influences on joint ventures. The use of fixed forms of compensation is deeply entrenched in many Chinese companies as part of the socialist heritage of state-controlled enterprises.

It is likely that institutional influences from Chinese parent companies will have a greater effect on the jobs of managers who have spent longer periods in those companies prior to transferring to the joint ventures. Definitions of jobs, controls, reward systems, and other structural features of organizations acquire the character of "socially-constructed, routine reproduced programs or rule systems" (Jepperson, 1991, p. 149) with institutionalization. Rule systems of this type take time to become institutionalized and they are not quickly changed (DiMaggio & Powell, 1983). Isomorphism with the Chinese parent can be expected to be stronger in situations where jobs and the incumbents of jobs have a longer history in the Chinese company. Institutional effects of this type lead to the expectation that managers with longer personal histories in Chinese parent companies are more likely to have jobs in joint ventures that reflect the practices of the Chinese companies—such as the use of fixed forms of compensation.

Controlling the analysis of programmability and fixed compensation for the effects of tenure in the Chinese parent company makes it possible to look at the separate effects of two different institutional influences on a single feature of control systems. The relationship between programmability and fixed compensation relies on the institutional influence of foreign parent firms—no similar relationship exists in Chinese state-owned companies, where fixed compensation generally has been a political imperative. The relationship between tenure in the Chinese parent company and fixed compensation relies on the institutional influence of Chinese parent companies. Examining these two variables together in a single model provides an indication of each of these institutional influences net of the other. Tenure was measured based on direct report of the number of months respondents had been in the Chinese parent firm and recorded in the variable PTENURE.

Validity

In addition to the analysis of construct validity described above, potential context effects such as common method variance were a subject of concern. The use of single-respondent self-report data is inescapable in confidential surveys, but it necessarily raises questions about artifactual variance due to context effects. However, a number of steps can be taken to reduce the likelihood of context effects such as common method variance in this type of survey data. Following Harrison, Mclaughlin, and Coalter (1996), the instrument was designed to avoid the use of overtly similar items or the contiguous placement of independent and dependent items. The use of multiple-indicator constructs also helps to reduce potential context effects (Harrison, Mclaughlin, & Coalter, 1996), and reverse coding of a number of scales provided a partial check on consistency effects (Podsakoff & Organ, 1986). Post-hoc analysis of validity also was carried out using Harman's single-factor approach (Podsakoff & Organ, 1986). Independent and dependent items did not load in a common factor, suggesting that common method variance was not a substantial problem.

Table 1. Means, Standard Deviations, and Correlations

Variables	Means	S.D.(n)	1	2	3	4
Sino-Japanese Companies						
1. FIXCOMP	5.32	1.04(35)				
2. EVALUAT E	4.81	.99(34)	-.21(34)			
3. MONITOR	5.75	.85(34)	.06(34)	-.00(33)		
4. PROGRA M	4.57	1.20(34)	-.12(34)	.26(33)	.29(33)	
5. PTENURE	112. 26	99.42(31)	.54(31)	.01(30)	.15(30)	-.06(31)

Variables	Means	S.D.(n)	1	2	3	4
Sino-American Companies						
1. FIXCOMP	5.64	.94(45)				
2. EVALUAT E	4.63	1.30(44)	.21(43)			
3. MONITOR	5.78	.82(46)	.25(45)	.34(44)		
4. PROGRA M	4.59	1.25(46)	.30(45)	.18(44)	.07(46)	
5. PTENURE	122. 51	105.42(43)	.36(42)	.22(41)	.28(43)	.07(43)

Note: Pairwise deletion is used. Number of cases are in parentheses.

Definition of Sub-populations

Before analyzing agency relations and institutional effects, it was necessary to look at a preliminary question—whether respondents could be treated as a single population for analytical purposes. The same institutional logic that drives the research also suggests that managers in Sino-Japanese and Sino-American joint ventures may be fundamentally different populations. If respondents are treated as a sample from a single population, differences between the two groups may violate basic assumptions of inferential statistics.

Tests for homogeneity of variance across the two groups indicated that heteroscedasticity was a significant issue. Homogeneity of variance for managers in Sino-Japanese and Sino-American companies was rejected at $\alpha = .07$ for the dependent measure EVALUATE using Levene's test. The sample was split into two groups in response to this finding, and parallel analyses were run for Sino-Japanese and Sino-American managers with separate testing of the significance of statistical relationships for each group. Treating the two groups as samples from independent populations represents a conservative analytical strategy under these conditions, but it does allow evaluation of the significance of relationships within each of the two groups. Intercorrelations, means, and standard deviations for the two groups are reported in Table 1.[2]

Analysis

Programmability and Rewards in Joint Ventures

As noted above, the relationship between the programmability of jobs and the form of rewards used for jobs is one of the most fundamental implications of agency theory for organizational control. Jobs that are more highly programmable also will tend to have compensation that does not vary with the economic performance of outputs. If agency theory accurately describes organizational control systems, a positive relationship should exist between programmability and fixed forms of compensation.

This relationship was modeled for Chinese managers in Sino-Japanese and Sino-American joint ventures as the effect of job programmability (PROGRAM) on fixed forms of compensation (FIXCOMP). The analysis was controlled for the effects of managers' tenure in Chinese parent companies prior to joining the joint venture. As indicated above, institutional effects associated with the control systems of Chinese parent companies can be expected to militate in favor of fixed compensation for managers with long tenure in those companies. The introduction of PTENURE into the models made it possible to examine the impact of programmability net of those effects. Separate models were estimated for Sino-Japanese and Sino-American joint ventures by regressing FIXCOMP on PROGRAM and PTENURE.

The effects of programmability on fixed forms of compensation were estimated with OLS regression. Separate models were estimated for managers in Sino-Japanese and Sino-American joint ventures, with and without control for tenure in the parent organization. Results of the regressions are reported in Table 2.

Programmability of jobs proved to be related to the importance of fixed forms of compensation in Sino-American joint ventures but not in Sino-Japanese joint ventures, as anticipated by Proposition 1a and Proposition 1b. The model was sig-

Table 2. Regression Models for FIXCOMP

	Model 1		Model 2	
Variables	Sino-Japanese Coefficient	Sino-American Coefficient	Sino-Japanese Coefficient	Sino-American Coefficient
Constant	-.15	.10	-.12	.06
PROGRAM	-.12	.25**	-.12	.25**
PTENURE			.43****	.24**
N	34	45	31	42
R^2 (adjusted)	.00	.07	.26	.18
P (model)	.49	.04	.01	.01

Notes: Pairwise deletion is used. * $p < .10$, ** $p < .05$, *** $p < .01$.

nificant in explaining variance in FIXCOMP in Sino-American joint ventures, and the slope coefficient for programmability was positive and significantly different from zero (*t*-statistic, $\alpha = .05$). The model for programmability and fixed compensation was not significant for Sino-Japanese joint ventures. These findings support the general premise of Proposition 1, suggesting that important differences may exist between the two types of organizations and that agency theory may have some applicability to control systems in Sino-American companies.

Tenure in parent organizations proved to be a significant predictor of the importance of fixed forms of compensation in both Sino-Japanese and Sino-American organizations. However, the effects of PTENURE also appeared to be independent of the effects of programmability of jobs in both cases. PROGRAM made a significant contribution to explained variance in FIXCOMP for managers in Sino-American joint ventures regardless of whether PTENURE was controlled. The introduction of PTENURE had no effect on the significance of PROGRAM for Sino-Japanese joint ventures; programmability does not appear to be related to the use of fixed forms of compensation in those companies, regardless of the effects of PTENURE.

The fact that tenure in Chinese parent organizations is a significant predictor of fixed forms of compensation reinforces the importance of institutionalization, suggesting that joint ventures are subject to important institutional effects from the local Chinese side. Control systems institutionalized within Chinese parent companies also influence practices in international joint ventures. This finding underscores the institutional complexity of joint ventures in China; they appear to represent amalgams of ideas and attitudes drawn from both parent companies.

Responses to Control Systems

The views of individual managers about controls were analyzed by modeling the effects of programmability and monitoring on attitudes toward evaluation systems. As indicated above, agency theory suggests that the combination of programmability and monitoring offers an efficient solution to problems of control, while mismatch between the two factors can create dis-utilities that reduce approval of control systems. In formal terms, this implies an interaction between programmability and monitoring. Thus, interaction effects were analyzed as well as the main effects of programmability and monitoring. Once again, separate models were estimated for managers in Sino-Japanese and Sino-American joint ventures.

The interaction between programmability and monitoring was analyzed by evaluating the significance of the product-term interaction effect for PROGRAM and MONITOR. Following methods suggested by Cronbach (1987), variables were centered to reduce multicollinearity in the model. As Jaccard, Turrisi, and Wan (1990) have pointed out, multicollinearity is the primary problem associated with the use of product term interactions in regression models and a major reason

Table 3. Regression Models for EVALUATE

	Model 3		Model 4	
Variables	*Sino-Japanese Coefficient*	*Sino-American Coefficient*	*Sino-Japanese Coefficient*	*Sino-American Coefficient*
Constant	.07	-.05	.05	-.07
MONITOR	-.08	.37**	-.09	.39**
PROGRAM	.23	.15	.23	.04
MONITOR x PROGRAM			.07	.39*
N	32	44	32	44
R^2 (adjusted)	.01	.10	.00	.15
P (model)	.32	.05	.51	.02

Notes: Pairwise deletion is used. * $p < .10$, ** $p < .05$, *** $p < .01$.

for rejection of the significance of interaction effects under conditions where they may be present. The transformation suggested by Cronbach (1987) minimizes problems due to multicollinearity while retaining the statistical power of significance testing.[3]

The significance of the interaction term was tested using methods suggested by Jaccard, Turrisi, and Wan (1990). The incremental contribution to explained variance in EVALUATE due to inclusion of the interaction term was analyzed, as well as the main effects and full models for both Sino-Japanese and Sino-American joint ventures.

The full model including the interaction term was significant for managers in Sino-American joint ventures (F-statistic, $\alpha = .05$). The incremental contribution to explained variance associated with the interaction term also was significant (F-statistic, $\alpha = .05$), suggesting that the combination of programmability and monitoring has an effect on managers that goes beyond the separate effects of the two variables. Neither full models nor main effects were significant for managers in Sino-Japanese joint ventures (Table 3).

The interpretation of regression coefficients in models using product term interactions is unlike their interpretation in simple additive models (Jaccard, Turrisi, & Wan, 1990). In the model for managers in Sino-American joint ventures, the coefficient for the main effect of monitoring is significantly different from zero, while the coefficient for programmability is not (Table 3). This indicates that monitoring has a significant effect on attitudes toward evaluation systems independent of programmability, in addition to its effect in combination with programmability. However, the effect of programmability is entirely through interaction with monitoring. The programmability of jobs does not, in itself, influence managers' views of evaluation systems.

These relationships are illustrated in Figure 1. The figure shows a plot of the relationships among programmability, monitoring, and managers' views of eval-

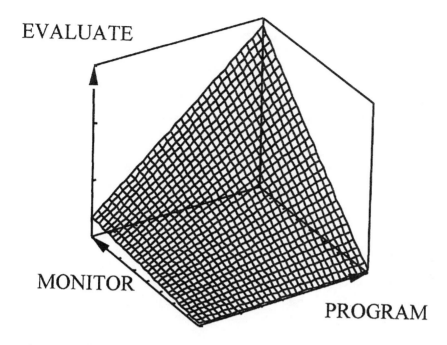

Figure 1.   Illustration of the Relationships Among EVALUATE, MONITOR,
and PROGRAM for Sino-American Joint Ventures

uation for Sino-American joint ventures. The surface of the function represents
the interaction effect of programmability and monitoring, while each of the individual planes depicts a two-variable relationship with the third variable held constant.

If the relationship between PROGRAM and EVALUATE is examined at the
point where MONITOR is equal to zero, the function will be a straight line parallel to the axis for programmability. All values of programmability will result in
the same attitudes toward evaluation systems, if monitoring does not take place.
However, programmability has a positive effect on attitudes toward evaluation
systems at any point away from the zero level of monitoring. In graphic terms, this
is the equivalent of examining a vertical cross-section of the figure parallel to the
plane defined by PROGRAM and EVALUATE. Any cross-section taken at a
point where MONITOR has a value greater than zero will show a positive slope
for the relationship between PROGRAM and EVALUATE.

On the other hand, the two-variable relationship between MONITOR and
EVALUATE will be positive for values of PROGRAM that include zero. A
cross-section taken at any level of programmability—including the origin—will
show a positively sloped line for the relationship between MONITOR and EVAL-

UATE. Monitoring has a positive impact on managers' views of evaluation even if jobs have no programmability, and the positive effect also grows as the programmability of jobs increases.[4]

The analysis provides support for the general proposition (Proposition 2) that Sino-American and Sino-Japanese joint ventures differ in important ways. As anticipated by Proposition 2a and Proposition 2b, responses to control systems implied by agency theory appear to have some significance within Sino-American joint ventures, but there is no evidence of similar attitudes within Sino-Japanese joint ventures. Managers in Sino-American joint ventures who face a mismatch of monitoring and programmability generally are less satisfied with control systems, while managers in Sino-Japanese joint ventures do not appear to be affected by these issues.

The finding that monitoring also has an independent effect on satisfaction with evaluation in Sino-American companies was interesting. It appears that managers working in Sino-American joint ventures generally feel evaluation is better managed when they are subject to greater monitoring—even if their jobs are not highly programmable—but managers in Sino-Japanese companies do not share the sentiment. This underscores the fact that foreign parent firms may exert a variety of institutional influences on joint ventures in China.

DISCUSSION

The most striking finding of this study is the fact that there appear to be significant differences between Sino-Japanese and Sino-American joint ventures in China, both in their control systems and in the way managers respond to those controls. Those differences suggest that foreign parent firms influence joint ventures in important ways and that the influences of foreign parent firms become institutionalized within joint ventures. The effects of foreign parent companies are reflected not only in the management practices of joint ventures, but in the attitudes of Chinese managers as well.

These institutional differences between Sino-American and Sino-Japanese joint ventures have direct bearing on many long-standing questions about the scope of theories that are rooted in liberal utilitarian traditions. The research provides an important indication that agency theory may offer insight into social relations within certain types of organizations in China. Control systems in Sino-American organizations and the attitudes of Chinese managers toward those controls show some evidence of conforming to expectations suggested by agency theory. The fact that the managers are Chinese and the organizations operate in China does not exert a superordinate influence that eliminates these effects. This is consistent with findings reported by Chia (1995) and raises questions about arguments about local influences offered by Shenkar and von Glinow (1994) and others.

However, it also is noteworthy that support for agency theory could be found only within Sino-American joint ventures. No evidence could be found of similar control relationships or attitudes in joint ventures involving Japanese companies. This highlights the fact that the theory appears to have important sociocultural roots and it indicates that agency theory may not provide the general analysis of exchange behavior sought by proponents of the idea of universal social and economic theories. At the same time, the research also suggests that theories of this type are not peculiar to any single locality or national society; their relevance varies among organizations operating within Chinese society as it does among organizations in Western societies. This underscores the fact that ideologies have become less firmly fixed to any group of people or place, as national boundaries have become more permeable and organizations have emerged that owe allegiance to no single society. However, these changes do not necessarily herald the type of movement toward homogenous attitudes and ideas or universal forms of economic or social relations once anticipated by work on modernization and the logic of industrialization (e.g., Inkeles & Smith, 1974). On the contrary, it appears that institutional features of organizations matter more than ever and that they are not readily encapsulated in global generalizations about people or places.

These observations are particularly important when they are viewed in the context of long-standing debates over the generality of and scope of social and organizational theory. More than a hundred years ago, the *methodenstreit* split European political economy into warring camps around the question of whether economic relations could be understood independent of culture (Barkai, 1996; Milford, 1995). The division between sociology and economics grew out of that dispute, and the underlying issue remains a subject of contention between the fields. Similar questions have remained important throughout the history of the social sciences, helping to shape more recent debates such as the disputes between formalist and substantivist economic anthropologists in the 1960s and 1970s (e.g., Sahlins, 1972).

During the last two decades, the comparative study of organizations has emerged as the area that addresses these issues most directly. Organizational researchers have brought together ideas from cross-national research on modernization and more recent work on culture and management to formulate a broad range of questions about relationships between organizations and the societies in which they operate (Lammers & Hickson, 1979). The underlying concern about the universality of analysis of social relations remains the same, but it has been focused on specific questions about the effects of local society or culture on organizations (Cheng, 1994).

The research reported here extends the comparative approach to begin to take account of the increased complexity and variety of modern international organizations. It suggests that the equation of sociocultural influences to locality may divert attention from important features of the contemporary global economy. A broad range of international organizations now exist that may be subject to important social and cultural influences from multiple societies, including—but not confined to—the societies in which they are located. However, the existence of these trans-societal institutional influences does not imply the type of global convergence that traditionally has been seen as the alternative to local influence (e.g., Lammers & Hickson, 1979). On the contrary, the fact that international organizations may be subject to multiple influences from local societies, foreign affiliates, and global markets suggests new levels of organizational complexity within and among societies.

CONCLUSION

The existence of institutional effects that bridge national boundaries provides a strong argument for expanding the scope of international and comparative research on management and adopting a more detailed view of international organizations. International research has been dominated by concern with the effects of national societies and local cultures (Earley & Singh, 1995), and this has favored analytical perspectives that often are less complex than the approaches used for analysis of organizations within Western industrial nations. As research in North America and Western Europe has moved away from deterministic models—and toward the view that organizations are embedded within multilayered systems of social institutions—national institutions have come to be seen as just one of many levels of social structure that shape and sustain organizations (Scott, 1987). The depth and complexity of this approach need to be more fully incorporated into comparative research.

The empirical findings described in this paper barely scratch the surface of these issues, and the research is more provocative than conclusive. The findings reported here do provoke some important questions about the generality of theories of economic organization and the nature of the categories that are used to qualify organizational theories in comparative research. A choice between universal theories of exchange and cultural balkanization inevitably impoverishes research. The decline of nationality in important segments of modern societies and the rise of international organizations have created global changes in social relations and an interweaving of norms and traditions among societies. These changes simultaneously challenge the homogeneity of local cultures and raise profound questions about the universality of social and economic theories.

APPENDIX A

Composition of Indices

FIXCOMP

Survey Questions:
How important are the following factors in determining your total compensation? Please circle a number using the scale from 1 = "No Importance" to 7 = "Very Important".
- Fixed salary (daily, weekly, monthly or annual);
- Standard annual or holiday bonuses (distributed to all employees).

EVALUATE
Survey Questions:
Do you agree with the following statements about the way performance is evaluated in your company? Please circle a number using the scale from 1 = "Strongly Disagree" to 7 = "Strongly Agree."

- People usually are evaluated on the right criteria;
- Hard work usually is rewarded in this company;
- The company usually does a good job of matching pay to performance;
- My pay accurately reflects the work I do.

MONITOR
Survey Questions:
How important are the following forms of performance evaluation in determining the rewards you receive (pay or promotion)? Please circle a number using the scale from 1 = "No Importance" to 7 = "Very Important."

- Individual work evaluation carried out by supervisor;
- Work evaluation of business unit as a whole carried out by supervisor;
- Work group's evaluation carried out by supervisor.

PROGRAM
Survey Questions:
How difficult would it be to accomplish the following things related to your job in this company? Please circle a number using the scale from 1 = "Very Difficult" to 7 = "Very Easy."

- Explain your job to other people in the company;
- Describe how your work affects the quality or cost of goods and services produced by your business unit;
- Define an objective measure of how well you have done your job.

PTENURE
Survey Question:
Length of your work in the parent company prior to working in this company (in month)?

ACKNOWLEDGMENTS

We would like to thank the editor, Joseph Cheng, and two anonymous reviewers for their constructive comments throughout the review process. Thanks also go to Madan Pillutla for providing helpful suggestions on an earlier version of the manuscript and Yihong Yu of Fudan University of China for assistance in data collection.

NOTES

1. Constraints to conform to organizational models established by parent firms may be less prominent in cases where joint ventures were established to undertake innovative activities that parents are ill-suited to carry out in house—although parent firms still may experience difficulty accepting necessary levels of autonomy for their joint ventures. However, joint ventures of this type are more typical of firms operating within highly developed industrial societies than emerging economies. While some of the joint ventures examined in this study did undertake relatively sophisticated product development activities, none of the companies could be characterized as doing highly innovative work.

2. As indicated above, there were strong theoretical and statistical grounds for believing that respondents in Sino-Japanese and Sino-American joint ventures represented samples from two different populations. In consequence, the two samples were analyzed separately, and propositions about each population dealt with independently. An analysis that pooled the two different samples would have violated necessary statistical assumptions.

The fact that the respondents from Sino-Japanese and Sino-American joint ventures represented two different populations therefore precluded any direct statistical testing of differences between regression coefficients or other cross-population comparisons based on treatment of the groups as samples from a common population. However, a rough comparison was carried out using nonparametric techniques. Confidence intervals for OLS coefficients were estimated using jacknife resampling techniques on the combined group of respondents from the two samples. Jacknife estimators are robust when assumptions are violated, although the probability of rejection of the null hypothesis tends to be substantially lower.

Based on the non-parametric estimates, intervals for regression coefficients for the two populations generally did not overlap at a $\alpha = .05$ level, except in the case of PTENURE. For PTENURE we could not reject the hypothesis that the coefficients for Sino-Japanese and Sino-American respondents were the same. Confidence intervals for PROGRAM in MODEL 1 did not include zero for Sino-American respondents and did include zero for the Sino-Japanese respondents, thus lending support to the proposition that PROGRAM had a significant effect on FIXCOMP in Sino-American ventures but not in Sino-Japanese ventures. Similar findings applied to MODEL 2: the hypothesis that the coefficient for PROGRAM was equal to zero could be rejected for Sino-American joint ventures but not for Sino-Japanese joint ventures. Findings for the analysis of EVALUATE mirrored findings for MODELS 1 and 2. In MODEL 3 and MODEL 4 it was possible to reject the hypothesis that the coefficients for MONITOR were equal to zero only for Sino-American respondents. While this additional analysis is by no means conclusive, it provides further support for the fact that the two populations have fundamentally different characteristics of the sort discussed in the text.

3. Cronbach (1987, p. 415) contrasts product term models with predictor variables that have means substantially different from zero to models where means for predictor variables have been set equal to zero. Centering variables with means equal to zero will alter the signs of below mean-observations. Relatively large values of the product term will be created by pairing of either large negative or large positive values. This will reduce the correlation between predictors and the product term and relieve problems of multicollinearity. At the same time, the sum of squares for the full models in both centered and non-centered cases will be identical. Sums of squares for the two types of models also

will be identical when product terms are removed. In consequence, significance testing for the inclusion of the product term is unaffected by the transformation of the predictor variables. At the same time, the statistical power of the analysis is increased by the reduction of multicollinearity.

4. The algebraic form of these relationships can be described in relatively simple fashion. Let the product term equation have the general form:

$$Y = a + b_1X_1 + b_2X_2 + b_3X_1X_2$$

Assume the product term and the main effect of X_2 are significant, but the main effect of X_1 is not significant, that is, $b_1 = 0$. In that case, the equation reduces to:

$$Y = a + b_2X_2 + b_3X_1X_2$$

which can be rewritten as:

$$Y = a + (b_2 + b_3X_1)X_2$$

When that expression is evaluated at the point where $X_2 = 0$, it reduces to $Y = a$, and the effect of X_1 on Y is constant for all values of X_1. If we evaluate the expression at the point where $X_1 = 0$, then it takes the form:

$$Y = a + b_2X_2$$

and Y is an increasing linear function of X_2.

For any fixed value of X_2 greater than zero, the terms b_2X_2 and b_3X_2 will be positive constants. The expression for Y as a function of X_1 can be rewritten as:

$$Y = (a + b_2X_2) + (b_3X_2)X_1$$

In general, the slope of the function and the intercept in the YX_2 plane will both depend on the value of X_2.

For any fixed value of X_1 greater than zero, the expression $(b_2 + b_3X_1)$ will be a positive constant. As indicated above, the basic equation can be written as:

$$Y = a + (b_2 + b_3X_1)X_2$$

Y therefore will again be a linear function of X_2. The slope of the function will depend upon the value of X_1, but the intercept in the YX_1 plane will be an invariant line parallel to the X_1 axis at a.

REFERENCES

Abo, T. (1994). *Hybrid factory: The Japanese production system in the United States.* Oxford University: New York.

Adler, N. J., Cambell, N., & Laurent, A. (1986). In search of appropriate methodology: From outside the People's Republic of China looking in. *Journal of International Business Studies, 70,* 61-74.

Azumi, K., Hickson, D., & Horvath, D. (1984). Structural conformity and cultural diversity in organizations: A comparative study of factories in Britain, Japan and Sweden. In K. Sato and Y. Hoshino (Eds.), *The anatomy of Japanese business* (pp. 101-120). Armonk, NY: M. E. Sharpe.

Barkai, H. (1996). The Methodenstreit and the emergence of mathematical economics. *Eastern Economic Journal, 22,* 1-19.

Bird, A., & Wiersema, M. (1996). Underlying assumptions of agency theory and implications for non-U.S. settings: The case of Japan. In S. Bacharach (Ed.), *Research in the sociology of organizations,* (Vol. 14, pp. 149-180). Greenwich, CT: JAI Press.

Bond, M. (Ed). (1986). *The psychology of the Chinese people.* London: Oxford University Press.

Boyacigiller, N. A., & Adler, N. J. (1991). The parochial dinosaur: Organizational science in a global context. *Academy of Management Review, 16,* 262-290.

Bricker, R., & Chandar, N. (1998). On applying agency theory in historical accounting research. *Business and Economic History, 27,* 486-499.

Brown, C., Nakata, Y., Reich, M., & Ulman, L. (1997). *Work and pay in the United States and Japan.* New York: Oxford University.

Cheng, J. L. C. (1994). Notes: On the concept of universal knowledge in organizational science: Implications for cross-national research. *Management Science, 40*(1), 162-168.

Chia, Y-M. (1995). The interaction effect of information asymmetry and decentralization on managers' job satisfaction: A research note. *Human Relations, 48,* 609-625.

Conlon, E. J., & Parks, J. M. (1990). Effects of monitoring and tradition on compensation arrangements: An experiment with principal-agent dyads. *Academy of Management Journal, 33,* 603-622.

Contractor, F., & Lorange, P. (Eds.) (1988). *Cooperative strategies in international business.* Lexington, MA: Lexington Books.

Cronbach, L. J. (1987). Statistical tests for moderator variables. *Psychological Bulletin, 102,* 414-417.

Davis, G., & Thompson, T. (1994). A social movement perspective on corporate control. *Administrative Science Quarterly, 39,* 141-173.

DiMaggio, P., & Powell, W. W. (1983). The iron cage revisited: Institutional isomorphism and collective rationality in organizational fields. *American Sociological Review, 48,* 147-60.

Donaldson, L. (1990). The ethereal hand: Organizational economics and management theory. *Academy of Management Review, 15,* 369-381.

Dunphy, D. (1987). Convergence/divergence: A temporal review of the Japanese enterprise and its management. *Academy of Management Review, 12,* 445-459.

Earley, C., & Singh, H. (1995). International and intercultural management research: What's next? *Academy of Management Journal, 38,* 327-340.

Eisenhardt, K. (1985). Control: Organizational and economic approaches. *Management Science, 31,* 134-149.

Eisenhardt, K. (1989). Agency theory: A review and assessment. *Academy of Management Review, 14,* 57-74.

Geringer, M., & Hebert, L. (1989). Control and performance of international joint ventures. *Journal of International Business Studies, 20,* 235-254.

Granovetter, M. (1985). Economic action and social structure: The problem of embeddedness. *American Journal of Sociology, 91,* 481-510.

Harrison, D. A., Mclaughlin, M. E., & Coalter, T. M. (1996). Context, cognition, and common method variance: Psychometric and verbal protocol evidence. *Organizational Behavior and Human Decision Processes, 68,* 246-261.

Hirsch, P., Friedman, R., & Koza, M. (1990). Collaboration or paradigm shift?: Caveat emptor and the risk of romance with economic models for strategy and policy research. *Organization Science, 1,* 87-98.

Hofstede, G. (1983). The cultural relativity of organizational practices and theories. *Journal of International Business Studies, 63,* 75-89.

Hunt, H. G., & Hogler, R. L., III. (1990). Agency theory as ideology: A comparative analysis based on critical legal theory and radical accounting. *Accounting, Organizations and Society, 15,* 437-454.

Inkeles, A., & Smith, D. B. (1974). *Becoming modern: Individual change in six developing countries.* Cambridge, MA: Harvard University.

Jaccard, J., Turrisi, R., & Wan, C. K. (1990). *Interaction effects in multiple regression.* Newbury Park, CA: Sage.

Jensen, M. C. (1983). Organization theory and methodology. *Accounting Review, 50,* 319-339.

Jensen, M. C., & Meckling, W. (1976). Theory of the firm: Managerial behavior, agency costs and ownership structure. *Journal of Financial Economics, 3,* 305-328.

Jepperson, R. L. (1991). Institutions, institutional effects, and institutionalism. In W. W. Powell & P. J. DiMaggio (Eds.), *The new institutionalism in organizational analysis* (pp. 143-163). Chicago, IL: University of Chicago.

Kagono, T., Nonaka, I, Okumura, A., Sakahibara, K., Komatsu, Y., & Sakashita, A. (1984). Mechanistic v. organic management systems: A comparative study of adaptive patterns of American and Japanese firms. In K. Sato & Y. Hoshino (Eds.), *The anatomy of Japanese business* (pp. 27-69). Armonk, NY: M.E. Sharpe.

Kaplan, R. (1983). The evolution of management accounting. *Accounting Review, 59,* 390-418.

Kaplinski, R., & Posthuma, A. (1994). *Easternization: The spread of Japanese management techniques to developing countries.* Essex, England: Frank Cass.

Kogut, B. (1988). Joint ventures: Theoretical and empirical perspectives. *Strategic Management Journal, 9,* 319-332.

Lammers, C. L., & Hickson, D. J. (Eds.) (1979). *Organizations alike and unlike: International and interinstitutional studies in the sociology of organizations.* London; Boston: Routledge & Kegan Paul.

Levinthal, D. (1988). A survey of agency models of organizations. *Journal of Economic Behavior and Organization, 9,* 153-185.

Lin, Z., & Hui, C. (1999). Should lean replace mass organization systems: A theoretical examination from a management coordination perspective. *Journal of International Business Studies, 30*(1), 45-80.

Lincoln, J. R., & Kalleberg, A. L. (1990). *Culture, control, and commitment: A study of work organization and work attitudes in the United States and Japan.* Cambridge, UK; New York: Cambridge University Press.

Lytle, A., Brett, J., Barsness, Z., Tinsley, C., & Janssens, M. (1995). A paradigm for confirmatory cross-cultural research in organizational behavior. In L. L. Cumming & B. Staw (Eds.), *Research in organizational behavior* (Vol. 7, pp. 167-214). Greenwich, CT: JAI Press.

Maruyama, M. (1984, January). Alternative concepts of management: Insights from Asia and Africa. *Asia Pacific Journal of Management,* 100-111.

Milford, K. (1995). Roscher's epistemological and methodological position—Its importance for the Methodenstreit. *Journal of Economic Studies, 22,* 26-52.

Mill, J. S. (1909). *Principles of political economy.* London: Longmans, Green.

Moe, T. (1984). The new economics of organization. *American Journal of Political Science, 28,* 739-777.

Nilakant, V., & Rao, H. (1994). Agency theory and uncertainty in organizations: An evaluation. *Organization Studies, 15,* 649-672.

Parks, J. M., & Conlon, E. J. (1995). Compensation contracts: Do agency theory assumptions predict negotiated agreements? *Academy of Management Journal, 38,* 821-838.

Parsons, T. (1956). Suggestions for a sociological approach to the theory of organizations. *Administrative Science Quarterly, 1,* 63-85.

Perrow, C. (1986). Economic theories of organization. *Theory and Society, 15,* 11-45.

Podsakoff, P. M., & Organ, D.W. (1986). Self-reports in organizational research: Problems and prospects. *Journal of Management, 12,* 531-544.

Robins, J. A. (1993). *A critical interpretation of agency theory as an approach to economic control.* Working Paper ST93014, Graduate School of Management, University of California, Irvine.

Sahlins, M. (1972). *Stone age economics*. Chicago: Aldine-Atherton.

Sapienza, H. J., & Gupta, A. K. (1994). Impact of agency risks and task uncertainty on venture capitalist-CEO interaction. *Academy of Management Journal, 37*, 1618-1632.

Schaan, J. L., & Beamish, P. W. (1988). Joint venture managers in LDC's. In F. Contractor & P. Lorange (Eds.), *Cooperative strategies in international business* (pp. 279-299). Lexington, MA: Lexington Books.

Scott, W. R. (1991). Unpacking institutional arguments. In W. W. Powell & P. J. DiMaggio (Eds.), *The new institutionalism in organizational analysis* (pp. 164-182). Chicago, IL: University of Chicago.

Shenkar, O., & von Glinow, M. (1994). Paradoxes of organizational theory and research: Using the case of China to illustrate national contingency. *Management Science, 40*, 56-71.

Tallman, S., Fladmoe-Lindquist, K., & Robins, J. (1997). Alliance strategies of US firms in Mexico. In H. Thomas (Ed.) *Strategic discovery*. New York: Wiley.

Tinker, T. (1988). Panglossian accounting theories: The science of apologising in style. *Accounting, Organisations and Society, 13*, 165-189.

Tosi, H. L., & Gomez-Mejia, L. R. (1989). The decoupling of CEO pay and performance: An agency theory perspective. *Administrative Science Quarterly, 34*, 169-189.

Triandis, H. (1989). Cross-cultural studies of individualism/collectivism. In J. Berman (Ed.), *Handbook of intercultural training: Issues in theory and design* (Vol. 1, pp. 82-117). New York: Pergamon Press.

Wellbourne, T. M., Balkin, D. B., & Gomez-Mejia, L. R. (1995). Gainsharing and mutual monitoring: A combined agency-organizational justice interpretation. *Academy of Management Journal, 38*, 881-899.

White, H. C. (1985). Agency as control. In J. Pratt & R. Zeckhauser (Eds.), *Principals and agents: The structure of business* (pp. 187-212). Boston, MA: Harvard Business School Press.

Zucker, L. (1991)[1977]. Institutionalization and cultural persistence. In W. W. Powell & P. J. DiMaggio (Eds.), *The new institutionalism in organizational analysis* (pp. 83-107). Chicago, IL: University of Chicago. Originally published in *American Sociological Review, 42*, 726-43 [1977].

MANAGING INSTITUTIONAL AND CULTURAL CONTRASTS
THE CASE OF SANYO ELECTRIC IN THE UNITED STATES

Roger L. M. Dunbar and Suresh Kotha

ABSTRACT

This paper considers some of the issues that a Japanese firm deals with in establishing and then managing a presence in the United States. It highlights how adaptation to the United States involves understanding and responding to both cultural and competitive dynamics. Specifically, the Sanyo case suggests how these conditions co-evolved, interacted, and changed over time. The case also illustrates how foreign firms competing in the United States should not underestimate the importance of cultural and competitive dynamics and how these can co-evolve over time in unmanaged ways. These dynamics, generally not apparent at entry, can and do play an important role as a firm adapts in a foreign setting.

More generally we argue that cross-cultural research needs to explore "phenomenon in the making" in order to understand how adaptation to a foreign setting occurs. A more qualitative approach enables researchers to emphasize the impact of the foreign setting and the process by which a firm constructs a view of itself in an evolving

Advances in International Comparative Management, Volume 13, pages 149-173.
Copyright © 2000 by JAI Press Inc.
All rights of reproduction in any form reserved.
ISBN: 0-7623-0589-4

world. The paper concludes by discussing possible implications for future research and practice on foreign firms seeking to establish a presence in the United States.

INTRODUCTION

Important differences in social structures and cultural beliefs distinguish Japan and the United States. Their respective governments manage their economies in different ways (Fallows, 1994; Lodge, 1987). Underlying norms and managerial values (Abegglen & Stalk, 1985; Lincoln, Hanada, & Olson, 1981; Ouchi, 1981) differ. As a result, managers rely on contrasting approaches to structure firm work and have different expectations about the management processes (Aoki, 1990; Kotha, Dunbar, & Bird, 1995; Lincoln, Hanada, & McBride, 1986). These differences can lead to contrasts in how business is approached and in how operations are managed (Kagono et al., 1985).

As managers assess financial opportunities in other countries, the potential disruptions that may stem from cultural and management differences can be downplayed or even ignored. Yet such differences can be very important. For example, they may make it difficult for firm managers operating in another country to recognize when, how, and where they should change their approach to maintain success (Murtha & Lenway, 1994). Yet if a firm continues to rely on home country practices not accepted abroad, its managers may inadvertently become involved in unanticipated conflicts and losses (Kogut, 1991).

This paper focuses on Sanyo Electric's efforts to establish a corporate presence in the United States. The study describes how Sanyo entered the United States and established its television and microwave manufacturing facility in Arkansas and then examines various issues that emerged for Sanyo over a decade. It concludes by discussing implications for Japanese managers establishing a corporate presence in the United States.

BACKGROUND LITERATURE

A growing body of research has considered how Japanese firms become established in the United States. The evidence suggests that generally Japanese firms have preferred to establish greenfield subsidiaries rather than acquire established facilities (Hennart & Park, 1994). They may prefer greenfield startups because this choice means they do not have to take over or rely on unknown "foreign" management (Kogut & Singh, 1988). Further, since Japanese managers are in control from the start, the Japanese perceive the venture as less risky (Li, 1995). Cole and Deskins (1988) studied Japanese greenfield automobile startups to identify factors impacting plant location. They concluded that, "Japanese plant sitings [in the auto industry] reflected a pattern in which avoidance of blacks is *one* factor in their site location decision" (p. 17, italics in the original), with the NUMMI plant being an important exception.

Japanese electronic firms entering the United States have usually focused exclusively on core businesses where they have an established competitive advantage (Chang, 1995). This is typical of many MNCs that have manufacturing operations overseas and provide their overseas affiliates with technical know-how and firm-specific organizing capabilities (Buckley & Casson, 1976; Caves, 1982). The subsidiary imports the parent's technologies along with experienced firm managers; these managers then implement practices that have proven effective in the home country (Zaheer, 1995).

Other studies have considered how Japanese manufacturing firms manage in the United States after successfully establishing a subsidiary (Cole & Deskins, 1988). Adler (1993), for example, examined the impact of work practices introduced at NUMMI, a joint venture between General Motors and Toyota Corporation. He highlighted how managers were able to develop a social context emphasizing commitment to continuous improvement and an intense focus on standardization. Introducing this new set of cultural beliefs helped NUMMI become highly efficient and learn over time (Brown & Reich, 1989).

In contrast, Milkman (1991) examined the work practices of Japanese manufacturers not involved in the automobile industry. She found that these plants usually employed a few hundred employees to do simple fabricating and assembly work. She noted that so-called "Japanese" organization practices such as emphasis on teamwork, job rotation, cross training, quality circles, and so on were almost nonexistent in these plants. Most did not employ any of the "lean" manufacturing systems such as just-in-time inventory systems used at NUMMI. Instead, the work organization in these plants strongly resembled that of nonunion American firms. She also noted that within these plants, most labor-related decisions were assigned to American human resource executives who advocated policies designed to avoid unionization (see also Beechler & Yang, 1994).

We add to these studies of Japanese adaptation patterns in the United States by examining Sanyo Manufacturing Company. Our purpose is to explore how a Japanese firm adapts to the U.S. environment and works toward overcoming its "liability of foreignness" (Hymer, 1976). Of specific interest is what happens after the Japanese firm has successfully entered the U.S. market and has implemented the parent firm's organizing practices. *How may these operating practices brought from Japan evolve as they are implemented by a U.S. workforce with different beliefs and work expectations?*

MNCs must also find ways to support and maintain the firm-specific competitive advantages and capabilities located in their overseas affiliates (Buckley & Casson, 1976; Caves, 1982; Zaheer, 1995). This becomes an important issue over time since the competitive dynamics of global industries inevitably erode firm-specific advantages. The parent must introduce new capabilities and advantages into the local subsidiary, or the local firm must develop new technical capacities and advantages to replace the aging ones that served it well in facilitating market entry. This leads to the additional question: *How may changes in competitive global dynamics impact the relationship between Japanese parent firms and their U.S. subsidiaries?*

METHODOLOGY

Our broad purpose is to explore how cultural and competitive dynamics may impact Japanese firms operating in the United States and how these effects evolve over time. To do this, we must rely on case material (Yin, 1994). The present research involves a longitudinal case study of Sanyo Electric, a Japanese firm that started U.S. manufacturing operations in 1977. To understand the context, we describe Sanyo's history before it established itself in the United States and then outline the specific issues Sanyo encountered as it attempted to cope with both U.S. cultural contexts and globally changing competitive conditions.

The processes Sanyo used to establish itself in the United States are necessarily unique, and this raises questions about the extent it is possible to generalize from them. While the specific events are unique to Sanyo, the underlying processes, priorities, and values used to manage them are not, and it is these that provide a basis for generalization (Tsoukas, 1989). The analytical task is to identify these underlying processes, priorities, and values that may have affected how Sanyo adapted, for they may have implications for other firms. The approach should enable us to tease out the multiplicity of factors that may have exerted influence, delineate linkages, and draw implications. A case study approach is well suited for this type of work (Kotha, 1998; Yin, 1994).

We chose Sanyo because it is an example of a firm based in a high-technology industry that had the support of many favorable conditions when it first entered the United States. The Japanese government had supported consumer electronics firms that, like Sanyo, had developed export capabilities to compete against U.S. manufacturers. Sanyo had also built up a mutually beneficial distribution relationship with Sears Corporation. When a government-managed marketing agreement limited television imports but placed no limits on Japanese firms manufacturing televisions in the United States, Sears helped Sanyo establish a manufacturing facility in the United States.

Despite these initially favorable conditions, questions linger about how long sources of competitive advantage will last in a globally competitive market. In the 1980s this became a concern for Sanyo and other industry participants as they faced severe competition that made it necessary to find new ways to compete. These later developments provided an opportunity for us to examine how Sanyo handled adversity. While flexibility is most often needed in times of adversity, differences in cultural values and management beliefs tend to reduce flexibility.

We were interested in how issues reflecting such differences might have arisen for Sanyo.

Data Collection

Following Campbell's (1975) dictum that multiple sources of inference about a phenomenon are analogous to degrees of freedom in statistics, we focused on multiple sources of data, including industry reports, business publications, and interviews. For data on Sanyo's operations in the United States, we identified approximately 40 newspaper and magazine articles in the Nexus/Lexus database that focused on the firm.[1] We drew on case studies of the firm (Hayes & Clark, 1981) and the TV industry (Choate, 1991; Dertouzos, Lester, & Solow, 1989; Porter, 1983). We also drew on a case describing the competitive situation faced by the Consumer Electronics Group of General Electric (Collis, 1988).

By phone, we interviewed Benny Goolsby of the International Union of Electrical Workers in Memphis, who briefed us about the union's relationship with Sanyo and provided material on his union's position in the various disputes. We also interviewed a reporter from the *Daily Times-Herald*, the newspaper in Forrest City, Arkansas that had covered Sanyo's TV manufacturing facility. He provided us with insights into why he thought Sanyo made certain decisions. Data from these different sources gave us a sense for what had happened at the Sanyo plant and the sorts of issues that had arisen. Together, these sources served as the basis for our case study of Sanyo's U.S. operations.

SANYO ELECTRIC CORPORATION

Sanyo Electric is a Japanese electronics firm headquartered in Osaka, Japan. Until the 1970s the firm had no manufacturing facilities in the United States. During the 1960s, however, it exported large numbers of TVs to the United States, to Sears, Roebuck & Co (Sears) in particular. At that time, Sears had a joint television production venture with Warwick Electronics, a subsidiary of the Whirlpool Corporation. It employed as many as 2,500 people in the venture's production facility located in Forrest City, Arkansas. The venture was 25 percent owned by Sears and served as a captive supplier of color TVs.

The Warwick facility found it difficult to meet the new quality and technology standards and the much more competitive prices when Japanese competition arrived in the mid-1960s. As customer returns increased, Sears became dissatisfied with Warwick and turned to Japanese producers to obtain TV sets. Four of the five assembly lines at the Warwick plant had been closed by the early-1970s, and employment had been cut to less than 400 people (Hayes & Clark 1981). Losses mounted to over $9 million in 1975 on sales of $71 million as demand ebbed and employee morale fell. An employee described the Warwick situation as follows (quoted in Hayes & Clark, 1981):

> This was really a desolate place.... People were continually being laid off, and the handwriting was on the wall for every one to see. There was no money, so we were letting equipment run down. We were having terrible quality problems and spending nights and weekends reworking sets so that we could keep up with our delivery schedules. The management group was working as hard as it could, and yet things kept getting worse. It was really demoralizing.

The TV Industry

In the 1950s U.S. television technology was state-of-the-art and U.S. manufacturers dominated world output. At the time, U.S. firms were buying cheap TV parts from Japanese partner firms and actively supported these firms in efforts to improve their ability to manufacture TV components (Dertouzos et al., 1989, p. 223). To increase the components the Japanese firms could make, the U.S. firms transferred their monochrome technology to these firms in the 1950s, and then their color technology in the 1960s. They did so because they anticipated that with these increased technology transfers, the range of components their partners could manufacture at low cost would increase still further. The goal from the standpoint of the U.S. manufacturers was to decrease costs (Porter, 1983).

In 1956 the fledgling Japanese television manufacturers formed the Home Electronic Appliance Market Stabilization Council. The council promoted Japanese TV producer growth and set minimum price levels for televisions designated for domestic sale. These minimum price levels guaranteed profit margins for televisions sold in Japan, while tariff and nontariff barriers effectively blocked foreign firms from entering this protected market. The Japanese firms used the resulting profits to invest in and improve the television-design knowledge transferred to them by U.S. firms.

In the early 1960s MITI decided to target the Japanese consumer electronics industry with governmental support to help it sell overseas. Supported by MITI, the Japanese firms worked to establish a product presence in the U.S. TV market. To coordinate their export efforts, they organized the Television Export Council in 1963. Their sources of competitive advantage at the time included superior technology, superior manufacturing processes, and high-quality products (Porter, 1983). They offered these superior TVs to importers like Sears and other retailers at prices well below those of U.S. producers.[2] By the late 1960s Japanese TVs were flooding into the United States and they quickly gained a dominant share of the U.S. market (Porter, 1983).

In 1968 the U.S. manufacturers requested protection from the U.S. government, alleging Japanese TV sets were being dumped in the United States.[3] Three years later the Treasury Department responded to these complaints and charged Japanese firms with dumping TVs.[4] By 1975 a minefield of proceedings and investigations faced Japanese firms (e.g., Hitachi, Mitsubishi, Sanyo, Sharp, and

Table 1. US Color TV Production by Japanese Firms

	1973	1974	1975	1976	1977	1978	1979
Sony	130	250	275	370	400	450	475
Matsushita	-	-	300	400	460	600	700
Sanyo	-	-	-	-	300	600	680
Toshiba	-	-	-	-	-	60	175
Mitsubishi	-	-	-	-	-	60	120
Hitachi	-	-	-	-	-	-	20
Sharp	-	-	-	-	-	-	100
	130	250	575	770	1160	1770	2270

Source: Porter, M. E. 1983. The U.S. Television Set Market, 1970-1979.

Toshiba). To represent them in resolving these cases, the Japanese firms hired Harald Malmgren, who had been the deputy special-trade representative for the Nixon and Ford administrations. In three months he worked out a compromise that became known as the Orderly Marketing Agreement (OMA). The Japanese would limit their television exports from Japan to the United States to 1.5 million units annually for three years. They would be permitted to use whatever manufacturing facilities they established in the United States to fill any demand that exceeded this quota. Many Japanese television makers quickly responded by establishing manufacturing facilities in the United States (see Table 1).

Sanyo Enters the United States

Sanyo had manufactured many of the TVs imported by Sears. Sears discussed with Sanyo the idea of providing technical help to its failing Warwick facility. Both were aware of the new import restrictions and Sanyo's consequent need for U.S. manufacturing facilities (Krisher, 1981). The discussions soon moved to the possibility that Sanyo might buy out Whirlpool's share of the Warwick venture. Sears arranged a buyout for $10.3 million and provided Sanyo with a loan arrangement to underwrite the purchase. A Sanyo Electric subsidiary, the Sanyo Manufacturing Company (SMC), was established on January 1, 1977 at Forrest City.

Forrest City is located in Northeast Arkansas, west of Memphis in the Mississippi cotton delta.[5] The city population is stable at 15,000 residents with around 50 percent white and 50 percent black. Around a third of the city population are illiterate, 30 percent are on welfare, incomes are generally low, and unemployment has hovered for many years around 20 percent.[6]

Sanyo was welcomed to Forrest City. People were afraid that the town's main employer, Warwick, would disappear, as had in fact been gradually happening. To manage the facility, SMC sent 26 managers and technicians from Japan. They were instructed to live throughout the city and to do, eat, play, and go to school just as the Americans did. It appears that all of these men knew the technology and business practices of Sanyo Electric, their parent corporation, very well. It is not clear whether they had considered or even knew much about what it might be like to live in a cultural and social environment like Forrest City.

Mr. Satoshi Iue from Osaka was SMC's president. He managed relations between the SMC subsidiary and Sanyo's Headquarters in Osaka. Mr. Tanemichi Sohma, a Japanese national, was appointed Vice President for Administration and Personnel and put in charge of day-to-day plant operations. He had attended the University of Southern California in the 1950s, and his English language ability was better than most of his colleagues. He managed the relations between the Japanese managers and local employees and between the plant and the local community. Five of the new top SMC executives, including Sohma, came from Japan. The other four SMC executives were Americans inherited from Warwick's previous management group. The Japanese managers and technicians supervised operations at different levels and throughout the plant.

Establishing Control and Commitment

Sohma wanted to build a cooperative relationship between plant workers and management, and he launched many initiatives within SMC to make good relations a reality. The new management also sought to win the trust and confidence of Forrest City's citizens. To announce their arrival, Sanyo invited everyone in Forrest City to a welcome party. They quickly cleaned, painted, and renovated the run-down plant. When they needed new hires, they specifically sought to rehire workers who had previously worked for Warwick and had been laid off.

Quality Emphasis

SMC imported many of its transistor components from Japan to Forrest City where the workers assembled them into TVs. Within the plant, SMC's new management consistently emphasized that their primary concern was improved product quality. According to a worker at the factory (Hayes & Clark, 1981, p. 3):

> The first thing Sanyo did when they took over [was that] they retained essentially all employees and managers who were there.... They did move some people around, though. For example, they took the former manager of Quality Control—who really had been taking a lot of heat from everybody during the previous two years, because of the quality problems we were having—and made him the plant manager. That, by the way, was just one of the signals they gave that the number-one priority for the plant was improving quality. All they talked about was quality.

In pursuing quality, many of the Japanese managers and technicians spent their time standing very close to the employees, watching what they did, correcting them, and providing training. The managers thought this was necessary. Some workers reported that at times they thought this behavior was amusing, and most found the Japanese to be very fussy always wanting everything done exactly the particular way that they thought was right. The workers were well aware of how the Japanese had installed quality checks everywhere. They admitted, however, that the Japanese approach had vastly improved product quality.

Building a Happy Family

More than 60 percent of the workers at the SMC plant were black, and the International Union of Electrical Workers (IUE) organized these hourly workers. Sohma met with the union and explained that the company wanted to build a partnership with them. He emphasized Sanyo's intent to improve quality. To help achieve this goal, he asked the union to discuss production policies, methods, and goals with management, and to join management in implementing a start-to-finish quality program that would guarantee no defective TV would ever leave the plant. Initially, the union was pleasantly shocked at this approach but also somewhat at a loss to know how to respond. They had difficulty because they recalled how Warwick's management had always insisted production policies were management's prerogative. Workers had learned to close their eyes carefully to the many defective TVs leaving the plant. They saw the new approach as a big and positive change.

The work style that developed at SMC was noisy, busy, and casual. Believing little things counted, Sohma and his managers tried to notice and respond to anything and everything that could cause employees discomfort. Whenever they could, they remedied the matter immediately. In turn, they expected the workers to correct anything they noticed was wrong on the assembly line and also to do this immediately. Managers tried to be sensitive to both manufacturing requirements and workers' needs. When equipment was lacking, it was immediately purchased. When workers made mistakes, they were immediately counseled rather than discharged. In the first year, "Sanyo set out to create a 'big happy family' atmosphere to enhance morale" (Reid, 1977).

Firm loyalty was also very important to Sohma, the Japanese managers, and SMC. Sohma recognized how some of Warwick's established labor practices destroyed rather than encouraged loyalty. It had been Warwick's custom, for example, to let people go immediately after the Christmas production season. Sohma pledged to the union that Sanyo would seek to smooth production to phase out the need for repeated layoffs and recalls. Local employees were impressed by this commitment. They saw it as demonstrating a cooperative attitude toward workers and a willingness to use power and authority to change things in ways that benefited everyone.

Yet while Sohma consistently preached mutuality and shared responsibility for the production process, he did not give up the hierarchical power or the privileges that he and the other SMC executives enjoyed.[7] The authority accorded Japanese managers and technicians always distinguished them from the rest of the plant workforce. Sanyo also made little effort to modify other labor practices inherited from Warwick. For example, practices associated with Japanese firms such as lifetime employment or seniority-based pay systems were not introduced.

Operating Management

To facilitate sharing the management process, a management supervisory committee was appointed, including three managers from the United States and three from Japan. Decision making within this committee turned out to be slow and difficult. The U.S. managers thought the Japanese managers alluded to or implied what they wanted rather than giving explicit instructions. Not sensitive to the subtle cues offered by the Japanese managers, they would wait for instructions not realizing that these had already been given. This frustrated all sides. The difficulties were never resolved, and the committee was eventually abandoned. There were similar difficulties with attempts to introduce quality circles and other teamwork practices, and Sanyo managers eventually abandoned these efforts.

Building Control and Commitment

The 1979 Strike

Though Sohma seemed to be the person in charge at Forrest City, many decisions had to be referred back to headquarters in Japan for approval. This requirement could cause delays and misunderstandings, in part because many Japanese executives at Sanyo Electric's headquarters were not familiar with business life in the United States.

This became an issue in 1979 when a union strike lasting eight weeks was called. The strike was concerned with cost-of-living increases that had been promised but never implemented by the previous Warwick management. The union considered these increases a commitment that had been won and hence kept. SMC's local management thought that given the many contributions they had made to improve the workers lot in Forrest City, the union should not be holding Sanyo responsible for agreements made with Warwick. Both sides needed a clearer understanding of the expectations each had for the other. As the strike entered its third week, headquarters management in Osaka became worried, suspecting something was terribly wrong in Forrest City.[8] Reasoning based on their Japanese experience that such a long strike must mean Sohma had gravely offended the workers, they directed him to call his workforce together, humble himself before them, and apologize for the terrible things he had done. In touch with the realities of the local situation, Sohma refused. His Osaka bosses did not understand these realities, and they rebuked Sohma, believing he had become too Americanized and was proving untrustworthy. Eventually, Sohma was able to resolve the issues amicably. SMC also entered into a new five-year contract with Sears commencing in 1980.[9]

Sanyo imported the major components for its U.S. models, allowing Osaka to leverage its home-country scale advantages. The managers' job at Forrest City was to persuade workers to increase their production rate so this facility could also achieve the cost advantages associated with high volume. The Japanese managers were well aware, for example, that Sanyo's plants back in Osaka achieved the same quality as Forrest City but were 25 percent more efficient. Forrest City needed to achieve these standards for Osaka to effectively implement its global strategy based on volume and low costs.

This meant continuing pressures to reduce costs. It also meant that SMC management could not always keep the well-intentioned promises it had made to workers. According to Mr. Nakai, a Japanese manager for SMC (Krisher, 1981):

> Given different American conditions, we haven't been totally able to transplant the Japanese way to America. There are good periods and also slow periods, with heavy sales focused on November and December for the Christmas season. We've naturally had to adjust our production schedule and lay off some workers, as do other American manufacturers.

In discussing the emerging differences between Japanese managers and U.S. workers, Mr. Nakai said (Krisher, 1981):

> American workers maintain a much looser relationship toward their company compared with the Japanese.... However, we learned some lessons from that [1979 strike] and are now trying to improve the situation. In Japan, the union lives with the company and never pulls the trigger unless it finds itself in an extremely serious situation. It tries as much as possible to work with us on the same ground, because its members' future and prosperity are directly linked to ours. The important question for us right now is how to instill this concept in our American workers.

For their part, the U.S. workers had seen the vast improvements in quality, efficiency, and volume achieved at the plant since the takeover by Sanyo. The continual pressure for production improvements was gradually generating doubts about whether the Japanese managers would ever be satisfied.

As production rates were increased as much as tenfold and workforce numbers were increased only threefold, Sanyo increased its commitment to the facility. One step was to add microwave ovens to the product mix. By 1981 the plant employed 1,750 workers making televisions, 350 working in a furniture shop, and 250 making microwave ovens. Sanyo invested in total around $60 million in the Forest City plant.

As well as increasing its commitment by working with local suppliers, Sanyo worked with local political leaders to attract additional Japanese investment to the area. In 1981, for example, Sanyo helped orchestrate a Far East tour by Arkansas Governor White to persuade Asian firms to establish plants in the area. Responding to Sanyo's recommendations, several Japanese and Far East firms located manufacturing and servicing facilities around Memphis and in the North East Arkansas area. In 1982 the union contract was successfully renegotiated without further incident.

Losing Control and Commitment

Competition Intensifies

In 1984 production capacity in the United States was 13.1 million TV sets while actual production was 11.5 million sets, around 89 percent of capacity. But TV

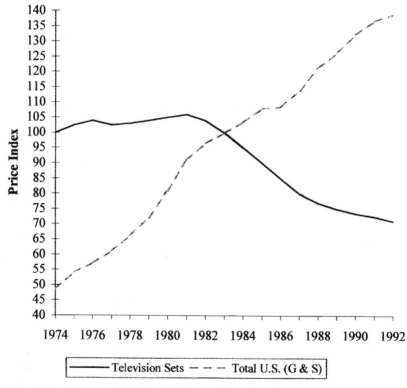

Annual Consumer Price Index U.S. 1974-1992

Source: Based on figures provided in The U.S. Consumer Electronics Industry in Review—1993 edition.

Figure 1.   Television Set Prices versus Total Sales of All Goods and Services 1974-1992

U.S. Imports of TVs

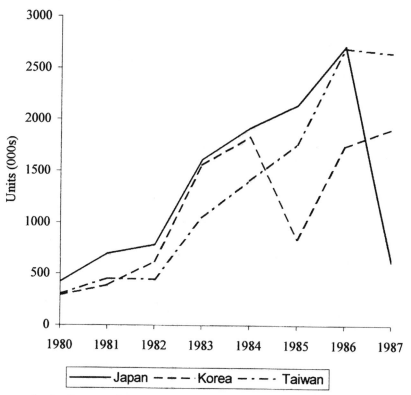

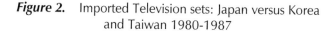

Source: Based on figures provided in Collis (1988).

Figure 2.   Imported Television sets: Japan versus Korea
and Taiwan 1980-1987

manufacturers from South Korea and other Asian countries were about to enter the U.S. market. They offered products of comparable quality to the Japanese televisions, but lower price. The timing of their entry also coincided with efforts by Japanese firms to expand their production capacity. At the time, however, demand for televisions was actually leveling off. With slowing demand and growing over capacity, firms started to employ price-cutting strategies to increase market share. SMC found itself less protected and facing more market challenges than it had ever experienced since coming to the United States. Forced to lower prices, managers now felt greatly increased pressure to improve their efficiency. Like most industry participants at the time, Sanyo had moved from a position where it had been making profits to a new position where it was forced to sustain losses.

Two years later U.S. industry production capacity had grown by 50 percent and was more than 17 million TV sets. This reflected the large capacity expansions undertaken by Japanese firms producing in the United States and new entrants coming from Korea and Taiwan. In contrast, actual television production had dropped to 11.2 million sets or just 66 percent of the expanded capacity. A shake out was about to occur among the 20 or so firms producing televisions in the United States (Porter, 1983) (see Figures 1 and 2).[10]

The 1985 Strike

Observing these changing competitive conditions, SMC had to renegotiate with its labor union in 1985. Knowing the competitive pressures it faced, Sanyo pressed the union to relax its rules relating to seniority rights and worker flexibility. They also proposed reductions in medical benefits and insurance costs. But the union resisted. Wilford W. Banks Jr., president of local 1106 of the IUE, was convinced that Sanyo just wanted more production and didn't want to have to pay for the extra effort. The atmosphere became bitter and for a short time, it was also violent (Byrne, 1988):

> The demands [of Japanese management] sparked a 21-day strike. Pickets carried signs that read: "Japs go home" and "Remember Pearl Harbor." Windows were broken, guns were fired, a car was overturned, and at one point the plant was nearly overrun by strikers.

Police arrested the picketers, and they hit the strikers. Eventually, a new 42-month contract ended the strike, but the union and the firm felt the strike had left a bitter legacy.

By 1986 SMC employed 1,700 people who produced 1.2 million TV sets and 500,000 microwave ovens. SMC was the largest Japanese TV producer in the United States with annual sales of $40 million. Yet due to increased competition reflecting industry overcapacity and price competition, the firm also lost $14 million. SMC asked the union to accept a 20 percent wage cut as a sign of solidarity and loyalty to the firm. In response the union agreed to forgo a 3 percent wage increase along with cost-of-living increases and to allow SMC some flexibility in reassigning employees.[11] After most of its requests had been rejected, SMC began examining other ways to achieve cost reductions and reestablish cost competitiveness. With continuing industry overcapacity, intense competition, and sinking prices, Sanyo headquarters in Osaka considered whether it should keep the Forrest City facility open. Given competitive pressures and the union's intransigence, it seemed imperative to relocate production to where it would be possible to reduce costs to compete successfully. According to Darrell Carter, VP for operations (Risen, 1988):

All the Japanese consumer electronics companies [with plants in the United States] are being faced with difficult decisions on job security.... They can't compete with imports from Korea and Taiwan, and so they are setting up feeder plants in Mexico, building parts and products they used to make in the U.S.

Sanyo decided to scale back its operations in Forrest City drastically and shift its labor-intensive production to a Maquiladora in Tijuana, Mexico where the labor costs were about an eighth of those in Arkansas. According to Annette Bradley, a worker at SMC (Risen, 1988):

I don't know if it was bad management, or bad parts, but I know one thing was they could get cheaper labor in Mexico.... I feel bad. They're taking jobs from the U.S. to Mexico because of cheaper labor, and it hurts the States and it hurts the people. I know they're human, they're out to make a dollar just like the rest of us are, but it's just that it would have been better if they would have just tried to work a little bit more with us, instead of just ship everything out.

Employment dropped from 1,200 in 1986 to 650 in 1988 including just 190 hourly workers. Sanyo may well have intended to withdraw from Arkansas completely, but Governor Bill Clinton made a successful appeal to Sanyo Electric's chairman in Osaka (*Economist*, 1993).[12]

Locally, Sanyo Japanese management had become increasingly frustrated with the "way of thinking" of American workers. Sanyo had faced fierce competition for years and had attempted to work with the union, improve product quality, and build workforce loyalty and commitment. The Sanyo managers were therefore frustrated that at a time of obvious firm need, there was no corresponding readiness on workers' part to make any sacrifice whatsoever on behalf of SMC.

DISCUSSION AND IMPLICATIONS

The way Sanyo entered the United States, the actions it took to establish good relations with its workforce, and the processes that then led to labor-management conflict at a critical juncture are worthy of discussion. The case illustrates how Sanyo's initial competitive advantage drawn from its parent and its trading relationships was eroded as its superior organizing principles and technological capabilities diffused to competitors in the United States and other parts of the world. It also illustrates how cultural and competitive dynamics interact and co-evolve to create new and unanticipated issues for a Japanese firm adapting to the U.S. environment.

Cultural Dynamics

Sanyo's Entry Process

Sanyo's impetus for establishing U.S. facilities can be traced to the Orderly Marketing Agreement of 1976 that effectively limited Japanese television exports. The agreement meant that if Japanese firms were to maintain their sales they had to produce their televisions in the United States. Sanyo implemented its entry into the United States strongly influenced by its established relationship with Sears.

Sears' actions reflect U.S. and not Japanese institutional and cultural norms. From Sears' point of view, its agreements with Sanyo reflected efforts to secure control and power over a committed and reliable supplier of a critical good (Porter, 1983). The Orderly Marketing Agreement threatened this relationship, and Sears wished to ensure a steady supply of high-quality TVs for its stores. Therefore, it encouraged Whirlpool to relinquish control of the Warwick facility to Sanyo and then guaranteed to buy a significant portion of Sanyo's television output from the Forrest City plant. These generous terms encouraged Sanyo to export its organizing methods and technologies directly from Osaka to Forrest City. It did this following the location and sales path presented to it by Sears.

Sears may be an unusual partner for Sanyo to follow because many of Sears' behaviors are in stark contrast to the institutional norms and culturally sanctioned behaviors Sanyo would expect from Japanese firms. A joint venture partnership (with Whirlpool) would certainly not have been thrown aside so easily in Japan. If a Japanese industry were threatened by foreign competition, government agencies would have held discussions with firms to assess how the consumer benefits of higher quality and cheaper TVs, for example, should be weighed against the national cost of losing an entire manufacturing industry. The fact that the basic technology had been created and developed by the firms now being forced to leave the industry would also have been discussed, and it would have been argued that this contribution justified a case for special consideration and support. Japanese post-World War economic history suggests a consistent preference for decisions that preserve industries as opposed to those that protect and favor consumer benefits (Fallows, 1994).

How Did Sanyo Establish Control and Commitment at the Warwick Facility?

The changes undertaken by Sanyo after its entry into the United States suggest that it sought to upgrade its Forrest City facility by directly transferring and imposing the parent company's technology and organizing practices on to its new subsidiary. Initially Sanyo focused on changing plant conditions and worker behaviors to improve TV quality and reliability. To staff the plant, Sanyo did not hesitate to employ members of the unionized workforce of the previous owner. In fact, they even went further, rehiring workers the previous owner had laid off. This policy is consistent with Brannen's (1995) observations that many Japanese top managers have great faith in plant workers. They believe that if these people are shown appropriate respect, they willingly work hard, cooperate, and produce. This new attitude was also in strong contrast to the Whirlpool approach that had shown little respect for workers while emphasizing volume and ignoring quality. The workers in Forrest City liked the contrasting approach introduced by Sanyo. The Japanese changes were intended to institutionalize a different approach to work. While the initial focus placed an emphasis on quality, this was to be just the beginning. The approach was expected to extend to an emphasis on quantity and culminate in processes directed toward continuous improvement. Sohma was the interface between the Japanese managers, the American workers, and the union, and so his role in the change effort was critical. Through his efforts, Sanyo effectively communicated its changed approach and won support from the labor force. It is likely that the historic unemployment in Forrest City and the low employee morale associated with Warwick's final days gave Sanyo management more power and also made the union more cooperative to management's initial requests (Beechler & Yang, 1994).

How Did Sanyo Lose Control and Commitment of Its Workforce?

As their initial concerns about their jobs faded and the improved output quality became accepted as normal, workers became more aware of how relentlessly the Japanese managers pursued increased efficiency. In work areas the managers were never satisfied and always wanted improvements. U.S. workers noted that while the Japanese de-emphasized status distinctions to improve work performance, they claimed special privileges in other areas. Yet they also expected the same organizational loyalty and sacrifice from workers as well as managers. The union felt that the Japanese did not appreciate how the combination of unrelenting pressures for work improvements, obvious privileges reserved for supervisors, and demands that everyone should be equally loyal to Sanyo were perceived as inconsistent conditions.

This state of affairs seems similar to the "bicultural alienation" discussed by Brannen and Sanyal (1993). The items in their "bicultural alienation scale" examine apparently positive aspects of supervisory behavior. These include the following assessments: supervisors seeking input from workers, workers feeling like valued group members, suggestions being valued, Japanese and Americans placing a similar value on hard work, and workers' participation and contributions at group meetings being valued. Yet Brannen and Sanyal (1993) found that as Japanese managers exert pressures for continual improvement and also emphasize their own privileged status, U.S. workers associate the scale behaviors with exploitation and new tricks to get more for less out of workers.

Such perceptions may be particularly likely in the United States where, unlike in Japan, the legal environment sanctions a competitive relationship between management and unions. In addition, people with individualistic values like U.S. workers may not respond well to organizational pressures for additional improvement unless they are provided with incentives that assure them additional individual (mostly financial) rewards. Given the increasingly competitive situation that

Sanyo's managers found themselves in and their expectations of employee loyalty, however, they did not consider offering further financial incentives. In fact, they asked for wage cuts. They reasoned that if the Forrest City workers were loyal to Sanyo, as the Japanese managers believed they should be, they would make needed extra efforts without need of further reward. But as Brannen and Sanyal (1993) note, if U.S. workers perceive themselves to be subject to continual and unfair pressure, they can become alienated rather than loyal.

When this culminated in a strike, many of Sanyo's Japanese managers were no longer optimistic about their ability to motivate U.S. workers. They reverted to negative stereotypes. As summarized by Brannen (1995), these stereotypes include beliefs that Americans "only think of themselves," and "only do things for money." The result can become a mutually negative cycle involving negative stereotyping on the one hand, and alienation and noncooperation on the other. This seems to be what eventually led to an embittered relationship between the union and SMC management after the second strike. Subject to direct market pressures and confronted with striking workers expressing no firm loyalty, Sanyo's managers became more self-centered and abandoned the idea and their ideal of "family" and community building.

Competitive Dynamics

Another area of interest is the way the competitive dynamics of the global television industry evolved and how this affected Warwick facility's competitive advantage. In 1977 Japanese electronic manufacturers had competitive advantages over U.S. firms based on their superior technology, superior manufacturing processes, higher-quality products, and prices that were significantly lower than those of U.S. manufacturers (Porter, 1983). But so far as Sanyo was concerned, industry competitive dynamics were not particularly significant at the time it entered the United States. With its superior product technology and demand guaranteed by Sears, SMC was initially buffered from the competitive dynamics of the U.S. industry.

This protection did not last, however. As the 1980s moved forward, the competitive pressures that plagued television manufacturers in particular, and electronic goods manufacturers in general, led to important changes. Increasingly, industry attention focused on financial returns enhanced by identifying those components that "added value" and could be priced to generate profits. The industry, including Sanyo, organized itself increasingly around component production. Components that required high skill and added high value were built most often in developed countries like Japan. Simpler, more standardized, or assembly line tasks were done in locations where labor costs were low such as Mexico and low-cost Asian countries. From a financial standpoint, these developments raised questions about the desirability of maintaining the SMC assembly plant in Arkansas.

Given this new competitive situation with new suppliers ready to offer the same quality but at lower prices than Sanyo (*Economist*, 1993), Sears was ready to abandon SMC in the same way it had abandoned its U.S. suppliers two decades earlier. This was a significant threat to SMC since Sears took 70 percent of its total output. With industry competition growing and price cuts the norm, Sears was no longer a reliable or a patient partner. Forced to lower prices, Sanyo managers felt enormous pressure to secure cost reductions and improve efficiency. They passed on this pressure directly to the workforce, but the U.S. workforce did not have the loyalty that Sanyo might have been able to count on from its Japanese employees in times of organizational need. The U.S. workers would not tolerate any increased managerial pressure, and in Forrest City, most didn't care about global competitive dynamics.

Building Competitive Advantage

Facing new competitive pressures, Sanyo needed to find new sources of competitive advantage. Taylor, Beechler, and Napier (1996) argue that a firm can use three generic orientations to build competitive advantage in a foreign country. When it entered the United States, Sanyo adopted an "exporting" approach, establishing the firm's competitive advantage through parent technology and organizing practices. A theoretical alternative is an "adaptive" approach where a firm imitates the local practices. This didn't make sense for Sanyo in 1977 because its technology and manufacturing practices were superior to those of U.S. firms. The third alternative is an "integrative" approach where a firm identifies the best ideas in its separate locations and then develops and builds its own unique integrative approach. This third approach was ultimately needed in Forrest City if SMC was to develop U.S.-based sources of competitive advantage.

Our analysis of Sanyo indicates that the three alternatives may not always be clear to managers, and in practice, the appropriate choice probably changes in response to competitive conditions (Beechler & Yang, 1994). In Sanyo's case, its exporting approach initially made sense. Later, however, Sanyo's increasing difficulties in implementing its Osaka practices in Forrest City and the mounting competitive pressures signaled that the firm's initial sources of competitive advantage might be eroding. Some form of integration accommodating the different values and priorities of the Japanese and U.S. workforces probably needed to be considered. Yet Sanyo management does not seem to have recognized the context-specific nature of some of the practices it attempted to transfer and did not take steps to explore the implications when they failed to transfer. Instead, Sanyo management simply abandoned elements that didn't transfer and sought no replacement for the functions performed by these abandoned elements. As the original sources of competitive advantage Sanyo brought to Forrest City eroded over time, the firm became increasingly vulnerable. The resource that Sanyo seems to have assumed it could rely on was employee loyalty. But when firm managers called for firm loyalty, none was there.

A comparison of Sanyo with NUMMI may be useful. Both firms took over an established U.S. plant and workforce and worked with American unions. Adler (1993) notes that success at NUMMI was due to two important factors. One aspect is the emphasis on standardized practices; both Sanyo and NUMMI plants shared this characteristic. Additionally, Adler (1993) reports that NUMMI established a social context committed to continuous improvement. Sanyo wanted this too, but failed to implement it. Perhaps the status differences and privileges that remained in Forrest City but were eliminated at NUMMI were symbolically important enough in an American context to sabotage implementing a continuous improvement culture. In addition, training programs explaining the continual improvement programs were reportedly extensive at NUMMI, while they were absent at Sanyo.

Implications

The Sanyo case highlights issues that come up when a Japanese firm enters the United States. Adaptation in a foreign setting involves understanding and responding to both cultural and competitive dynamics. The Sanyo case suggests how these conditions co-evolve, interact, and change over time. More generally, cross-cultural research needs to explore "phenomenon in the making" to understand how adaptation in a foreign setting evolves. A more qualitative approach enables researchers to emphasize the impact of the foreign setting and the process by which a firm socially constructs its evolving world in this context.

Our analysis suggests that partner relationships are sensitive to and change in response to competitive pressures. U.S. partner commitments may be focused on the short term and what is currently convenient. Also, the U.S. personnel who originally negotiated such deals are less likely to be with their firm when times change. Japanese partners are, in addition to short-term commitments, concerned about loyalty and longer-term issues. These contrasting perspectives can lead to misunderstandings at times of growing competitive pressure when worker sacrifices and loyalty might help a firm survive, but these expectations are simply not part of a short-term view. Therefore the success of foreign alliances with U.S. firms is affected by changing competitive dynamics (i.e., the speed at which foreign superior practices and technology diffuse in the United States) and other societal-level factors (cf. Cheng, 1994). This suggests the following proposition:

Proposition 1.   The success of alliances is affected by how the respective parties interpret the short-term and long-term consequences of changing competitive and social dynamics.

Our analysis of Sanyo's U.S. operations indicates that U.S. workers welcome worker participation in the production process. They may perceive unfairness, however, if there are continual pressures for improvement and management receives obvious privileges the workforce does not enjoy. Such inconsistencies may sabotage efforts to establish a continuous improvement culture. In addition since a continuous improvement culture is not the norm in U.S. unionized firms, implementing it may require support from an extensive training program. Learning from the experiences of other ventures such as NUMMI can help Japanese managers put in place mechanisms to make continuous improvements efforts successful (Adler, 1993).

Proposition 2. Japanese firms that adopt work practices accounting for both plant- and societal-level factors are more likely to succeed in sustaining the commitment of their U.S. workforce.

More generally, managers going abroad make decisions that balance a reliance on what they know from their home country with what they learn, and must adapt to, in the new country. This is an area of cross-cultural research which seems critical to practitioners (cf. Taylor, 1991). We suspect that firms from different countries use different approaches reflecting their cultural origins in successfully transferring home country practices to a foreign setting. We also suspect they differ in the extent to which they adapt the home country practices to the local environment. The parameters that influence these decisions are an important area for future research.

We also found that the changing nature of competitive dynamics affects firm competitive advantages. The Sanyo case indicates that while parent-based competitive advantage was needed to enter the U.S. market, it eroded over time. If a firm is in a foreign country for some time, it will probably need to develop a more integrated base of competitive advantage that draws in ideas from both the local facility and the parent. In other words, successful adaptation in a foreign setting involves understanding and responding to both the cultural *and* competitive dynamics.

Proposition 3. Foreign firms that explicitly develop an integrated base of competitive advantage drawing on local conditions are likely to be more successful than firms that only emphasize transferring parent-based competitive advantage.

We suspect that firms from different countries use different approaches reflecting their cultural origins in deciding the extent to which to invest efforts in developing an integrated base of competitive advantage. These bases will include a combination of social and technical factors and are likely to vary across industry. While initially, Sanyo's human resources practices were appealing to its U.S.

workforce, later events uncovered difficulties in adaptation that probably made an integrated base of competitive advantage impossible to achieve for this firm. As Sanyo's experience is limited to the consumer electronics industry, it is hard to generalize to other industries. Other firm case studies will probably be necessary to identify how an integrated base of competitive advantage can be developed in other industries.

CONCLUSIONS

Sanyo is an example of a Japanese firm that imposed Japanese ways of doing things when it established its facilities in the United States and then assessed the ongoing developments based on Japanese values. Though the Sanyo managers had great confidence in their methods and values and succeeded in bringing about many important improvements supported by their U.S. workforce, eventually these efforts reached an upper bound. The Japanese managers had difficulty accepting this state of affairs, for their corporate strategy was based on expansion and the lowering of production costs. But Sanyo's continual push for improvement led to worker alienation, strikes, and rejection right at the time that continued strategic success for Sanyo required worker loyalty, commitment, and sacrifice. The Sanyo case illustrates that foreign firms competing in the United States should not underestimate the importance of cultural and competitive dynamics and how these co-evolve over time in unmanaged ways. These dynamics, generally not apparent at entry, can and do play an important role as a firm adapts in a foreign setting.

ACKNOWLEDGMENTS

Authors are listed alphabetically. We thank Allan Bird, Anil Nair, Myles Shaver, and D. Eleanor Westney for their helpful comments on the earlier versions of this paper.

NOTES

1.   We also contacted Mr. Naoki Nakamura, president of Sanyo's operations in the United States. He responded to our request in a gracious manner but noted, "because of some past incidents that have occurred it would be in our best interests that you choose another Japanese company." We informed him that while we were disappointed in his unwillingness to partake in the study, we intended to continue with our focus on Sanyo Electric's U.S. operations.

2.   The Japanese firms not only offered TVs to importers at prices U.S. manufacturers believed were below cost, in addition, they offered rebates of up to $40 per set and additional payments for "market research." While these Japanese tactics appalled U.S. manufacturers, U.S. importers liked them and willingly agreed to import Japanese TVs.

3.   In 1951 there were over 90 U.S.-owned firms that manufactured TVs. By 1968, 28 firms manufactured TVs. By 1976 only six U.S.-owned firms remained. As a result of the Japanese imports, U.S.

employment in television production dropped 50 percent between 1966 and 1970, another 30 percent between 1971 and 1975, and a further 25 percent between 1977 and 1981.

4.   This finding meant that anti-dumping levies could be collected from firms to offset the advantage they had gained. The calculation of such levies required accurate information from the Japanese firms, however, and they would not provide this data. Although it was possible to impute the figures, to do so would have invited retaliation and a trade war.

5.   General Nathan Bedford Forrest, a flamboyant hero of the confederate cavalry, founded Forrest City in 1866. General Forrest is remembered for several reasons. During the Civil War he is reputed to have had approximately 20 horses shot out from under him. After the war, he settled in Forrest City, where he became the first grand wizard of the Ku Klux Klan (KKK). He later resigned as the KKK became too violent for him.

6.   The media has periodically highlighted the racial tensions that have historically pervaded Forrest City and the surrounding county. Court-ordered school integration directly impacted the area in 1965. In 1969, for example, students at a black high school rioted after a favorite teacher was fired for "insubordination." A private school, Forrest City Academy, was founded in the 1970s for whites only. Its closure in the 1980s reflected the greater tolerance characteristic of more recent times. In 1988 the Forrest City High School held its first integrated prom. The media watching closely not only reported no incidents but pronounced it an outstanding success.

7.   As an example, Sohma explained to the union that Japanese managers found it repulsive when workers smoked on the production line. With union cooperation he phased out smoking among line workers. Some Japanese executives reasoned that because they were not workers on the line, this agreement did not apply to them and they continued to smoke in the plant. They also claimed special parking privileges and other perks. In this way Sohma supported distinctions and privileges accorded to Japanese managers but not to workers.

8.   Strikes in Japan are usually symbolic expressions of a breakdown in relations between management and workers. Having effectively signaled their concerns by wearing armbands and working even harder than usual, for example, workers most often then call off their strike.

9.   Under the terms of the contract, Sears "agreed to purchase at least 70% of its annual requirements of color televisions receivers for sale in the United States from SMC.... During 1980 about 82% of the company's production went to Sears; the remainder was sold through SMC's parent company" (Hayes & Clark, 1981, p. 3).

10.   Most of the firms producing in the United States were foreign-owned. Many were Japanese subsidiaries but several were more recently established subsidiaries of Korean and Taiwanese multinationals. The Korean and Taiwanese firms were prepared to compete just as fiercely on quality and price criteria as the Japanese had done two decades earlier.

11.   The union had asked its auditor to check SMC's books and assess whether a request to cut wages by 20 percent was justified. The auditor's perspective was in terms of Sanyo's relative labor costs and not in terms of Osaka's need to establish a strategic advantage through cost competitiveness. When he reported Sanyo's problems were not located in its relative labor costs, the union rejected SMC's request.

12.   The *Economist* noted (1993, p. A29): "Some say that Sanyo did not pull out altogether only because Mr. Clinton, on a trip to Japan, appealed to Sanyo's chairman in person to save the plant. He intervened again when Sears cut back on its Sanyo orders, arranging a new retailing deal with Wal-Mart chain (which is based in Arkansas)."

REFERENCES

Abegglen, J. C., & Stalk, G. (1985). *Kaisha.* Basic Books, New York.

Adler, P. S. (1993, January-February). Time and motion regained. *Harvard Business Review*, 97-109.

Aoki, M. (1990). Towards an economic model of the Japanese firm. *Journal of Economic Literature,* *28,* 1-27.

Beechler, S., & Yang, J. Z. (1994). The transfer of Japanese-style management to American subsidiaries: Contingencies, constraints and competencies. *Journal of International Business Studies,* *25* (3), 467-79.

Brannen, M. Y. (1995). Does culture matter? Negotiating a complementary culture to support technological innovation. In J. K. Liker, J. E. Ettlie, & J. C. Campbell (Eds.), *Engineered in Japan.* New York: Oxford University Press.

Brannen, M. Y., & Sanyal, A. (1993). Bicultural alienation in Japanese-Owned companies: A preliminary study in scale development. Paper presented at the *Academy of International Management Meetings,* October 20-24, Maui, Hawaii.

Brown, C., & Reich, M. (1989, Summer). When does union Management cooperation Work? A look at NUMMI and GM-Van Nuys. *California Management Review,* 26-41.

Buckley, P. J., & Casson, M.C. (1976). *The future of the multinational enterprise.* London: MacMillan.

Byrne, J. A. (1988, July 14). At Sanyo's Arkansas plant the magic isn't working. *Business Week.*

Campbell, D. (1975). "Degrees of freedom" and the case study. *Comparative Political Studies, 8* (2), 178-193.

Caves, R. (1982). *Multinational enterprise and economic analysis.* New York: Cambridge University Press.

Chang, S. J. (1995). International expansion strategy of Japanese firms: Capability building through sequential entry. *Academy of Management Journal, 38* (2), 383-407.

Cheng, J. L. C. (1994). On the concept of universal knowledge in organizational science: Implications for cross-national research. *Management Science, 40* (1), 162-168.

Choate, P. (1991, September 30). Japan and the big squeeze. *The Washington Post,* p. D1.

Cole, R. E., & Deskins, D. R., Jr. (1988, Fall). Racial factors in site location and employment patterns, *California Management Review.*

Collis, D. J. (1988). General Electric—Consumer electronics group. *Harvard Business School case #* *389-048.* Boston, MA: Harvard Business School Press.

Dertouzos, M. L., Lester, R. K., & Solow, R. M. (1989). *Made in America: Regaining the Productive Edge.* Cambridge, MA: MIT Press.

Economist (1993, March 6). The limits of success: East Arkansas: American survey, A29+.

Fallows, J. (1994). *Looking at the sun: The rise of the new East Asian economic and political system.* New York: Pantheon.

Hayes, R., & Clark, K. (1981). Sanyo Manufacturing Corporation—Forrest City, Arkansas. *Harvard Business School Case # 9-682-045.* Boston, MA: Harvard Business School Press.

Hennart, J. F., & Park, Y. (1994). Location, governance, and strategic determinants of Japanese manufacturing investment in the United States. *Strategic Management Journal, 15,* 419-436.

Hymer, S. H. (1976). *The international operations of national firms: A study of direct investment.* Cambridge, MA: MIT Press.

Kagono, T., Sakakibara, K., Nonaka, I., & Okumura, A. (1985). *Strategic Vs. Evolutionary Management: A U.S.-Japan Comparison of Strategy and Organization.* Amsterdam: North-Holland.

Kogut, B. (1991). Country capabilities and the permeability of borders. *Strategic Management Journal, 12,* 33-47.

Kogut, B., & Singh, H. (1988). The effect of national culture on the choice of entry mode. *Journal of International Business Studies, 19,* 411-432.

Kotha, S. (1998). Competing on the Internet: How Amazon.com is rewriting the rules of competition. *Advances in Strategic Management, 15,* 239-265.

Kotha, S., Dunbar R. L. M., & Bird, A. (1995). Strategic action generation: A comparison of emphasis placed on generic competitive methods by U.S. and Japanese managers. *Strategic Management Journal, 16,* 195-220.

Krisher, B. (1981, June 15). How the Japanese Manage in the U.S. *Fortune*, pp. 97-99.

Li, J. (1995). Foreign entry and survival: effects of strategic choices on performance in international markets. *Strategic Management Journal, 12*, 33-47.

Lincoln, J. R., Hanada, M., & Olson, J. (1981). Cultural orientations and individual reactions to organizations: a study of employees of Japanese-owned firms. *Administrative Science Quarterly, 26*, 93-115.

Lincoln, J. R., Hanada, M., & McBride, K., (1986). Organizational structures in Japanese and US manufacturing. *Administrative Science Quarterly, 31* (3), 338-364.

Lodge, G. C. (1987). Introduction: Ideology and country analysis. In G. C. Lodge & E. F. Vogel (Eds.), *Ideology and national competitiveness: An analysis of nine countries* (pp. 1-28). Boston: Harvard Business School.

Milkman, R. (1991). *Labor relations and economic globalization*. LA: UCLA Institute of Industrial Relations.

Murtha, T. P., & Lenway, S. A. (1994). Country capabilities and the strategic state: How national political institutions affect multinational corporations' strategies. *Strategic Management Journal*, Special Summer Issue, *15*, 113-129.

Ouchi, W. (1981). *Theory Z: How American business can meet the japanese challenge*. Addison-Wesley, Reading, MA.

Porter, M. E. (1983). The U.S. television set market, prewar to 1970 (pp. 449-481). and the U.S. television set market, 1970-1979 (pp. 482-511). *Cases in Competitive Strategy*. New York: Free Press.

Reid, T. R. (1977, September 2). A curious marriage. *The Washington Post*, p. A1+.

Risen, J. (1988, August 16). Disillusionment grows at Japanese-owned plants in U.S. *The Los Angeles Times*, C1+.

Taylor, W. (1991, March-April). The logic of global business:An interview with ABB's Percy Barnevik. *Harvard Business Review*, 91-105.

Taylor, S, Beechler, S., & Napier, N. (1996). Towards an integrative model of strategic international human resource management. *Academy of Management Review, 21* (4), 959-985.

Tsoukas, H. (1989). The epistemological status of idiographic research in the comparative study of organizations: A realist perspective. *Academy of Management Review, 14* (4), 551-561.

Yin, R. K. (1994). *Case study research: Design and methods* (2nd ed.). Thousand Oaks, CA: Sage Publications.

Zaheer, S. (1995). Overcoming the liability of newness. *Academy of Management Journal, 38* (2), 341-363.

CORPORATE GOVERNANCE AND GLOBALIZATION

IS THERE CONVERGENCE ACROSS COUNTRIES?

Mauro F. Guillén

ABSTRACT

Proponents of the globalization thesis argue that cross-national patterns of corporate governance are converging or will converge on either the Anglo-Saxon, shareholder-centered model or some hybrid between the shareholder and stakeholder models. Other scholars, however, observe that corporate governance models cannot be seen in isolation of the rest of the institutional underpinnings of the economy and predict no convergence in corporate governance across countries. They make three interrelated arguments. First, corporate governance is tightly coupled with path-dependent legal traditions that are unlikely to change in the near future. Second, corporate governance models interact in complex ways with other institutional features directly related to the ways in which firms compete in the global economy. Third, the variety of economic, social, and political actors involved in corporate governance across countries makes it hard to envision convergence as the result of global pressures because they may attempt to shape and oppose changes adverse to their interests. Longitudinal evidence on various corporate governance dimensions drawn

Advances in International Comparative Management, Volume 13, pages 175-204.
Copyright © 2000 by JAI Press Inc.
All rights of reproduction in any form reserved.
ISBN: 0-7623-0589-4

from both advanced and newly industrialized countries shows little convergence over the last 20 years.

INTRODUCTION

A corporate governance system is the "set of incentives, safeguards, and dispute-resolution processes used to order the activities of various corporate stakeholders" such as owners, managers, workers, creditors, suppliers, and customers (Kester, 1996, p. 109). Corporate governance provides a framework for the division of labor and of financial results in the firm. Corporate governance plays a key role in any economy. A well-functioning corporate governance system can contribute to economic efficiency, and perhaps even social equity. A poorly conceived system can wreak havoc on the economy by misallocating resources or failing to check opportunistic behaviors. Moreover, different corporate governance systems are associated with peculiar managerial decision-making criteria and temporal orientations (Bühner et al., 1998; Kester, 1996; Lazonick & O'Sullivan, 1996).

Most conceptual analyses of corporate governance to date make comparisons between the shareholder-centered models of the United States or the U.K., and the stakeholder-centered models of Japan or Germany (Bühner et al., 1998; Lazonick & O'Sullivan, 1996; Macey & Miller, 1995; Roe, 1993). Other researchers also propose the French and Scandinavian systems as separate models due to their different legal origins (La Porta et al., 1998). Corporate governance patterns continue to differ markedly across countries in spite of decades of economic globalization and 20 years of intense financial globalization. The literature has documented great cross-national differences in terms of such essential aspects of corporate governance as the importance of large stockholders, the legal protection of shareholders, the extent to which relevant laws are enforced, the treatment of stakeholders such as labor, suppliers or the community, the reliance on debt finance, the structure of the board of directors, the way in which executives are compensated, and the frequency and treatment of mergers and takeovers, especially hostile ones. Concentrated, not dispersed, ownership is still the rule rather than the exception throughout the world, and so is family control of even the largest corporations or business groups in most countries (Becht & Röell, 1999; La Porta et al., 1998, 1999; Loredo & Suárez, 1998; Shleifer & Vishny, 1997; Thomsen & Pedersen, 1996).[1]

This paper focuses on the question of whether globalization is reducing the diversity in corporate governance practices across countries or not. The effects of globalization on corporate governance have important social, economic, and political as well as managerial implications. Intuitively, globalization is a process related to increasing cross-border flows of goods, services, money, people, and information. Globalization appears to be associated with a disjunction of space and time (Giddens, 1990, p. 64, 1991, p. 21), a shrinking of the world (Harvey,

1989; Mittelman, 1996). The global economy—driven by increasing technological scale, alliances between firms, and information flows (Kobrin, 1997, pp. 147-
148)—is one "with the capacity to work as a unit in real time on a planetary scale"
(Castells, 1996, p. 92). It is also one in which national economies become more
interdependent in terms of trade, finance, and macroeconomic policy (Gilpin,
1987, p. 389).

While only a few skeptics doubt the existence of a process of globalization,
there is little agreement as to what the consequences are (for reviews, see Guillén,
2001b; Waters, 1995). Some management scholars (Prahalad, 1997) and sociologists (Meyer et al., 1997) argue that convergence in organizational patterns is taking place as a result of globalization. Other researchers see globalization as
promoting diversity in the world as opposed to homogeneity (Guillén, 2001a,
2001b; Macey & Miller, 1995). Among others, the argument is made that companies in different countries will tend to adopt corporate governance practices consistent with free capital markets and geared toward maximizing shareholder
value. The increase in foreign direct and portfolio investment—with the concom-
itant rise of powerful multinational corporations and institutional investors—are
commonly cited as pressures tending toward convergence. Companies and countries that do not bend to this trend are predicted to decline in terms of global competitiveness (Bishop, 1994; Charkham, 1995; Ibbotson & Brinson, 1993; Loredo
& Suárez, 1998; OECD, 1998a; Useem, 1996). As recently as 1999, the World
Bank and the OECD have joined forces to "improve global corporate governance
practices" with the creation of the Global Corporate Governance Forum, an initiative that may increase the pressure on developing countries to reform their corporate governance systems, although it has thus far only recommended increasing
transparency rather than uprooting long-standing practices (Sargent, 1999, p. 3;
O'Sullivan, 1999).

Examining the impact of globalization on organizational patterns such as corporate governance systems is a delicate task because scholars do not agree as to
when globalization started and to what extent it has made inroads (Guillén,
2001b). While some scholars date the beginning of globalization with the first cir-
cumnavigation of the Earth or the rise of the European-centered world economy
in the early sixteenth century, others would rather wait until the turn of the twentieth century, World War II, the oil crises of the 1970s, the rise of Thatcher and
Reagan, or even the collapse of the Soviet Union in 1989. This paper focuses on
trends in corporate governance since the mid-1970s. The proponents of the convergence thesis and its detractors coincide in observing that little convergence, if
any, took place prior to 1973. Hence, they both focus on the rise in foreign trade,
foreign direct investment, and cross-border portfolio investment since the late
1970s as factors potentially shaping corporate governance practices.

Surprisingly, the extant literature has not produced longitudinal evidence documenting changes in corporate governance practices for a number of countries
large enough to tell whether there is convergence in the world or not. This paper

is the first to systematically compare the arguments for and against convergence in corporate governance, and to provide longitudinal empirical evidence on patterns of corporate governance for both rich and emerging countries. The paper focuses on aggregate trends at the country level of analysis since the mid-1970s or the early 1980s (depending on the indicator) rather than on concrete events affecting specific companies. I start by presenting the arguments for and against convergence. Then I present longitudinal quantitative evidence, including the influence of foreign investment from different home countries, the presence of institutional investors, the distribution of listed corporate equity by type of shareholder, the debt-equity ratios of nonfinancial firms, the adoption of long-term incentives in CEO remuneration, and the occurrence of hostile takeovers. The evidence presented shows that little convergence has taken place since 1980 although some countries have adopted certain isolated features of the shareholder-centered model. In the conclusion I propose to intensify our research efforts on cross-national patterns of corporate governance from a comparative approach that takes national diversity and its consequences seriously into account.

ARGUMENTS FOR CONVERGENCE

Proponents of the "globalization thesis" about convergence in corporate governance systems see the rise of foreign direct and portfolio investment as a force tending toward homogeneity. However, they do not agree on the outcome of such a process of convergence. Some scholars and observers argue that globalization will cause corporate governance practices to converge on the American shareholder-centered model whereas others sustain that there will be convergence half way between the shareholder and stakeholder models. A third group of convergence proponents argues that it is hard to predict the final outcome of convergence. Let us analyze each argument in turn.

Convergence on the Shareholder-Centered Model

Early students of corporate governance argued that secure shareholder rights and the sharp separation of (dispersed) ownership from (managerial) control were inevitably more "efficient" and "modern" than alternative models such as those underpinning family firms, conglomerates, bank-led groups, or worker cooperatives, and would accordingly become widespread (Berle & Means, 1932; Kerr et al., 1964). These models developed historically in the United Kingdom and the United States, the two dominant world powers of the nineteenth and twentieth centuries, and spread to other countries that adopted English common law, largely the former colonies of the British Empire (La Porta et al., 1998). Given the dominance of American business from the end of World War II to at least the 1970s, one would have expected the American corporate governance model—dispersed ownership, strong legal protection of shareholders and indifference to other stakeholders, little reliance on bank finance, relative freedom to merge or acquire—to have been adopted as the best practice throughout the world.

The globalization of financial investment and money-managing starting in the early 1980s has spurred another round of arguments predicting a convergence on the American model because it is based on market principles. Most financial and money managers would prefer companies throughout the world to observe shareholder rights, maximize shareholder value, and be transparent in their reporting of corporate activities and results (Useem, 1996). The rise of globally diversified mutual funds seems to create "pressures for the standardization of information on companies" (Ibbotson & Brinson, 1993, p. 321; see also Shleifer & Vishny, 1997, p. 757).[2]

Convergence on a Hybrid Model

A second group of convergence proponents seized on the rise of Germany and Japan as formidable manufacturing powers from the 1960s to the 1980s to argue that there is a trend toward a hybrid model combining features from both the shareholder and the stakeholder models (Fleming, 1998; OECD, 1998a). The OECD's report on corporate governance—written by six prominent managers or directors from the United States, France, Britain, Germany, and Japan—states that "as regulatory barriers between national economies fall and global competition for capital increases, investment capital will follow the path to those corporations that have adopted efficient governance standards.... Philosophical differences about the corporation's mission continue, although views appear to be converging" (1998a, p. 83). Unlike the first group of convergence proponents, however, the experts assembled by the OECD point out that convergence is not toward the U.S. approach but toward a middle ground between the shareholder- and stakeholder-centered models.

The argument about convergence on a hybrid model is based on the premise that no single model is optimal along each and every dimension. "It is not productive to argue whether any system of governance is inherently superior to others...systems are 'path specific'" (OECD, 1995, p. 29). Therefore, this second group of convergence proponents argues that market forces will eventually encourage firms and countries to select features from existing models as they strive to remain competitive.

Convergence on an Undefined Model

The third group of proponents of convergence argues that it has become exceedingly difficult to predict whether the U.S. model or a hybrid will ultimately predominate. Thus, Matthew Bishop, writing in 1994 for *The Economist* magazine, admits that "predicting trends in corporate governance is a tricky business.

Five years ago the long-termism of the Japanese and Germans seemed the best course; and the turmoil caused by hostile bids in America and Britain seemed the opposite. Now things look different." After a detailed analysis of cross-national differences, Jonathan Charkham (1995, p. 363) leaves it up to the reader to decide which is the "best" model, assuming that the best or most efficient will eventually prevail.

ARGUMENTS AGAINST CONVERGENCE

There are at least three arguments in the extant literature that provide a rationale against the prediction that corporate governance practices are converging or will converge across countries. First, corporate governance systems are tightly coupled with path-dependent regulatory traditions in the areas of banking, labor, tax, and competition law that are unlikely to be modified in the near future. Second, corporate governance systems do not exist in isolation of other institutional features directly related to the ways in which firms formulate their strategy to compete in the global economy. Third, global pressures on corporate governance practices are mediated by domestic politics in ways that make convergence across countries rather unlikely.

The Legal Case Against Convergence

The legal argument against convergence in corporate governance notes that corporate law is intimately related not only to social custom but also to other legal areas, such as banking, labor, tax, and competition law. Such complex systems of laws and regulations evolve in a path-dependent way and are resistant to change (Bebchuk & Roe, 1999; Bühner et al., 1998). As Columbia law professor Mark Roe (1993) explains in detail, the American model of corporate governance emerged from a specific legal and law-making tradition prone to limiting the activities of banks, privileging managerial over worker rights, taxing the dividends obtained from cross-holdings of shares, and specifying tight constraints on collaborative arrangements between firms in the same industry. In Germany and Japan, by contrast, a different set of banking, labor, tax, and competition laws and regulations supports models of corporate governance that facilitate routine interactions between owners and managers, and extensive collaborative ties between financial institutions and firms or between firms themselves. In particular, executive compensation systems are unlikely to converge across countries because the tax treatment of perquisites, pension funds, and long-term incentives is so different. Similarly, the patterns of stockholding across different institutional actors such as financial intermediaries, nonfinancial firms, and households are also unlikely to converge because of competition and tax regulations specifying who can own what.

Economists La Porta, Lopez-de-Silanes, Shleifer, and Vishny argue in a series of influential papers (La Porta et al., 1998, 1999) that diversity in corporate governance around the world results from attempts by stockholders to surmount poor legal investor protection (see also Bühner et al., 1998, p. 147, prop. 1). Thus, ownership concentration is a frequent way in which investors try to gain power in order to protect their interests. Using detailed data from nearly 50 countries, La Porta and colleagues (1998) identify four legal traditions—French (which includes the French, Spanish, and Portuguese spheres of colonial influence), German (Central Europe and Japan), Scandinavian, and Common Law (the former British colonies)—which help explain patterns of variation. Thus, legal traditions with relatively weak investor protection (German, Scandinavian, French) have more concentrated ownership than the common-law countries. In another paper, La Porta and colleagues (1999) establish that in 27 wealthy countries, both the largest 20 firms in terms of market capitalization and the 10 firms with capitalization just above $500 million do not tend to have dispersed ownership, but are under the control of families, the state, or financial institutions, in that order of importance (see also Guillén, 2001a, chap. 3; Orrù, Biggart, & Hamilton, 1997).

Like La Porta and colleagues, Roe (1993, p. 1989) concludes that "the American governance structure is not inevitable, that alternatives are plausible, and that a flatter authority structure does not disable foreign firms." Rather than using agency costs or contract theory or judicial doctrine to explain this or that feature as mitigating or reflecting managerial deviation from the maximization of shareholders' wealth," he continues, "we must consider the role of politics, history, and culture" (1993, p. 1997). To those variables now we turn.

The Institutional Case Against Convergence

An institutional approach indicates that it is futile to attempt identifying the best practice or model in the abstract (Guillén, 1994; Whitley, 1992, 1999). Rather, countries and their firms are socially and institutionally equipped to follow different competitive strategies in the global economy. One such institutional equipment is the pattern of corporate governance prevalent in the country, which facilitates specific competitive strategies and temporal orientations (Bebchuk & Roe, 1999; Bühner et al., 1998; Kester, 1996; Kim & Hoskisson, 1996; Lazonick & O'Sullivan, 1996).

Thus, German, French, Japanese, and American firms are justly famous for their competitive edge, albeit following different strategies for different industries and market segments that are closely intertwined with their corporate governance systems. Germany's educational and industrial institutions—dual-apprenticeship system, management-union cooperation, dual-board corporate governance system, and tradition of hands-on engineering or *Technik*—enable companies to excel in high-quality, engineering-intensive industries such as advanced machine tools, luxury automobiles, and specialty chemicals. The participation of labor on the supervisory boards of German corporations is a key mechanism compelling firms to look for smart ways of employing the skills of their expensive though extremely productive and sophisticated workers (Hollingsworth et al., 1994; Murmann, 1998; Streeck, 1991, 1995; Soskice, 1998). The French model of elite engineering education has enabled firms to excel at large-scale technical undertakings such as high-speed trains, satellite-launching rockets, or nuclear power. French boards of directors tend to span the private and state-owned sectors of the economy, which play a key role in those industries (Storper & Salais, 1997, pp. 131-148; Ziegler, 1995, 1997). The Japanese institutional ability to borrow, improve, and integrate ideas and technologies from various sources allows its companies to master most categories of assembled goods such as household appliances, consumer electronics, and automobiles (Cusumano, 1985; Dore, 1973; Westney, 1987). In order to do so Japanese corporations rely on the stability and close ties afforded to them by the *keiretsu* structure of corporate governance (Gerlach, 1992; Kim & Hoskisson, 1996). Last, the American cultural emphasis on individualism, entrepreneurship, and customer satisfaction enables her firms to become world-class competitors in goods or services that are intensive in people skills, knowledge, or venture capital, such as software, financial services, or biotechnology (Porter, 1990; Storper & Salais, 1997, pp. 174-188). Undoubtedly, the capital market driven, shareholder-centered model of corporate governance fits this situation best.

Sociologists and political scientists have long noted the strong association between the stakeholder-centered model of corporate governance and social-democratic policymaking in Central European countries with extensive welfare states and strong labor market institutions (Hollingsworth et al., 1991; Streeck, 1991, 1995; Soskice, 1998). It is important to underline that most of the empirical evidence available demonstrates that this alternative is viable, even in the face of globalization. Noting the association between openness to the global economy and the size of the state, and using cross-national data for the advanced industrial democracies since 1960, Geoffrey Garrett (1998, pp. 1-2, 11, 107, 132-133, 157-158) empirically demonstrates the viability of social-democratic policymaking even with increasing exposure to globalization in the forms of cross-border trade and capital mobility. He also proves that it is possible to win elections with redistributive and interventionist policies, and that better economic performance in terms of GDP growth and unemployment obtains, though with higher inflation than in the laissez-faire countries (United States, Britain). Garrett (1998, p. 157) concludes that "big government is compatible with strong macroeconomic performance," and that markets do not dominate politics.

Political scientist Evelyne Huber and sociologist John Stephens (1999) advance an interesting argument about the linkage between the stakeholder-centered view of the firm and macroeconomic policies and performance. They begin by noting that countries with generous welfare states have generally done at least as well as countries with less generous welfare states in terms of unemployment and economic growth. They maintain that a configuration of mutually consistent and reinforcing generous welfare state programs and coordinated production regimes (high union density, low wage dispersion, active worker participation in the governance of the firm) allow countries to compete in world markets on the basis of high wages and high-quality products—the so-called "high road" to international competitiveness (see also Hollingsworth et al., 1991; Soskice, 1998; Streeck, 1991, 1995).

One finds a similar diversity of patterns among newly industrialized countries in Asia, Latin America, and Southern Europe. The distribution of organizational forms and corporate governance systems across these countries has grown more diverse over time, not less. In some countries cooperatives and small family firms thrive (Spain, Taiwan), while in others it is large business groups that predominate (Korea, Indonesia, Mexico, Turkey). Institutional scholars have documented with case studies and systematic quantitative evidence that organizations and patterns of corporate control diverge as countries develop and become more embedded in the global economy (Orrù, Biggart, & Hamilton, 1996; Biggart & Guillén, 1999; Guillén, 2001a; Aguilera, 1998). Moreover, such diversity is related in complex ways to each country's role in the global economy. Korea has made a dent in international competition in a way that is intimately related to the indigenous patterns of social organization and corporate governance underpinning the rise of large, capital-intensive, and diversified conglomerates known as *chaebol*. Thus, the Koreans export mass-produced automobiles, consumer electronics, chemicals, and steel. The Taiwanese *guanxiquiye* networks of small family firms, by contrast, are thriving in the global economy on the basis of their adaptability and flexibility. Taiwan is known for its exports of machine tools, auto parts, and electronic components. And the Spanish worker-owned cooperatives and family firms have succeeded by leveraging relationships with foreign multinationals and managing not to fall prey to the lending practices of the country's all powerful banks. They are known internationally for their components and branded consumer products (Orrù, Biggart, & Hamilton, 1996; Guillén, 2001a).

The institutional approach to the study of trends in corporate governance is useful to understand why the empirical literature has thus far failed to establish a clear link between corporate governance and economic performance using conventional multiple regression techniques. Quantitative studies have reported that differences in corporate governance across advanced industrial economies are not significantly associated with differences in financial or sales performance at the company level, after controlling for industry and firm size (Thomsen & Pedersen, 1996). Other researchers have found no evidence that differences in corporate governance systems affect GDP growth over the long run (La Porta et al., 1998). One may interpret these results as proof that corporate governance does not matter for economic performance. A second possibility is, however, that the different corporate governance systems enable firms and countries to excel at different kinds of activities in the global economy. The institutional argument against convergence would support such an interpretation.

The Political Case Against Convergence

The third counterargument about corporate governance and globalization observes that economic and financial globalization are shaped and contested by political interests. The literature on the diffusion of corporate governance and organizational forms in general is replete with detailed studies of how domestic political conditions affect outcomes (Djelic, 1998; Fligstein, 1990; Orrù, Biggart, & Hamilton, 1996). Domestic politics mediate in the relationship between external trends or shocks and outcomes. There is no a priori theoretical reason why the impact of globalization on corporate governance should be any different, as scholars (Macey & Miller, 1995; O'Sullivan, 1999) and policymakers (Binns, 1998) have recognized.

Examples from the vast literature on the historical transformation of corporations and corporate governance suffice to make the point. Djelic (1998) provides compelling historical evidence that, under pressure from Marshall planners and advisors, German and French politicians, industrialists, and labor leaders resisted the direct implementation of American corporate governance and industrial organization blueprints during the 1950s. Domestic actors were able to shape and mold American models to their own goals and priorities. Outcomes also depended on the mutual accommodations found by governments, employers, and unions. Guillén (1994) analyzes how domestic coercive and normative factors affected the transfer of models of management throughout the twentieth century, with no one country adopting a given model for the same reasons or with similar outcomes. Aguilera (1998) notes that even most similar cases such as Spain and Italy have diverged considerably over time because of regulatory and policy choices made a long time ago, whose effects endure because actors become entrenched in them.

Even in the United States, trends and changes in corporate governance have typically taken place in the midst of fierce political battles. Fligstein (1990) documents how the transitions from the manufacturing to the marketing and to the financial conceptions of corporate control over the twentieth century were punctuated by political and legislative struggles. A raging debate erupted in the 1990s between, on the one hand, managers, economists, and legal experts celebrating the efficiency of the separation of ownership from control (Easterbrook & Fischel, 1991; Romano, 1993), and, on the other, institutional investors and economists charging that the system is deeply flawed because it gives managers way too much discretion (Jensen, 1993). The outcome of this struggle is yet to be determined (O'Sullivan, 1999; Useem, 1996) as American managers and boards reacted to the rise of institutional investors and financial deregulation with a mixture of defensive measures (e.g., poison pills) and adaptive actions (e.g., managerial incentives). What seems clear is that top managers have both been harmed and benefited by this struggle. Although the rate of CEO forced succession has increased, average CEO compensation was in 1999 roughly 419 times greater than for the average manufacturing worker, up from a multiple of 44 in 1965 (O'Sullivan, 1999).

The data and analysis by La Porta and colleagues (1998, 1999) provide further credence to the argument that political forces will shape and perhaps derail the homogenizing effects of globalization. They argue that the internationalization of capital markets is not enough to unsettle the existing ownership structures, which are "primarily an equilibrium response to the domestic legal environments that companies operate in" (La Porta et al., 1999, p. 512). Given that concentrated ownership produces a centralization of power, La Porta and colleagues (1999, p. 513) are "skeptical about the imminence of convergence of corporate ownership patterns, and of governance systems more generally, to the Berle and Means model."

The creation of the single market among the European Union (EU) member countries illustrates how politics mediate in the relationship between globalization pressures and corporate governance outcomes. The process of European integration has so far failed to generate enough momentum to bring about a convergence in corporate governance laws and practices. In a revealing paper, Lannoo (1999, p. 270) observes that European legislators have fought "very hard" over the last 25 *years* "to bring some harmonization to standards for corporate control in the EU," but that their efforts have been thwarted by "irresolvable disagreements among member states." Instead, he maintains, "either industry or the European Commission should take the initiative to come up with a European-wide code of best practice, in the light of the improbability that any significant harmonization of corporate governance standards will occur at the European level." However, Susan Binns (1998), of the European Commission, notes that researchers are "still searching for economic evidence that one approach [to corporate governance] produces better results than another," and concludes that it is better to leave "these issues for regulation at the national level," albeit avoiding "too much divergence in national rules and practices."

Systems in which banks are successful players in corporate governance are unlikely to evolve toward the market-based system if only because banking interests will be opposed (O'Sullivan, 1999). Quantitative research on banking suggests that universal banks active in all sorts of financial services from commercial banking to investment banking and stock trading—a key component of the German corporate governance system—achieve "a better risk-return trade-off, due to superior monitoring and information collection capacity" than banks in market-based financial systems such as the American or the British (Steinherr & Huveneers, 1994, p. 271). It is not unusual for universal banks to be among the best managed and most profitable in the world, even when shareholders' return is the performance measure (*The Banker*, July 1998, p. 20; Guillén & Tschoegl, 1999; Guillén, 2001a, chap. 7). Scholars arguing against convergence observe that if universal banks with strong ties to industry are so profitable in some countries they are unlikely to implement reforms detrimental to their interests.

Table 1. Dimensions of Corporate Governance in Selected Cross-National Empirical Studies

Dimension:	Useem 1984	Charkham 1995	Shleifer & Vishny 1997	La Porta et al. 1998, 1999	Bühner et al. 1998	OECD 1998a	Loredo & Suárez 1998	O'Sullivan 1999	Present study
Ownership structure	—	Yes	Yes	Yes*	Yes*	Yes	—	Yes*	Yes*
Impact of foreign investment	—	—	—	—	—	—	—	—	Yes*
Role of the banks	—	—	Yes	—	Yes	—	—	Yes	Yes*
Role of institutional investors	—	Yes	Yes	—	—	Yes	—	Yes*	Yes*
Role & nature of the board of directors	Yes	Yes	—	Yes	Yes	Yes	Yes*	—	—
Interlocking directors	Yes*	Yes	—	—	Yes	—	—	—	—
CEO pay components	—	—	—	—	—	—	—	—	Yes*
Market for corporate control (hostile takeovers)	—	—	Yes	—	Yes	—	—	—	Yes*
Number of countries	2	5	4	27-49	3	14	8	3	6-43

Note: * Quantitative indicator used.

CONVERGENCE OF CORPORATE GOVERNANCE SYSTEMS: THE EVIDENCE

Data

A key problem besetting the cross-national study of corporate governance is the dearth of empirical indicators for the relevant dimensions. Table 1 summarizes the indicators used by selected cross-national studies to capture differences in corporate governance. Previous studies vary in terms of the range of indicators used, the nature of the indicator (quantitative or qualitative), and the number of countries included. With the only exception of the recent papers by La Porta and colleagues (1998, 1999) and Shleifer and Vishny (1997), the extant literature on cross-national corporate governance practices is generally based on evidence drawn from a small number of countries. Moreover, previous studies tend to rely on qualitative indicators to a much greater extent than quantitative ones. No previous study has provided longitudinal indicators of the various dimensions of corporate governance.

The choice of empirical indicators for this paper was based on three criteria. First, the previous literature was consulted to develop a list of relevant aspects and indicators capturing the multidimensional character of corporate governance (see Table 1). Second, only indicators that speak to the tenets of the globalization thesis about convergence in corporate governance, and to the legal, institutional, and political cases against convergence were considered. Third, only quantitative indicators available for at least two points in time were included.

Six indicators met these criteria. The first two assess to what extent pressures toward convergence on the Anglo-Saxon model are present. The first indicator is the stock of foreign direct investment by firms under the influence of various corporate governance systems in their home countries, while the second is the presence of institutional investors in each country, which measures pressures toward convergence on a transparent and shareholder-friendly model like the Anglo-Saxon system. The remaining four indicators capture specific dimensions of corporate governance as reflected in the extant literature: the proportion of listed corporate equity held by different types of shareholders, which gives an indication of the various groups with a claim on the corporation; the balance between debt and equity financing struck by nonfinancial firms, which speaks to the influence of banks in corporations; the adoption of long-term incentives in CEO remuneration, which is indicative of attempts by shareholders to align the interest of the CEO with their own; and the occurrence of hostile takeovers, which indicates the existence of a market for corporate control. These six indicators cover essential dimensions of corporate governance as identified in the existing empirical literature (Table 1). Unfortunately, data on two of the dimensions reflected in Table 1—the role and nature of the board of directors and the prevalence of interlocking direc-

Table 2. The Origin of Foreign Direct Investment by Type of Home-Country
Corporate Legal Tradition, 1980 and 1997

	Foreign Direct Investment Outward Stock (% of world total)	
Country	1980	1997
Anglo-Saxon legal tradition:	65.57	49.55
Australia	0.43	1.48
Canada	4.53	3.89
Hong Kong	0.03	3.88
India	0.00	0.02
Ireland	...	0.16
Israel	0.01	0.16
Malaysia	0.08	0.44
New Zealand	0.25	0.19
Nigeria	0.00	0.36
Pakistan	0.01	0.01
Singapore	1.84	1.23
South Africa	1.09	0.34
Thailand	0.00	0.11
United Kingdom	15.33	11.67
United States	41.97	25.63
French legal tradition:	15.58	21.07
Argentina	0.01	0.03
Belgium	1.15	2.72
Brazil	0.12	0.25
Chile	0.01	0.16
Colombia	0.03	0.04
Egypt	0.01	0.01
France	4.50	6.40
Greece	...	0.02
Indonesia	...	0.12
Italy	1.40	3.53
Mexico	0.03	0.09
Netherlands	8.03	6.02
Peru	0.00	0.00
Philippines	0.03	0.03
Portugal	0.02	0.15
Spain	0.23	1.38
Turkey	...	0.01
Venezuela	0.00	0.10
German legal tradition:	16.20	23.57
Austria	0.10	0.42
Germany	8.22	9.21
Japan	3.74	8.04
South Korea	0.03	0.51
Switzerland	4.10	4.43
Taiwan	0.02	0.97
Scandinavian legal tradition:	1.96	4.32
Denmark	0.39	0.73
Finland	0.14	0.57

(continued)

Table 2. (Continued)

	Foreign Direct Investment Outward Stock (% of world total)	
Country	1980	1997
Norway	0.36	0.91
Sweden	1.07	2.11
Total four legal traditions	99.31	98.51
World Outward FDI Stock ($bn)	524.6	3,541.4

Source: UNCTD (1998); La Porta et al. (1998, pp. 1130-1131).

tors—are not available for a sufficiently large number of countries and for at least two points in time.

It is also important to note two further features of the data. First, they are always aggregated at the national level of analysis, which may conceal some interesting within-national differences. For example, not all firms in Japan find themselves under the governance structure of a *keiretsu*, and not all German companies have a bank as a main shareholder. Second, given that measurement of the various dimensions was performed independently, convergence of corporate governance may be assessed for each dimension individually, without assuming that all dimensions have to evolve in unison.

The tabular data are presented for individual countries grouped according to the legal tradition underpinning its corporate governance system. The influential classification developed by La Porta and colleagues (1998) was followed to group countries. It distinguishes among the Anglo-Saxon, French, German, and Scandinavian legal traditions. Taken together, these four categories account for virtually every capitalist country in the world. Classifying countries in groups of legal traditions facilitates assessing the evidence presented. In particular it makes it easier to see if trends over time are toward convergence or divergence.

Results

The globalization thesis argues that the spread of foreign multinationals will force a convergence of corporate governance models. While it may be true that multinationals are a homogenizing force, it is not at all clear why it should produce a worldwide convergence of corporate governance on the American model as opposed to another model or a hybrid. The reason is that the impact of foreign investment originating from countries with an Anglo-Saxon legal tradition and a shareholder-centered corporate governance system is waning. Table 2 presents some telling statistics. Following La Porta and colleagues' (1998) classification of countries in terms of legal tradition, it turns out that the proportion of the world's stock of outward foreign investment accounted for by the Anglo-Saxon countries is *falling*, from 66 percent in 1980 to just over 50 percent in 1997. Meanwhile, the combined shares of the countries influenced by the German, French, or Scandina-

Table 3.   Financial Assets of Institutional Investors
(Insurance Companies, Pension Funds, and Investment Companies)

Country	Total financial assets (% GDP)		Financial assets held in shares (% GDP)	
	1990	1995	1990	1995
Anglo-Saxon legal tradition:				
Australia	47.5	75.9	18.5	38.0
Canada	58.6	87.9	11.7	21.1
United Kingdom	114.5	162.3	75.6	112.0
United States	127.4	170.8	29.3	61.5
French legal tradition:				
Belgium [a]	44.8	59.4	8.5	11.3
France	52.9	75.3	11.6	16.6
Greece [b]	6.5	23.0	0.7	1.4
Italy	13.3	20.6	2.1	3.5
Mexico [c]	8.6	3.9	1.4	0.8
Netherlands	133.4	158.4	18.7	36.4
Portugal [d]	9.2	35.3	0.2	2.5
Spain [e]	16.3	38.3	1.8	2.3
Turkey	0.6	0.7	0.1	0.0
German legal tradition:				
Austria [f]	24.5	35.2	1.2	3.2
Germany	36.5	46.1	3.3	5.5
Japan	81.7	77.4	18.8	13.9
South Korea	48.1	57.7	9.1	7.5
Switzerland [g]	120.2	78.1	19.2	39.1
Scandinavian legal tradition:				
Denmark	57.4	66.8	11.5	18.7
Finland	33.2	50.0	5.6	10.0
Norway	36.0	42.6	5.0	6.8
Sweden	85.7	114.8	24.0	40.2
Transition economies:				
Czech Republic [h]	...	24.0	...	11.5
Hungary	...	4.5	...	0.1
Poland [i]	...	1.6	...	0.4
Unweighted mean [j]	52.59	67.30	12.63	20.56
Standard deviation [j]	41.31	47.85	16.46	26.37

Notes: [a] Exc. pension funds in 1995; [b] Exc. insurance and investment companies; [c] Exc. pension funds; [d] Exc. insurance companies in 1995; [e] Exc. non-autonomous pension funds; [f] Exc. pension funds in 1990; [g] Exc. pension funds in 1995; [h] 1994 data for 1995; [i] Exc. pension funds for 1995; [j] Exc. the transition economies.

Source: OECD, *Institutional Investors: Statistical Yearbook 1997.*

vian legal traditions has grown from 34 to 49 percent over the same time period. It seems, therefore, that if there is convergence in corporate governance it may not be on the shareholder-centered model characteristic of the U.K or the United States but rather on some kind of hybrid.

Table 4. Listed Corporate Equity by Type of Shareholder (in percentages)

Type of Shareholder	USA 1986	USA 1993	USA 1996	UK[c] 1976	UK[c] 1993	UK[c] 1996	Germany 1985	Germany 1993	Germany 1996	France 1982	France 1993	France 1996	Sweden 1993	Sweden 1996	Japan[d] 1983	Japan[d] 1993	Japan[d] 1996
Households	51	49	49	28	18	21	17	17	15	38	19	23	16	19	27	24	20
Financial sector:	46	...	47	60	61	68	15	29	30	24	8	30	23	30	42	44	42
Banks	...	...	6	...	1	1	...	14	10	...	3	7	1	1	...	22	15
Pension funds [a]	...	31	28	...	51	50	...	7	12	...	1	9	8	14	...	18	12
Investment funds [b]	...	11	12	...	7	8	...	8	8	...	2	11	14	15	...	3	-
Other financial firms	...	4	1	...	2	9	...	-	-	...	2	3	-	-	...	1	15
Nonfinancial firms	15	-	-	5	2	1	51	39	42	22	59	19	34	11	25	24	27
State	0	-	-	3	1	1	10	4	4	0	4	2	7	8	0	1	1
Foreign	6	5	5	4	16	9	8	12	9	16	11	25	9	32	5	7	11
Other	-	-	-	-	2	-	-	-	-	-	-	-	10	-	-	-	-
Total	100	100	100	100	100	100	100	100	100	100	100	100	100	100	100	100	100

Notes: - not applicable.
    ... not available.
    [a] Includes insurance companies.
    [b] Includes mutual funds.
    [c] UK figures are for end of 1994 instead of the end of 1996.
    [d] For Japan, pension and investment funds are included under other financial institutions.

Source: OECD (1995, p. 17, 1998b, p. 16); Berglof (1988).

Also contrary to the predictions of the globalization thesis, institutional investors such as insurance companies, pension funds, and investment companies have
a very unequal presence across countries. Moreover, the differences across countries are growing, not shrinking. Table 3 presents the available data for over 20
rich countries plus Mexico, South Korea, the Czech Republic, Hungary, and
Poland. The influence of institutional investors—as measured by their financial
assets held in shares of companies as a percentage of GDP—is the highest in the
UK (at 112%), followed by the United States (62%; see Useem, 1996), and a
handful of relatively small countries within the 30-50 percent range (Australia,
Netherlands, Switzerland, and Sweden). Most countries shown in the table have
ratios below 20 percent, and over half of them do not even reach 10 percent.
Between 1990 and 1995 the influence of institutional investors barely grew in
many countries (Greece, Italy, Portugal, Spain, Austria, Germany, Norway), and
actually decreased in a few others (Mexico, Turkey, Japan, South Korea). Overall,
differences in the presence of institutional investors across countries are widen-
ing, as revealed by the standard deviations, which have increased from 41 to 48 in
the case of total financial assets, and from 16 to 26 in the case of assets held in
shares.

Patterns of stockholding are proving to be remarkably resilient. Table 4 presents the breakdown for countries belonging to each of the four legal traditions.
The Anglo-Saxon tradition differs sharply from the German and Scandinavian
ones. Moreover, the differences are not getting smaller over time. It is only in the
case of France that one observes a clear shift toward a greater presence of institutional investors, but this is coming at the expense not of banks but of households.
Thus, large stockholders (banks and other financial institutions, and nonfinancial
firms) continue to be the norm in countries whose legal tradition does not protect
shareholder rights above and beyond those of other stakeholders. As hypothesized
by La Porta and colleagues (1998, 1999) and Bühner and colleagues (1998, p.
147, prop. 1), large organizational actors are major shareholders in countries that
did not adopt the common law provisions of the Anglo-Saxon tradition.

The role of banks as providers of funds to industry is another key aspect in
which countries differ from one another. Figure 1 presents the debt-equity ratios
of nonfinancial firms over the last three decades. Only the trend lines for such
small countries as Austria, Belgium, Finland, and Norway show a convergence on
the Anglo-Saxon pattern of relatively balanced debt and equity. German, Italian,
Japanese, South Korean, and French nonfinancial firms show few signs of convergence over the last two decades. Figure 2 shows the unweighted means and standard deviations for each year between 1975 and 1995. Mean debt-equity ratios
dropped during the mid-1980s from about 270 to about 160 percent, and the standard deviation from 160 to 100 percent, approximately. Since 1987, however, neither the mean nor the standard deviation have dropped any further in spite of the
rapid increase in trade, foreign direct investment, and capital mobility across bor-

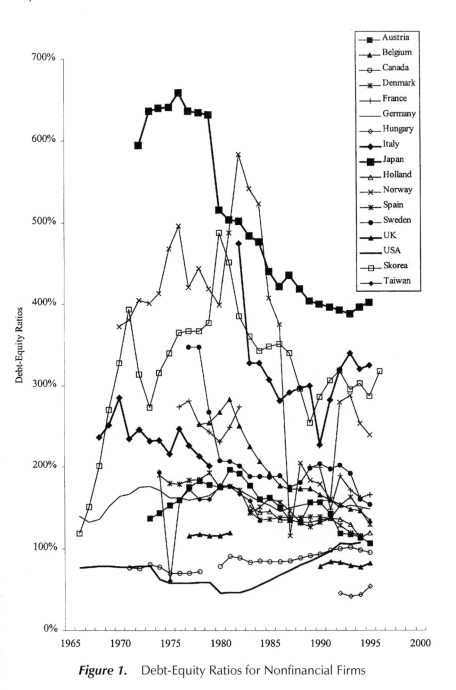

Figure 1.   Debt-Equity Ratios for Nonfinancial Firms

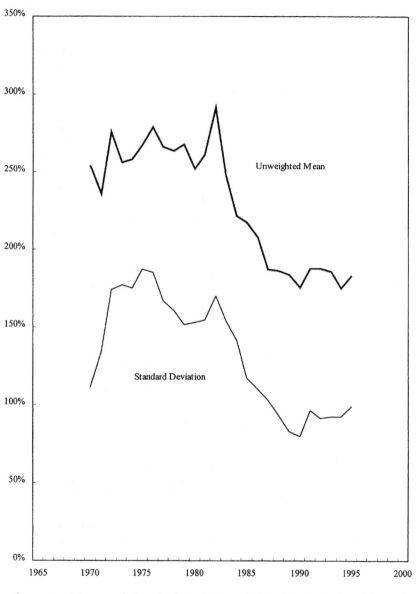

Figure 2.   Mean and Standard Deviation of Debt-Equity Ratios, Selected
Countries, 1975-1995

Table 5. Long-Term Incentives in CEO Pay

Country	Long-Term Incentives As % of Total Remuneration		
	1988	*1993*	*1998*
Anglo-Saxon legal tradition:			
Australia	0	1	2
Canada	14	16	14
Hong Kong	0	0	12
Malaysia	...	...	12
New Zealand	...	...	0
Singapore	0	0	12
South Africa	...	...	10
United Kingdom	15	15	17
United States	28	34	36
French legal tradition:			
Belgium	0	0	6
Brazil	0	0	11
France	15	16	14
Italy	0	4	6
Mexico	0	0	0.1
Netherlands	0	0	9
Spain	0	0	0
Venezuela	0	0	0
German legal tradition:			
Germany	0	0	0
Japan	0	0	0
South Korea	0	...	0
Switzerland	1	4	3
Scandinavian legal tradition:			
Sweden	0	0	0
Unweighted mean [a]	4.06	5.00	7.89
Standard deviation [a]	8.17	9.32	9.17

Note: [a] Excludes countries with missing data, that is, Malaysia, New Zealand, South Africa, and South Korea.
Source: Towers Perrin, *Worldwide Total Remuneration*, various years.

ders. Thus, there is little evidence that the patterns of financing by nonfinancial firms are changing as a result of globalization.

In the shareholder-centered model of corporate governance, there is a tendency to introduce incentives to align the interests of the managers with those of the shareholders. The adoption of long-term incentives to encourage CEOs to maximize shareholder wealth is extremely heterogeneous across countries. Not surprisingly, only the Anglo-Saxon countries have a strong tendency to use such incentives (Table 5). Among those in the French legal tradition, only France, Brazil, and the Netherlands have adopted such incentives. In the case of France, O'Sullivan (1999) reports that CEOs, and not shareholders or directors, are behind the adoption. Countries in the German or Scandinavian legal traditions

Table 6.   Announced Hostile Corporate Takeovers

| | Transaction Value (% of World Total) | | | |
| | Targets | | Acquirers | |
Country	1980-1989	1990-1998	1980-1989	1990-1998
Anglo-Saxon legal tradition:	96.9	89.0	90.4	88.4
Australia	1.5	2.6	2.9	2.1
Canada	1.1	6.1	4.6	4.9
Hong Kong	.3	.8	.2	.0
India	.0	.0	.0	.0
Ireland	.1	.2	.0	.2
Israel	.0	.0	.0	.0
Malaysia	.1	.1	.1	.1
New Zealand	.0	.1	.0	.4
Nigeria	.0	.0	.0	.0
Pakistan	.0	.0	.0	.0
Singapore	.0	.1	.0	.1
South Africa	.0	.1	.0	.2
Thailand	.0	.0	.0	.0
United Kingdom	18.4	18.2	18.6	17.5
United States	75.3	60.7	63.9	63.0
French legal tradition:	2.1	6.5	5.0	6.5
Argentina	.0	.0	.0	.0
Belgium	.0	.0	.0	.1
Brazil	.0	.0	.0	.0
Chile	.0	.0	.0	.0
Colombia	.0	.0	.0	.0
Egypt	.0	.0	.0	.0
France	1.9	5.4	2.9	3.6
Greece	.0	.0	.0	.0
Indonesia	.0	.0	.0	.0
Italy	.0	.7	.3	2.5
Mexico	.0	.0	.1	.0
Netherlands	.1	.0	1.6	.1
Peru	.0	.0	.0	.0
Philippines	.0	.0	.0	.0
Portugal	.0	.2	.0	.2
Spain	.0	.1	.0	.1
Turkey	.0	.0	.0	.0
Venezuela	.0	.0	.0	.0
German legal tradition:	.7	2.1	2.7	3.1
Austria	.0	.1	.0	.1
Germany	.2	1.8	.2	2.2
Japan	.5	.0	.4	.0
South Korea	.0	.0	.0	.1
Switzerland	.0	.1	2.1	.7
Taiwan	.0	.0	.0	.3
Scandinavian legal tradition:	.1	1.3	.3	1.1
Denmark	.0	.0	.0	.0

(continued)

Table 6. (Continued)

	Transaction Value (% of World Total)			
	Targets		Acquirers	
Country	1980-1989	1990-1998	1980-1989	1990-1998
Finland	.0	.1	.0	.0
Norway	.0	.6	.0	.4
Sweden	.1	.6	.2	.7
Unweighted mean	2.32	2.30	2.28	2.32
Standard deviation	11.74	9.60	10.06	9.88
World Total (million $)	805,440	423,652	805,440	423,652

Note: Dollar figures have been adjusted for inflation using the U.S.'s GDP deflator (1992=100).
Source: SDC Platinum (Securities Data Company).

remain oblivious to the trend toward long-term incentives in CEO pay, although there are indications that shareholders are reasserting their influence (O'Sullivan, 1999). As with the presence of institutional investors, differences in the use of long-term incentives have grown slightly between 1988 and 1998, as revealed by the increase in the standard deviation.

Perhaps the clearest indicator that corporate governance models are not converging has to do with the market for corporate control. The shareholder-centered model has historically been more susceptible to hostile takeover activity. During the 1980s shareholder activism and financial deregulation in the United States and U.K. contributed to a sharp rise in hostile takeovers (O'Sullivan, 1999; OECD, 1998b). The occurrence of hostile takeovers, however, is not a worldwide phenomenon, but one largely confined to the Anglo-Saxon countries, both in terms of targets and acquirers (Table 6). Companies in the United States and U.K. alone accounted for 94 percent of worldwide hostile targets in terms of transaction value in 1980-1989, and 79 percent in 1990-1998. American and British acquirers were responsible for roughly 80 percent of worldwide hostile takeovers during the 1980s and 1990s.

Among countries in legal traditions other than the Anglo-Saxon, only France stands out for its relatively high (and rising) level of hostile takeover activity targeting its companies. French companies, however, have become less likely to launch hostile bids. Italian, German, Norwegian, and Swedish acquirers have become more active in the 1990s than in the 1980s, but their absolute level of activity is still very low compared to the Anglo-Saxon countries, even after the decline of hostile activity in the United States and the U.K. during the 1990s. Hostile takeover activity remains stagnant at relatively low levels or has decreased in such countries as the Netherlands, Spain, Switzerland, and Japan, and even in some countries influenced by the Anglo-Saxon tradition, for example, Ireland and Malaysia. The rest of the world remains largely unaffected by hostile takeovers. Compared to the 1980s, differences across countries in the incidence of hostile takeovers have dropped slightly during the 1990s (from a standard deviation of 11.74 to 9.60), but remained approximately the same in terms of the home country of the acquirer firm.

DISCUSSION

The literature on corporate governance and globalization contains important theoretical disagreements. Scholars, however, have found very little evidence suggesting convergence. Except for the cases of France and, to a lesser extent, Belgium, the Netherlands, and the Scandinavian countries, there are no discernible shifts in stockholding, debt-equity ratios, long-term incentives in CEO pay, or hostile takeovers. Moreover, changes in the composition of foreign direct investment suggest that if there is convergence, it may not be on the shareholder-centered model but on a hybrid. One should keep in mind, however, that the trend toward globalization will continue and that it may be too early to tell the extent to which national corporate governance models are resistant to it. At any rate, it seems safe to conclude that, given the trends over the last 20 years, the wholesale convergence of corporate governance systems across countries is unlikely in the near future. Convergence along selected aspects or dimensions is more likely, although it has thus far affected only a handful of countries.

The lack of convergence in indicators of corporate governance in the face of growing globalization is consistent with the findings of previous studies focusing on other economic and organizational variables. The varieties of capitalism research tradition in political science has contributed innumerable case studies and quantitative analyses demonstrating that, in spite of globalization, there is little convergence in terms of economic policymaking across countries (Garrett, 1998, 1999; Hollingsworth et al., 1991; Soskice, 1998; Streeck, 1991, 1995). Comparative organizational sociologists have also presented qualitative and quantitative evidence to the effect that firms pursue different modes of economic action and adopt different organizational forms depending on the institutional and social structures of their home countries even as globalization increases (Orrù, Biggart, & Hamilton, 1996; Biggart & Guillén, 1999; Guillén, 2001a). Taken together, the empirical evidence provided by sociologists and political scientists supports well the case for diversity, or at least resilience, in cross-national organizational patterns in the midst of globalization. This paper adds to this growing body of comparative literature by documenting little convergence in patterns of corporate governance even with growing globalization. As Thomsen and Pedersen (1996) observe, there is no clear relationship between differences in corporate governance and differences in firm-level performance across countries. These findings invite further theoretical work to specify how exactly corporate governance practices affect firm strategy, and, in turn, how differences in strategy due to corporate governance translate into levels of performance. As the extant literature suggests, future theoretical work may aim at conceptualizing how different governance practices enable firms to pursue different strategies leading to comparable levels of high performance in the global economy (Bühner et al., 1998; Kim & Hoskisson, 1996; Lazonick & O'Sullivan, 1996).

The absence of discernible convergence as a result of globalization invites a reconsideration of the effects of increasing cross-border economic activities. The social science literature on globalization provides two useful ways of addressing this apparent problem. First, the reason why globalization does not seem to produce convergence in corporate governance may have to do with the fact that increasing economic exchange across borders does not necessarily force actors to adopt similar patterns of behavior. Social scientists have underlined that what is perhaps most distinctive about globalization is that it intensifies our consciousness of the world as a whole, making us more aware of each other, and perhaps more prone to be influenced by one another, although not necessarily more like each other (Robertson, 1992, p. 8; Albrow, 1997, p. 88; Waters, 1995, p. 63; Guillén, 2001a).

The second way to better understand the effects of globalization on an organizational variable is to reconsider the nature of globalization itself, without denying its existence. A variety of social scientists have argued and documented with empirical evidence that globalization is far from being a uniform process or an inexorable trend. Rather, it seems to be a more fragmented, incomplete, discontinuous, and contingent process than the proponents of convergence generally admit because it affects different sectors of the economy and regions of the world in different ways and to different degrees (Hirst & Thompson, 1996). Social and political theorists as well as historians and anthropologists have elaborated a comprehensive theoretical and empirical critique of the presumed convergent consequences of globalization that may provide the foundation for a better understandings of its impact on cross-national organizational patterns (Cox, 1996, p. 28, 30 n. 1; Mazlish, 1993, p. 4; Giddens, 1990, pp. 64, 175, 1991, pp. 21-22; Albrow, 1997, pp. 86, 144, 149, 189; Friedman, 1994, pp. 210-211; McMichael, 1996, pp. 177, 190-197, 234-235; Robertson, 1992, pp. 27, 145).

CONCLUSION: TOWARD A COMPARATIVE ANALYSIS OF CORPORATE GOVERNANCE

The three arguments against convergence in corporate governance—legal, institutional, political—provide enough reason to cast serious doubt on the idea that there is convergence in corporate governance, whether on the shareholder-centered model or a hybrid. Globalization seems to encourage countries and firms to be different, to look for a distinctive way to make a dent in international competition rather than to converge on a best model. In a global context, corporate governance must support what a country and its firms can do best in the global economy. Globalization seems not to be about convergence to best practice, but rather about leveraging difference in an increasingly borderless world. This argument and the empirical findings reported in this paper are consistent with previous research on how different corporate governance systems enable firms to pursue different strategies (Bühner et al., 1998; Kester, 1996; Lazonick & O'Sullivan, 1996).

The complexity of both globalization and corporate governance certainly invites additional research. We are in great need of further theoretical work to clarify how corporate governance affects competitiveness and the well-being of various groups in society. We also need better data and on more countries. Better indicators will facilitate making comparisons on specific dimensions as opposed to looking for wholesale convergence of entire corporate governance systems. Given the infancy of our efforts to understand the impact of globalization on corporate governance, it seems sensible to ask for more studies using a comparative approach. We need to engage in comparative work in the dual sense of using multiple methods of data collection and analysis, and of applying our theoretical and empirical tools to a variety of research settings defined at various levels of analysis (Cheng, 1989, 1994a, 1994b; Skocpol, 1984; Smelser, 1976; Tilly, 1984). The differences and similarities across such settings ought to give us a handle on the patterns according to which the effects of globalization change from one setting to another.

ACKNOWLEDGMENTS

The author thanks the University of Pennsylvania's Research Foundation for funding. He is also grateful to Work Study research assistants Anne Chun, Yi Jun, and Gina Mok for their constancy and precision. Gerald Davis, Michael Useem, Edward Zajac, two anonymous referees, and the editor, Joseph Cheng, provided useful comments.

NOTES

1.   One exception to the large literature on cross-national differences in corporate governance is Corbett and Jenkinson (1996), who document that there are only small differences in the financing patterns of firms across countries.

2.   It is not at all clear, however, that financial and money managers would prefer to see a wholesale convergence in patterns of corporate governance across the world. The reason lies in that different corporate governance systems are associated with peculiar competitive strategies and responses to the business cycle (Kester, 1996; Kim & Hoskisson, 1996; Lazonick & O'Sullivan, 1996; Bühner et al., 1998). Accordingly, the chances that stock markets in the world are uncorrelated with each other increase with the diversity in patterns of corporate governance. Uncorrelated stock markets "enrich the menu" for diversification because they provide greater opportunities for global portfolio investment, one of the key ways in which financial managers achieve superior performance over the long run (Malkiel & Mei, 1998, p. 23; Siegel, 1998, pp. 139, 286; Ibbotson & Brinson, 1993; *Financial Times*, 1995, pp. 447-453).

REFERENCES

Aguilera, R. V. (1998). *Elites, corporations and the wealth of nations: historical institutional patterns in Italy and Spain.* Ph.D. Dissertation, Department of Sociology, Harvard University.

Albrow, M. (1997). *The global age.* Stanford, CA: Stanford University Press.

Bebchuck, L. A., & Roe, M. J. (1999). A theory of path dependence in corporate ownership and governance. *Stanford Law Review, 52,* 127-170.

Becht, M., & Röell, A. (1999). Blockholdings in Europe: An international comparison. *European Economic Review, 43,* 1049-1056.

Berglof, E. (1988). Capital Structure as a mechanism of control: A comparison of financial systems. In M. Aoki, B. Gustafsson, & O. Williamson (Eds.), *The firm as a nexus of treaties.* Newbury Park, CA: Sage.

Berle, A., & Means, G. (1932). *The modern corporation and private property.* New York: MacMillan.

Biggart, N. W., & Guillén, M. F. (1999). Developing difference: Social organization and the rise of the auto industries of South Korea, Taiwan, Spain, and Argentina. *American Sociological Review, 64,* 722-747.

Binns, S. M. (1998). A preliminary reply to the preliminary report. www.ecgn.ulb.ac.be/ecgn/docs/ html/PreliminaryReply.htm

Bishop, M. (1994). Watching the boss: A survey of corporate governance. *The Economist,* January 29.

Bühner, R., Rasheed, A., Rosenstein, J., & Yoshikawa, T. (1998). Research on corporate governance: A comparison of Germany, Japan, and the United States. In J. L. C. Cheng & R. B. Peterson (Eds.), *Advances in international comparative management* (Vol. 12, pp. 121-155). Stamford, CT: JAI Press.

Castells, M. (1996). *The rise of the network society.* Cambridge, MA: Blackwell.

Charkham, J. (1995). *Keeping good company: A study of corporate governance in five countries.* Oxford: Oxford University Press.

Cheng, J. L. C. (1994a). Toward a contextual approach to cross-national organization research: A macro perspective. In S. B. Prasad (Ed.), *Advances in international comparative management* (Vol. 4, pp. 3-18). Greenwich, CT: JAI Press.

Cheng, J. L. C. (1994b). On the concept of universal knowledge in organizational science: Implications for cross-national research. *Management Science, 40,* 162-168.

Corbett, J., & Jenkinson, T. (1996). The financing of industry, 1970-1989: An international comparison. *Journal of the Japanese and International Economies, 10,* 71-96.

Cox, R. W. (1996). A perspective on globalization. In J. H. Mittelman (Ed.), *Globalization: Critical reflections* (pp. 21-30). Boulder, CO: Lynne Rienner Publishers.

Cusumano, M. (1985). *The Japanese automobile industry: Technology and management at Nissan and Toyota.* Cambridge, MA: Harvard University Press.

Djelic, M.-L. (1998). *Exporting the American model.* New York: Oxford University Press.

Dore, R. (1973). *British factory—Japanese factory.* Berkeley, CA: University of California Press.

Easternbrook, F., & Fischel, D. (1991). *The economic structure of corporate law.* Cambridge, MA: Harvard University Press.

Financial Times. (1995). *FT global guide to investing.* London: FT Pitman Publishing.

Fleming, R. W. (1998, November-December). Worldwide changes in corporate governance. *The Corporate Board,* 1-4.

Fligstein, N. (1990). *The transformation of corporate control.* Cambridge, MA: Harvard University Press.

Friedman, J. (1994). *Cultural identity and global process.* London: Sage.

Garrett, G. (1998). *Partisan politics in the global economy.* New York: Cambridge University Press.

Garrett, G. (1999). *Trade, capital mobility and government spending around the world.* Working Paper, Department of Political Science, Yale University.

Gerlach, M. L. (1992). *Alliance capitalism: The social organization of Japanese business*. Berkeley, CA: University of California Press.

Giddens, A. (1990). *The consequences of modernity*. Stanford, CA: Stanford University Press.

Giddens, A. (1991). *Modernity and self-identity*. Cambridge, MA: Polity Press.

Gilpin, R. (1987). *The political economy of international relations*. Princeton, NJ: Princeton University Press.

Guillén, M. F. (1994). *Models of management: Work, authority, and organization in a comparative perspective*. Chicago: The University of Chicago Press.

Guillén, M. F. (2001a). *The limits of convergence: Globalization and organizational change in Argentina, South Korea, and Spain*. Princeton, NJ: Princeton University Press.

Guillén, M. F. (2001b). Is globalization civilizing, destructive or feeble? A critique of six key debates in the social-science literature. *Annual Review of Sociology*.

Guillén, M. F., & Tschoegl, A. T. (1999). At last the internationalization of retail banking? The case of the Spanish banks in Latin America. Working Paper. The Wharton School.

Harvey, D. (1989). *The condition of postmodernity*. Oxford: Blackwell.

Hirst, P., & Thompson, G. (1996). *Globalization in question*. London: Polity.

Hollingsworth, J. R., Schmitter, P. C., & Streeck, W. (1994). Capitalism, sectors, institutions, and performance. In J. Hollingsworth, P. Schmitter, & W. Streeck (Eds.), *Governing capitalist economies: Performance and control of economic sectors* (pp. 3-16). New York and Oxford: Oxford University Press.

Huber, E., & Stephens, J. D. (1999). *Welfare state and production regimes in the era of retrenchment*. Occasional Papers No. 1, School of Social Science, Institute for Advanced Study, Princeton, NJ.

Ibbotson, R. G., & Brinson, G. P. (1993). *Global investing*. New York: McGraw-Hill.

Jensen, M. (1993). The modern industrial revolution, exit, and the failure of internal control systems. *Journal of Finance, 48*, 831-880.

Kerr, C., Dunlop, J. T., Harbison, F., & Myers, C. A. [1960] (1964). *Industrialism and industrial man*. New York: Oxford University Press.

Kester, W. C. (1996). American and Japanese corporate governance: Convergence to best practice? In S. Berger & R. Dore (Eds.), *National diversity and global capitalism* (pp. 107-137). Ithaca, NY: Cornell University Press.

Kim, H., & Hoskisson, R. E. (1996). Japanese governance systems: A critical review. In J. L. C. Cheng & R. B. Peterson (Eds.), *Advances in international comparative management* (Vol. 11, pp. 165-189). Greenwich, CT: JAI Press.

Kobrin, S. J. (1997). The architecture of globalization: State sovereignty in a networked global economy. In J. H. Dunning *Governments, globalization, and international business* (pp. 146-171). New York: Oxford University Press.

La Porta, R., Lopez-de-Silanes, F., & Shleifer, A. (1999). Corporate ownership around the world. *Journal of Finance, 54*, 471-517.

La Porta, R., Lopez-de-Silanes, F., Shleifer, A., & Vishny, R. W. (1998). Law and finance. *Journal of Political Economy, 106*, 1113-1155.

Lannoo, K. (1999). A European perspective on corporate governance. *Journal of Common Market Studies, 37*, 269-294.

Lazonick, W., & O'Sullivan, M. (1996). Organization, finance, and international competition. *Industrial and Corporate Change, 5*, 1-49.

Loredo, E., & Suárez, E. (1998). Corporate governance in Europe: Is convergence desirable? *International Journal of Management, 15*, 525-532.

Macey, J. R., & Miller, G. P. (1995). Corporate governance and commercial banking: A comparative examination of Germany, Japan, and the United States. *Stanford Law Review, 48*, 72-112.

Malkiel, B., & Mei, J. P. (1998). *Global bargain hunting*. New York: Simon and Schuster.

Mazlish, B. (1993). An introduction to global history. In B. Mazlish & R. Buultjens (Eds.), *Conceptualizing global history* (pp. 1-24). Boulder, CO: Westview Press.

McMichael, P. (1996). *Development and social change: A global perspective.* Thousand Oaks, CA: Pine Forge Press.

Meyer, J. W., Boli, J., Thomas, G. M., & Ramirez, F. O. (1997). World society and the nation-state. *American Journal of Sociology, 103*, 144-181.

Mittelman, J. H. (1996). The dynamics of globalization. In J. H. Mittelman (Ed.), *Globalization: Critical reflections* (pp. 1-19). Boulder, CO: Lynne Rienner Publishers.

Murmann, J. P. (1998). *Knowledge and competitive advantage in the synthetic dye industry, 1850-1914: The coevolution of firms, technology, and national institutions in Great Britain, Germany, and the United States.* Book manuscript. Evanston, IL: Kellogg Graduate School of Management, Northwestern University.

OECD. (1995). Financial markets and corporate governance. *Financial Market Trends, 62*, 13-35.

OECD. (1998a). *Corporate governance: Improving competitiveness and access to capital in global markets.* Paris: Organization of Economic Cooperation and Development.

OECD. (1998b). Shareholder value and the market in corporate control in OECD countries. *Financial Market Trends, 69*, 15-37.

Orrù, M., Biggart, N. W., & Hamilton, G. G. (1997). *The economic organization of East Asian capitalism.* Thousand Oaks, CA: Sage.

O'Sullivan, M. (1999). *Corporate governance and globalisation.* Working Paper, INSEAD.

Prahalad, C. K. (1997). Corporate governance or corporate value-added? In D. H. Chew (Ed.), *Studies in international corporate finance and governance systems: A comparison of the U.S., Japan, and Europe* (pp. 46-56). New York: Oxford University Press.

Porter, M. E. (1990). *The competitive advantage of nations.* New York: Free Press.

Robertson, R. (1992). *Globalization: Social theory and global culture.* London: Sage Publications.

Roe, M. J. (1993). Some differences in corporate structure in Germany, Japan, and the United States, *Yale Law Journal, 102*, 1927-2003.

Romano, R. (1993). *The genius of American corporate law.* Washington, DC: American Enterprise Institute Press.

Sargent, J. (1999, October 1). World bank, OECD introduce global corporate governance forum. *The ISS Friday Report*, 3-4.

Shleifer, A., & Vishny, R. W. (1997). A survey of corporate governance. *Journal of Finance, 52*, 737-783.

Siegel, J. J. (1998). *Stocks for the long run.* New York: McGraw-Hill.

Skocpol, T. (Ed.) (1984). *Vision and method in historical sociology.* New York: Cambridge University Press.

Smelser, N. J. 1976. *Comparative methods in the social sciences.* Englewood Cliffs, NJ: Prentice-Hall.

Soskice, D. (1998). Divergent production regimes: Coordinated and uncoordinated market economies in the 1980s and 1990s. In H. Kitschelt, P. Lange, G. Marks, & J. D. Stephens (Eds.), *Continuity and change in contemporary capitalism* (pp. 101-134). New York: Cambridge University Press.

Steinherr, A., & Huveneers, C. (1994). On the performance of differently regulated financial institutions: Some empirical evidence. *Journal of Banking and Finance, 18*, 271-306.

Storper, M., & Salais, R. (1997). *Worlds of production: The action frameworks of the economy.* Cambridge, MA: Harvard University Press.

Streeck, W. (1991). On the institutional conditions of diversified quality production. In E. Matzner & W. Streeck (Eds.), *Beyond Keynesianism: The socio-economics of production and full employment* (pp. 21-61). Hants, England: Edward Elgar Publishing.

Streeck, W. (1995). *German capitalism: Does it exist? Can it survive?* Discussion Paper 95/5. Cologne: Max Planck Institut für Gesellschaftsforschung.

Thomsen, S., & Pedersen, T. (1996). Nationality and ownership structures: The 100 largest companies in six European nations. *Management International Review, 36*, 149-166.

Tilly, C. 1984. *Big structures, large processes, huge comparisons.* New York: Russell Sage Foundation.

Useem, M. (1984). *The inner circle: Large corporations and the rise of business political activity in the U. S. and U. K.* New York: Oxford University Press.

Useem, M. (1996). *Investor capitalism: How money managers are changing the face of corporate America.* New York: Basic Books.

Waters, M. (1995). *Globalization.* New York: Routledge.

Westney, D. E. (1987). *Imitation and innovation: The transfer of western organizational patterns to Meiji Japan.* Cambridge, MA: Harvard University Press.

Whitley, R. (1992). *Business systems in East Asia: Firms, markets, and societies.* London: Sage.

Whitley, R. (1999). Firms, institutions and management control: The comparative analysis of coordination and control systems. *Accounting, Organizations, and Society, 24*, 507-524.

Ziegler, J. N. (1995). Institutions, elites, and technological change in France and Germany. *World Politics, 47*, 341-372.

Ziegler, J. N. (1997). *Governing ideas: Strategies for innovation in France and Germany.* Ithaca, NY: Cornell University Press.

DETERMINING THE EFFECTS OF EXIT, VOICE, LOYALTY, AND NEGLECT ON CHANGING A DUBIOUS DECISION IN CANADA AND HONG KONG

Kevin Au and Brian Bemmels

ABSTRACT

Hirschman (1970) argued that employee behaviors signaling dissatisfaction with managerial decisions may provoke management to change their course of action, and that such changes may ultimately facilitate the recuperation of a declining organization. This paper includes two studies that test Hirschman's proposition, one in Canada and the other in Hong Kong, and compares the results to identify cross-cultural differences. Undergraduate subjects played the role of a marketing director and made an investment decision in part one of a scenario study. They were then informed in part two of the study that their investment was unsuccessful. Additionally, an important group of subordinates showed exit, voice, loyalty, or neglect (EVLN) behaviors in response to the poor decisions. Results showed that EVLN behaviors had little direct influence on the subjects' subsequent decisions in part two of the study. Further analysis suggests, however, that the EVLN behaviors of subor-

Advances in International Comparative Management, Volume 13, pages 205-225.
Copyright © 2000 by JAI Press Inc.
All rights of reproduction in any form reserved.
ISBN: 0-7623-0589-4

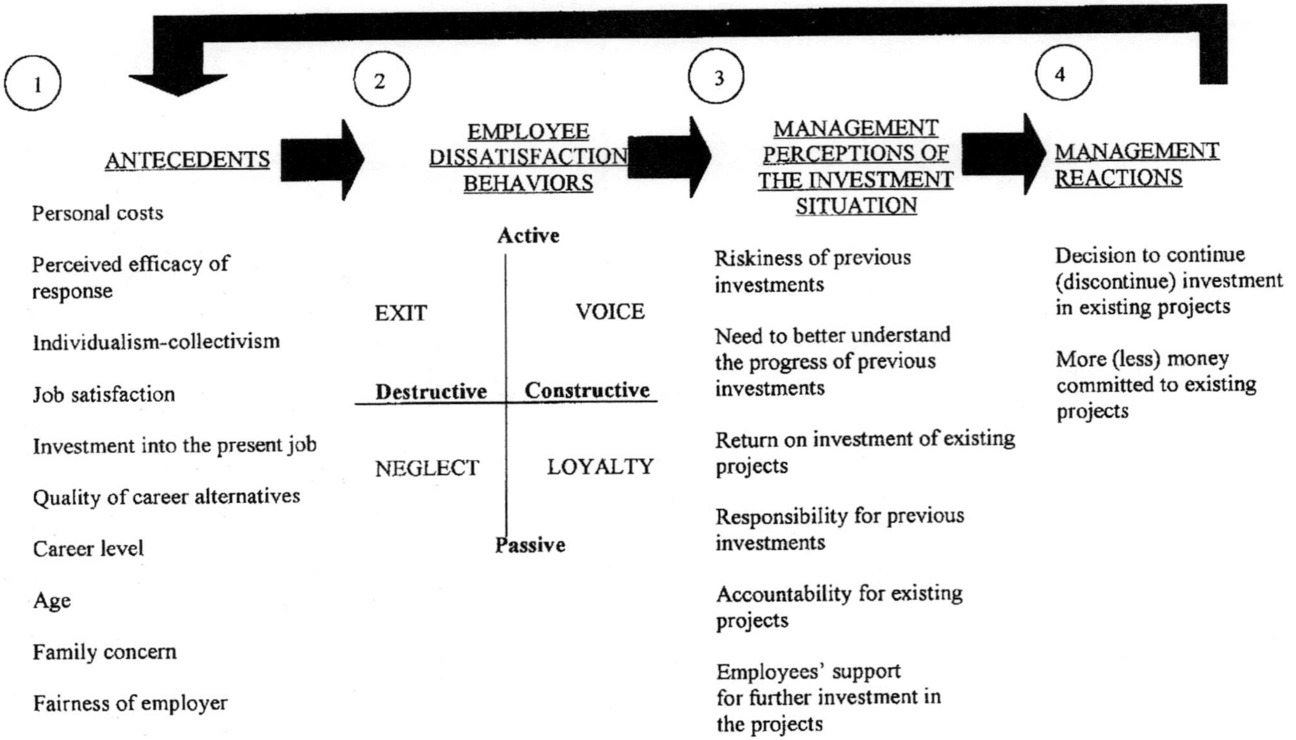

Figure 1. EVLN and Recuperation of Organization As a Dynamic Interactive Process

dinates did affect the subjects' cognitive evaluations of their own investment decisions, and this effect differed between Canadian and Hong Kong subjects. These findings are discussed in light of cultural differences, economic conditions, and organizational structure. Managerial and research implications are also discussed.

Hirschman (1970) suggested that organizational decline and employee discontent may spur employees to display various dissatisfaction behaviors. These behaviors may push organizational leaders to make changes that will facilitate recuperation. A model depicting this thesis is shown in Figure 1.

The employment relationship is a dynamic process and the display of dissatisfaction behaviors is only one stage in this process. The starting premise is a situation that provokes employees to feel dissatisfaction. Dissatisfied employees then choose to display dissatisfaction behavior—exit, voice, loyalty, and neglect (EVLN). Management observes the dissatisfaction behavior of the employees and may make changes in the organization. Such changes act as feedback to employees, affecting the state of their antecedents, and a new cycle begins.

To date researchers have focused on stages one and two, that is, to identify the different types of dissatisfaction behaviors and their antecedents. Other stages in the model are rarely studied. In particular, the extent to which employee dissatisfaction behaviors provoke managers to change their decisions, which is a crucial part of Hirschman's thesis, has not been tested (Bemmels, 1996).

This paper will first report a study in Canada that examined this sin qua non proposition of Hirschman (1970). We then examine two studies conducted in Hong Kong. The first preliminary study in Hong Kong was done to ascertain the conceptual validity of EVLN behaviors (van de Vijver & Leung, 1997). In general terms, we tested whether Hong Kong Chinese and North Americans comprehend the EVLN concepts analogously. The second study investigated whether Chinese reacted to EVLN behaviors differently from Canadians. Cross-cultural differences are discussed in light of differences in the societal contexts in the two cultures with an emphasis on further research issues (Cheng, 1989, 1994). The aim is to provide a basis for future research by documenting data systematically and supplying explanations. These are modest objectives for, as far as we know, ours is the first study that tests Hirschman's (1970) thesis across cultures.

TYPES OF DISSATISFACTION BEHAVIOR

Farrell (1983) classified four types of dissatisfaction behavior under two independent dimensions: constructive versus destructive and active versus passive. *Exit* is active and destructive. Employees displaying this behavior are unlikely to believe any change from the present situation will occur and, thus, quit or transfer. *Voice* is active and constructive. It is an attempt to change the situation by expressing opinions to upper-level managers rather than to escape from the objectionable state of affairs. *Neglect* is passive and destructive. It refers to lax and indifferent behaviors among workers. Last, *Loyalty* is passive and constructive, as employees remain silent and wait for management to change. Although Farrell (1983) found that people perceived loyalty as passive-destructive instead of passive-constructive, adding active elements, such as "giving something extra when the organization needs it," could restore its active meaning (Withey & Cooper, 1989, p. 537).

ANTECEDENTS OF DISSATISFACTION BEHAVIOR

Studies concerning the antecedent stage focus on predictors for EVLN (for a review, see Bemmels, 1996). Rusbult and Farrell (1983) and Rusbult and colleagues (1988) found that higher job satisfaction and more personal investments into the job encouraged voice and loyalty but discouraged exit and neglect. They also found that higher quality of employment alternatives stimulated exit and voice but stifled loyalty. Roberts and Coleman (1993) found that senior- and middle-level mangers are more likely to use voice than lower-level managers. They also found that managers with family responsibilities displayed less neglect as this behavior might affect their job security. In addition, Saunders and colleagues (1992) found that subordinates tended to voice to supervisors who they perceived as fair, easy to approach, likely to respond in time, and unlikely to retaliate against employees. Thus, the perception of subordinates about the supervisors is also important in determining which kind of dissatisfaction behavior is displayed.

Studies of personality variables found that internal locus of control is associated with exit and voice behavior whereas external locus of control is related to loyalty (Withey & Cooper, 1989). Parker (1993) also found that self-efficacy is related with voice behavior. The influence of individualism-collectivism (Singelis et al., 1995) was examined in a recent study. Thomas and Au (1998) found that students high on horizontal collectivism, that is, seeing oneself as merged with and equal to their peers, were more likely to engage in the active and constructive behavior of voice, but were less likely to engage in the passive activities of loyalty and neglect. Horizontal individualists had a higher tendency to use exit behavior. On the other hand, vertical collectivists who saw status differences among their peers had a lower propensity to respond with voice.

CONSEQUENCES OF DISSATISFACTION BEHAVIOR

A key element of Hirschman's (1970) theory is that exit and voice are mechanisms for organizational recuperation. These two types of dissatisfaction behavior signal to management that a problem exists, what the nature of the problem is, and that something should be done about it. In Hirschman's book (1970), voice is regarded as the preferred, but generally neglected, response to facilitate organizational recuperation. Hirschman (1976) explained that voice conveys more information than exit, articulates the sources of discontent, and indicates changes employees preferred. In contrast, exit usually conveys little information about the sources of discontent or what could be done to minimize discontent among other workers.

Although we could find no organizational study that tested whether voice behavior leads to better consequences than exit behavior, a study on adult romantic relationship suggests that this is the case. Rusbult (1986) found that those who used voice and loyalty behaviors to resolve conflicts with their partners reported more favorable outcomes, better immediate consequences, and greater satisfaction and commitment afterwards. On the contrary, those who used exit and neglect experienced less favorable long-term and short-term results. These results are consistent with Farrel (1983) and others (e.g., Withey & Cooper, 1989) that voice and loyalty behaviors are constructive but exit and neglect behaviors are destructive.

The positive effect of voice and loyalty and the negative effect of exit and neglect are also consistent with research on criticism. Constructive criticism has characteristics similar to voice and loyalty, such as specific information, the absence of threats, and being a considerate action. On the other hand, destructive criticism is similar to exit and neglect, as this is more general in content, contains threats, and is an inconsiderate action (Baron, 1992).

Baron (1992) argued that people process constructive criticism in their central persuasive route (Petty & Cacioppo, 1986) which deals with information carefully and in detail. As a result, reasonable arguments supported by evidence are likely to induce behavioral change. On the other hand, people process destructive criticism in their peripheral route where information is not processed thoroughly. Persuasion occurs only when the destructive criticism is accompanied by powerful peripheral cues, such as information relating to the expertise and attractiveness of the persuader. The cognitive processing of destructive criticism via this route is, however, easily interrupted by other reactions to the destructive aspects of the criticism. One reaction is self-serving bias which leads people to perceive that they are fairer when they deliver criticism than the others from whom they receive criticism (Messick et al., 1985). Another reaction is that people perceive their motive of delivering criticism as positive, but the motive of people who criticize them as negative or even malicious. Consequently, behavioral change through destructive criticism is less likely than through constructive criticism.

Another area that is relevant to understanding the consequence of dissatisfaction behavior is research on controversial decisions (Tjosvold, 1992, 1998). Tjosvold (1982) found that controversial views of subordinates may be incorporated into the decision making of superiors, depending on the approach to resolving the conflict. When superiors and subordinates avoided an open controversy, the superiors did not fully explore the others' argument, but found the argument reasonable and sometimes integrated it into their decision. When the parties were competitive and debated the controversy, the parties did not explore the other's argument, rejected the other's position, and made decisions based on their own point of view. Last, when the parties discussed the issues frankly and considered the benefits of the others' position, the superiors explored, accepted, and combined the other's argument with their own to make a decision.

Controversy avoidance is similar to neglect and loyalty behaviors where subordinates avoid discussion with their superiors. Competitive controversy is similar to exit where the superior finds no avenue for an open exchange of views with the subordinates, while experiencing threats and frustration with the actions of the subordinates. Cooperative controversy is similar to voice behavior where subordinates and the supervisors openly exchange their views on the issue.

STUDY 1

The subjects played the role of a marketing manager of a hypothetical company in a scenario study. They made an investment decision in the first part of this study. In the second part of the scenario they were informed that their decision was unsuccessful and that a key group of subordinates were displaying either exit, voice, loyalty, or neglect behaviors. The subjects made a second investment decision in the second part of the study. The amount invested in the second part was compared to test whether the EVLN behaviors of their subordinates affected their decision.

Based on Baron (1992) and Tjosvold (1992), constructive criticism and cooperative controversy, as embodied in voice and loyalty behavior, are likely to induce change. Like destructive criticism and competitive controversy, exit and neglect behaviors are processed via the peripheral route (Petty & Cacioppo, 1986). The subordinate status of the employees undermines the persuasiveness of these behaviors, and therefore little change in management behavior will be triggered.

Hypothesis 1. Voice and loyalty behaviors of the subordinates are more successful in changing the behavior of managers than exit and neglect behaviors.

In addition, self-serving bias and suspicion about the motives of subordinates, as suggested in Baron (1992), are likely to affect the psychology of the decision-making process. Subjects who find their subordinates exhibiting exit and neglect behaviors are likely to be more defensive because they perceive these behaviors as threatening and try to compete with the subordinates. On the contrary, subjects who find subordinates exhibiting voice and loyalty behaviors may be more open, honest, and willing to cooperate and engage in joint problem solving (Tjosvold, 1998).

Escalating commitment research has revealed several cognitive rationalizations that managers use to deny the folly of their investment decisions and continue to invest more money in dubious projects (Brockner, 1992). Based on this research, we can expect the subjects in this study faced with exit and neglect conditions to: (H2a) downplay their responsibility for the initial investment decision; (H2b) reduce the perceived significance of further investment; (H2c) deny the risk involved in further investment; and (H2d) stress that further investment will eventually make the project successful. The reverse is expected for the subjects facing voice and loyalty behaviors from subordinates.

Method

Design

This study is a 6 (conditions: exit, voice, loyalty, neglect, control 1, control 2) x 2 (product: skin care, makeup) factorial design experiment. The scenarios used were modeled on Simonson and Staw (1992) and Staw (1976). The condition factor was manipulated by randomly giving subjects a different description of subordinate behavior in part two of the scenario. The product factor was not manipulated.

Subjects

Ninety-eight business students were recruited from a large university on the west coast of Canada to participate in a 30-minute study. They each received C$10 and were fully debriefed after they finished. The median age of the subjects was 20, and 47 percent of the students were male.

Procedure

The study was run in small groups of six to 15 people. Undergraduates responded to notices posted on campus and came in the lab in groups every 45 minutes. When they arrived an experimenter explained to them that they would each do a case consisting of two parts. They were asked to raise their hand when they finished part 1, so that the experimenter could give them part 2. The case was modified from a Harvard case and was pretested using MBA students. They found the case to be a realistic and interesting business exercise.

Part 1 of the case described the entry of a cosmetic product from Canada to Japan. It described the cosmetic market and consumer preferences with forecast figures. The subjects were asked to choose investing in either makeup or skin care products given the limited company resources.

When the experimenter picked up part 1 from the subjects, he would take a look at the choice of each subject, pretending that he was checking to make sure the subject had completed part 1. He would then give the appropriate part 2 questionnaire that matched their choice of either skin care or makeup in part 1. All subjects except those in control 2 conditions received a part 2 questionnaire that indicated gloomy results regardless of the product they chose to invest in. For example, subjects who chose to invest in makeup products would receive a questionnaire indicating that makeup products performed more poorly than skin care products. However, subjects in control 2 condition would receive a part 2 questionnaire which indicated positive results for the product they chose.

The part 2 questionnaires of the exit, voice, loyalty, and neglect conditions contained a paragraph (excluded in the control conditions) explaining the behavior of a key group of employees—beauty consultants—of the company. The paragraph opened as such, "The dismal performance of makeup products is well-known among your subordinates in Japan, especially beauty consultants who have first-hand information of the market. Recently, …."

Then, the message went on differently depending on the conditions of the study. The exit condition stated "…you find that some of them have started looking for new jobs. Discussions about job openings in other companies were overheard and were relayed to you. Reading job ads during work hours has also been spotted. Some have already applied for transfers to concentrate on selling makeup (skin care) products. The number of employees quitting from the skin care department became more obvious."

In the voice condition, it said that, "…you have received suggestion letters from subordinates expressing their dissatisfaction and suggesting that you modify your efforts to promote skin care (makeup) products. In addition, some of them tell you in person of their dissatisfaction with the general direction of the company and discuss specific policies to change the situation. Vocal expression of dissatisfaction to the company seems obvious."

In the loyalty condition, it said that, "…you find that despite this poor performance beauty consultants continue to work extra time, volunteer to provide training sessions to new recruits, and recruit more beauty consultants. They also continue to help with administrative work for management. Their willingness to continue doing things beyond their normal duties seems obvious."

Last, in the neglect condition, it said that, "…you find that absenteeism and tardiness have increased among beauty consultants who are responsible for skin care (makeup) products. Some of them have found reasons to take long leaves. In addition, most of them have lost their interest in serving their customers, and have stopped attending new company courses and recruiting new beauty consultants for the company. Disregardful and lax behaviors seem obvious." A pre-test showed that students evaluated the behavior of employees corresponding to the theoretical definition of EVLN behavior (Au, 1993).

Several subjects were interviewed after the experiment. They reported no suspicion about the behavior of the experimenter when he checked their choice of investment. Neither did they report noticing that there were different versions of the part 2 questionnaire.

Dependent Variable

Subjects were asked to indicate how much additional money out of C$10m they were willing to invest into either skin care or makeup products. They were also asked to explain the rationale behind their decision in an open-ended question.

Perceived Effects of EVLN Behavior

To assess whether dissatisfaction behavior had influenced subjects' investment decisions, they were asked to answer a question on a five-point scale (one-agree, five-disagree): Do you agree that the behavior of the beauty consultants affected your decision?

Reasons for their Decision

Four five-point scales (one-agree, five-disagree) were used to tap the reasons behind subjects' decision: (1) Do you agree that you are responsible for the disappointing (successful) performance of the Japanese operation between 1992-1995? (2) Do you agree that investing more promotion funds would finally make the skin care (makeup) products profitable? (3) Do you agree that you have made a risky decision? (4) Do you agree that you have allocated a substantial amount of promotion funds for skin care (makeup) products?

Manipulation Check of Beauty Consultants' Behavior

Five items were used to check whether the behavioral descriptions of EVLN were valid. Subjects in the experimental conditions evaluated the behavior of the beauty consultants on five eight-point semantic differentials: (1) good to the company–bad to the company, (2) reactive–proactive, (3) ethical–unethical, (4) support your decision to increase funds for skin care (makeup) products–do not support your decision to increase funds for skin care (makeup) products, and (5) appropriate–inappropriate.

Results

Perceptions of Dissatisfaction Behavior

One-way ANOVAs of the evaluations of the beauty consultants' actions were all significant ($p < .01$), except the evaluation scores of the reactive-proactive scale (see Table 1 for means). Neuman-Keuls tests at $p < .05$ suggested that voice and loyalty behaviors were perceived as benefiting the company more and as being more appropriate than exit and neglect behaviors. Loyalty behavior was perceived as supporting more investment but the other three are not. Neglect was

Table 1.   ANOVA of Perceptions of the Beauty
Consultants' Dissatisfaction Behaviors

Variable	df	F	Exit	Voice	Loyalty	Neglect
Canada						
Benefit the company	3, 70	10.61	5.35	3.71	2.95	5.53
Proactive	3, 70	1.01	4.88	4.82	4.19	4.16
Moral	3, 69	5.16	4.47	3.81	3.52	5.16
Support you to invest more	3, 70	4.26	5.71	5.18	3.76	5.32
Appropriate	3, 70	17.54	4.94	3.76	2.95	6.00
Hong Kong						
Benefit the company	3, 77	27.34	4.52	2.91	2.60	5.52
Proactive	3, 78	10.85	3.27	2.00	1.90	3.88
Moral	3, 78	21.57	4.50	3.78	3.25	5.18
Support you to invest more	3, 78	10.20	4.95	4.35	2.80	4.53
Appropriate	3, 77	16.39	4.41	3.70	3.11	5.65

Note: Canadians worked on eight-point scales whereas Hong Kong subjects worked on seven-point scales. The smaller the figure, the stronger the degree of approval. All the F statistics are significant at $p < .01$.

perceived as unethical relative to voice and loyalty behaviors, but the difference between neglect and exit behavior is not significant. All four behaviors were perceived as somewhat proactive with no significant differences among them.

These results imply that Canadian students regarded loyalty and voice as positive to the company and exit and neglect as negative and unethical. In particular, loyalty is regarded as the most positive and neglect as the most negative. Overall, Canadian students found EVLN behaviors to align on the constructive-destructive dimension. They did not, however, perceive EVLN behaviors to align along the proactive-reactive dimension found in Farrel (1983).

Further Investment

A comparison of the amount invested by two control groups is significant ($t = 1.91, p < .05$). Subjects invested more if their investment was successful (control 2) than if it was unsuccessful (control 1). However, other comparisons are not significant. Hence, there is little support for the hypothesis (1) that exit, voice, loyalty, and neglect behaviors by subordinates will affect management decision differently (see Table 2).

Perceptions Regarding Investment

Comparisons between control 1 and control 2 are significant for scores of perceived responsibility of investment ($t = 1.88, p < .05$), future profitability of product investment ($t = 1.64, p < .10$), and perceived risk of investment ($t = 1.40, p < .10$). Subjects in the control 2 condition felt they were more responsible, the prod-

Table 2. Means of the Dependent Variables by Experimental Condition

Variable	Exit	Voice	Loyalty	Neglect	Control 1	Control 2
Canada						
Amount ($,000)	447	503	476	440	442	590
Influence of Subordinates' Action	2.47	2.35	2.43	2.32	2.42	2.70
Responsible	3.06	3.06	3.29	3.53	3.00	2.20
Profitability	2.88	2.59	2.71	2.78	2.92	2.20
Risky Decision	2.12	2.76	2.62	3.05	2.17	2.80
N	17	17	21	19	12	12
Hong Kong						
Amount ($,000)	502	539	508	500	524	531
Influence of Subordinates' Action	3.68	3.26	3.35	3.76	-	-
Responsible	3.64	3.52	3.75	3.94	3.59	3.19
Profitability	3.64	3.74	3.10	3.65	3.65	3.90
Risky Decision	3.59	3.35	3.55	3.53	3.12	3.62
N	22	23	20	17	17	21

Note: Canadian subjects worked on five-point scales whereas Hong Kong subjects worked on seven-point scales. The smaller the figure, the stronger the degree of approval.

ucts more likely to be profitable, and their investment less risky than those in the control 1 condition. More analyses found that subjects in the Neglect condition perceived their investment to be more risky ($t = 2.27, p < .01$) and that they were less responsible for their past investment decision ($t = 1.45, p < .10$) than subjects in control 1 condition.

Relationships between Investment Amount and Perceptions

Table 3 presents the correlations between amount invested and perceptions concerning the investment decision across all groups and for each group. The first observation is that investment amount correlates with potential profitability of products in almost all conditions. This means that subjects, except those in the loyalty condition, invested because they believed that investing more would finally make the products profitable.

Second, although the overall correlation between amount of investment and perceived significance of investment is close to zero, the correlation in the neglect condition is significant. Using Fisher's test of differences in correlations found that the correlations in the neglect and the control 1 condition are different ($z = 2.01, p < .05$). It implies that the more the subjects in the neglect condition invested, the less substantial they claimed their investment amount was. Third, subjects in the neglect condition perceived less risk the more money they invested. However, subjects in the voice, exit, and loyal conditions perceived more risk as the investment amount increased.

Table 3. Correlations between the Amount Being Invested
and Reasons for Investment by Experimental Condition

Variable	Exit	Voice	Loyalty	Neglect	Control 1	Control 2
Canada						
Substantial amount being invested	-37	23	13	**50**	-28	00
Decision being influenced by Beauty Consultants	-14	-05	-19	25	16	09
Being responsible for disappointing performance	-08	-04	-14	26	35	-23
More fund will make the investment final profitable	**-75**	**-57**	-01	**-51**	-35	-59
New Investment is risky	-20	-10	-36	17	01	11
Hong Kong						
Substantial amount being invested	-12	-04	-14	**-71**	**-52**	-37
Decision being influenced by Beauty Consultants	13	27	40	-30	-	-
Being responsible for disappointing performance	05	-09	30	07	09	-02
More fund will make the investment final profitable	-12	**-55**	**-52**	**-59**	**-62**	-26
New Investment is risky	16	-02	18	-22	-46	-03

Note: Figures are correlation coefficients. Bold coefficients are significant at $p < .05$.

When interpreting these results, keep in mind that the amount invested and the levels of perceptions are more or less the same across all the conditions, except control 2. Therefore, the dissatisfaction behavior of beauty consultants did not affect the means of these variables, but has a more subtle effect on the cognitive process of the subjects as it modifies the relationships between the amount invested and perceptions of that investment. Overall, hypotheses 2a, 2b, 2c, and 2d received some support.

Discussion

This study tested the recuperative functions of EVLN in the context of an investment decision. The results show that dissatisfaction behavior demonstrated by a group of key employees has little impact in changing management's investments. However, the results suggest that dissatisfaction behavior of employees does modify how respondents evaluated the subsequent decisions they made. Neglect behavior by the beauty consultants made respondents defend their decision by perceiving their further investment as less significant, seeing their further investment as less risky, and suggesting that further investment as more likely to be profitable. In comparison, loyalty behavior of beauty consultants made respondents more honest in their evaluations. Therefore, they evaluated their further investment as more risky when they had invested more money. Similarly, they acknowledged that they had invested more money when they had in fact done so. Also, they did not justify their further investment as more likely to be profitable. In sum, although dissatisfaction behavior caused no overt changes in investment decisions, it did affect the cognitive processes of the subjects when they made their decision. This effect may plant a seed for future changes when other circumstances lead managers to finally come to terms with the reality of the situation.

STUDY 2

Most studies related to Hirschman (1970) were done in North America (for an exception, see Ross, 1988), so testing whether Hong Kong Chinese also conceptualize dissatisfaction behavior in the form of EVLN is a necessary first step to testing our hypotheses in Hong Kong. If Chinese do not possess these concepts, subordinates who display EVLN behavior would make no sense to them and an experiment like the above would be invalid as well (Lonner & Berry, 1986).

Method

Subjects

One-hundred-thirty-eight undergraduates in libraries and hostels of a large university in Hong Kong were requested to fill out a short questionnaire by two male research assistants. The response rate was 45 percent. The students participated voluntarily and were given a debriefing note when the research assistants picked up the completed questionnaire.

Questionnaire

The questionnaire contained a short case about a company in crisis based on Garland (1990). The participants were instructed to imagine that they were researchers involved in a failing R&D project. After reading the case, they decided their likelihood of taking different types of action on five-point scales (one-very likely, five-very unlikely). The statements describing the types of action were adapted from Withey and Cooper (1989). The questionnaire took the students about 10 minutes to complete.

Results

Exploratory factor analyses were conducted to see whether the EVLN items clustered together as in Withey and Cooper (1989). This analysis revealed that four factor solutions (*eigen* > 1) were suitable for both cultures and can be inter-preted as the EVLN behaviors (Withey & Cooper, 1989). The exit and neglect factors were the same as in Withey and Cooper (1989), and the key items of the voice and loyalty factors also fit together. The scores of the four factors were compared in a one-way ANOVA. The ANOVA was significant, F (3, 411) = 65.95, $p < .01$. Newman-Keuls tests showed that Hong Kong subjects preferred voice ($M = 2.69$) to loyalty ($M = 3.04$), but exit ($M = 3.62$) and neglect ($M = 3.70$) are equally disliked.

Discussion

The results imply that Hong Kong students demonstrate the same perceptions about appropriate reactions to dissatisfaction. They suggest that EVLN concepts exist in the minds of Hong Kong subjects, and therefore, studying how they may respond to these behaviors makes sense in Study 3 (see below). Having said that, the finding proves merely that Hong Kong subjects categorize reactions to dissat-isfaction the same as those in Canada and the United States. It does not prove that they do not have their unique way of reacting to dissatisfaction other than EVLN. The design of this study precluded us from finding any indigenous dissatisfaction behaviors should they exist. In addition, the results suggest that Hong Kong stu-dents prefer to display voice and to a less extent loyalty, whereas the two negative reactions, neglect and exit, were equally disliked by them. The subjects were more interested in using positive responses to the disappointing situation of the company (Farrell, 1983).

STUDY 3

This study was designed to provide a cross-cultural comparison of the findings from Study 1. As suggested by other scholars (Adler, 1992), management theories developed in one culture may not be generalizable to other cultures. More impor-tant, the comparison is intended to identify cross-cultural differences that are caused by differences in societal context (Cheng, 1989, 1994). The hypotheses of this study are the same as those of Study 1.

Method

Subjects

One-hundred-and-twenty business undergraduates of a large university in Hong Kong participated in this study in small groups. They received HK$60 upon fin-ishing the questionnaire and were fully debriefed. Among them, 39 percent are male and their median age was 20.

Questionnaire

The questionnaires used in Canada were back-translated into Chinese. The country of the firm was changed from Canada to Hong Kong. A few MBA students of the university pre-tested the questionnaires and found them realistic and interesting to work on. The procedure is the same as in Study 1.

Results and Discussion

Perceptions of Dissatisfaction Behavior

As shown in Table 1, one-way ANOVAs of the evaluations of the actions of the beauty consultants were all significant ($p < .01$). Neuman-Keuls tests at $p < .05$ suggest that the actions described in the voice and loyalty conditions were evaluated as more favorable to the company, moral, proactive, and appropriate than those described in the exit and neglect conditions. Moreover, the action described in the loyalty condition was evaluated as supporting more investment than the action in the other conditions.

These results imply that Hong Kong students regarded loyalty and voice as positive to the company and exit and neglect as negative (consistent with Study 1). In particular, loyalty is regarded as the most positive and neglect as the most negative (see Table 1). By and large, Hong Kong students aligned EVLN behaviors on the favorable-unfavorable dimension, but seemed to ignore the proactive-reactive dimension found in Farrel (1983).

Further Investment on Products and Perceptions on Investment

An ANOVA of the amount invested was not significant. Even the mean amount invested in the control 2 condition is the same as that in the control 1 condition (see Table 2). Comparisons of the reasons for further investment were also insignificant. These results differ from our findings in Canada.

Consistent with our Canadian results, however, the dissatisfaction behavior of beauty consultants modifies the relationships between the amount invested and perceptions of that investment. The effects are not entirely the same as found in Canada, though.

In the neglect condition, the more money the subjects invested, the more they perceived that their investment was a more substantial amount of money. Indeed, this relationship is stronger in the neglect condition than in the exit ($r = -.71$ versus $-.12$, $z = 2.18$, $p < .05$), voice ($r = -.71$ versus $-.04$, $z = 2.21$, $p < .05$), and loyalty conditions ($r = -.71$ versus $-.14$, $z = 2.14$, $p < .05$). Hence, in contrast to Canadian subjects, Hong Kong subjects in the neglect conditions were less defensive than subjects in other conditions.

Also in the neglect condition, the less the subjects invested, the more they indicated that their decision was affected by the behavior of the beauty consultants. This relationship reverses in the other conditions. The correlations of the neglect ($r = -.30$) and loyalty ($r = .40$) conditions are different ($z = 2.22, p < .01$), and so are those of the neglect and voice ($r = .27$) conditions ($z = 1.68, p < .10$). The correlation of the neglect condition is, however, not significantly different from the correlation ($r = .13$) of the exit condition ($z = 1.25$, n.s.). A third observation is that the larger the amount invested, the more the subjects expected their further investment to eventually become profitable.

We would also expect a negative relationship between perceived risk and amount invested. This relationship was found in the neglect and control 1 conditions, but it was reversed for subjects in the exit and loyalty conditions. The correlations in the control 1 and exit conditions are different ($z = 1.85, p < .10$), and so are the correlations between control 1 and loyalty conditions ($z = 1.88, p < .10$). These results imply that subjects in the exit, loyalty, and, to a less extent, voice conditions decided to invest more even after acknowledging the risk involved. In contrast, subjects in the neglect and control 1 conditions recognized the risk and invested accordingly.

In sum, the findings provide little support that voice and loyalty are more effective than exit and neglect in changing the course of actions of managers (H1). Moreover, expected profitability of the investment is positively related to the amount of investment (H2d) in all the conditions. The other hypotheses received support in some of the conditions.

OVERALL DISCUSSION

Both studies in Canada and Hong Kong found that dissatisfaction behaviors of subordinates did not change the course of investment by management. Specifically, EVLN behaviors did not reduce the amount invested into a dubious project. Nevertheless, it was found that dissatisfaction behavior subtly affected management's views of the dubious project. For Canadians, neglect behavior by the beauty consultants made the decision maker more defensive, as they minimized the significance of the amount invested and the risk of the investment. Interestingly, although subjects perceived both exit and neglect behaviors as negative, exit behavior by the beauty consultants affected the decision makers in a way similar to voice and loyalty behaviors.

EVLN behaviors were found to exert different effects on student decision makers in Hong Kong. Neglect behavior by the beauty consultants did not induce decision-makers to be defensive. Quite the opposite, neglect behavior lead subjects to acknowledge the significance of their investment, the influence of beauty consultants' behavior on their decision, and that their investment was risky. The effects of exit and loyalty and, to a less extent voice, are quite different. They failed to trigger an honest assessment during the decision-making process.

There are several reasons for the weak effect of EVLN on changing the decisions of managers. One is that management may be reluctant to take advice from subordinates, especially advice contradicting their prior decisions. Literature on whistle-blowing documents numerous cases in which management not only deny wrong-doing but also retaliate against whistle-blowers (Westin, 1981). Similarly, although grievances filed by employees may provide information that can improve the organization, management generally interprets them in a negative way and ignores the messages of employees from this channel (Lewin & Peterson, 1988).

Another reason could be the nature of the scenario. Although beauty consultants were described as someone who knew the market, subjects who were asked to play the role of a marketing manager might not think so. They might instead regarded themselves as the ones who know the market and are in charge of business decisions. It is also possible that our scenario study did not provide powerful manipulations in spite of the success of other scenario studies, such as Staw (1976). Subjects did not receive the reaction from consultants as they would in real life, and the investment was not real money. Future studies may employ a different design to test this possibility. In addition, student subjects in the experiments might have limited experience with subordinates and attentive to the messages in the EVLN behaviors. Although several studies in this area showed that student subjects behaved similarly to adult subjects (e.g., Tjosvold, 1982; Withey & Cooper, 1992), readers should be cautious in generalizing the results to experienced, adult managers.

Cross-Cultural Differences on the Effects of EVLN Behavior

Hong Kong and Canadian subjects responded differently toward neglect behavior by the beauty consultants. Neglect behavior moderated the beliefs of the subjects toward their investment. Canadian subjects became more defensive, whereas their Hong Kong counterparts became more honest and open. The evaluations of neglect behavior are unfavorable in both groups (see Table 1).

These cross-cultural differences could be accounted for by several societal factors (Cheng, 1994). First, cultural individualism-collectivism, as applied in cross-cultural conflict resolution research, may be used to explain these findings. Individualists, such as Canadians, value the pursuit of truth in dispute resolution. Hence, they favor a process that allows open debate and acute questions and comments are typically exchanged (Leung & Wu, 1990). As neglect behaviors do not contribute toward disclosing the truth but inflict clandestine damage on the company, individualists may interpret neglect behavior as aggravating the problem or even "hitting below the belt." As a result, they may react to neglect with defensive behaviors and try their best to rationalize their decision.

On the other hand, avoidance and compromise are dominant conflict resolution procedures for collectivists, such as the Hong Kong Chinese (Leung & Wu, 1990). They do not want to disrupt the apparent harmony and cause animosity between disputing parties. Managers in Hong Kong are paternal leaders who oftentimes allow only top-down communication although they are obliged to act benevolently to subordinates (Redding & Wong, 1986). Many of them would see voice behavior as a challenge to their supremacy, and thus as conflict provoking. Indeed, most organizations in Hong Kong have centralized decision making and are structured for top-down rather than bottom-up communication (Redding & Wong, 1986). This organizational context makes the use of voice by subordinates more difficult. Exit behavior is equally ineffective in influencing Hong Kong managers.

Exit behavior is common in Hong Kong where workers jump from one company to another in a tight labor market. A strong economy has made its unemployment rate lower than 3 percent since the early 1980s. In contrast, Canada has suffered from a sluggish demand for natural resources. The unemployment rate was around 10 percent when the data was collected in Canada. When we consider these differences in economic and labor conditions with the fact that exit behavior is vague in its target and meaning (Hirschman, 1976), it is conceivable that Hong Kong subjects might find it hard to see a clear message in the exit behavior of subordinates. Neglect is probably the most explicit way for Hong Kong subordinates to express dissatisfaction to management.

Neglect behavior is detested by Hong Kong managers. Yet, it may be this little ache that subordinates inflict on them that can draw managers' attention. Paternal Hong Kong business leaders may be more willing to yield to subordinates who know how to convey dissatisfaction subtly in a manner that preserves their superiors' "face" (Redding & Wong, 1986). That may be why subjects become more honest about the situation in the neglect condition.

This discussion implies that "humble pie" is made from different recipes across cultures. Faced with neglect behavior from subordinates, individualistic managers toughen their commitment in their investment decision whereas collectivistic managers soften their commitment. One implication for cross-cultural workplaces is that collectivistic employees should not display neglect behavior to send a urgent message to individualistic managers. Likewise, individualistec employees should not display voice or exit behaviors, but rather neglect behavior to collectivistic managers.

A corollary implication is that Canadian managers, many of them individualists, should not discipline collectivist subordinates, such as those from East Asia and South America, who display neglect behavior as a means of expressing dissatisfaction. They should look deeper into the underlying cause of neglect behavior since it is simply a preferred way for these subordinates to show dissatisfaction and criticism to management (Roongrerngsuke & Chansuthus, 1998). The subordinates may not have any malicious motive to disrupt production or harm the organization.

As with exit behavior, neglect behavior is vague in its target and meaning, and encourages little interaction with management. A collectivist manager may benefit more from subordinates, at least in some situations, if they are involved in discussions with the managers. Such discussions can be promoted by organizational practices that underscore cooperative goals, promote group works, distribute common rewards, and facilitate constructive controversy dynamics, such as the ability to question, understand, integrate, and agree (Tjosvold, 1998, p. 292).

The findings of this study have several implications for future research. First, the studies in two different cultures were consistent in finding no support for the hypothesis that EVLN behaviors lead to change in managerial behaviors that could help recuperate a declining organization. In particular, no support was found for the notion that voice is a more effective mechanism than exit, loyalty or neglect (Hirschman, 1976). These findings cast doubt on Hirschman's well-known theory and call for further research to verify our findings. Moreover, our account of the findings suggests that societal factors, including economic conditions, organizational structure, and cultural individualism, should be tested in future studies. Incorporating these variables will be an important step toward a comprehensive theory on EVLN behaviors. One specific procedure in this direction is to ascertain differences in individualism-collectivism among the subjects by measuring this construct directly. This procedure will provide a more vigorous test of the arguments concerning cultural influences on individual behaviors (Bond & Smith, 1996).

To conclude, this study tested the fundamental predictions of Hirschman (1970) across cultures and proposes several societal variables to explain the findings. As a result, it aids our understanding on how criticism is received and processed by members of different cultural groups, and how such reception and processing can affect communication and management effectiveness. It is hoped that this study will act as a springboard to stimulate future research that extends Hirschman's theory across cultures.

ACKNOWLEDGMENTS

This study is funded by a research grant from the Centre for International Business Studies, University of British Columbia, and an Incentive Grant from the Faculty of Business Administration, Chinese University of Hong Kong. The authors would like to thank Bill Lau for assistance with collecting the data for this project. The authors would also like to thank Ilan Vertinsky for comments on an earlier draft of the paper.

REFERENCES

Adler, N. J. B. S. (1992). Academic and professional communities of discourse: General knowledge on transnational human resource management. *Journal of International Business Studies, 23,* 551-69.

Au, K. (1993). *Can dissatisfied employees curtail further commitment to dubious investment? An exploratory study on Hirschman (1970) argument*. Vancouver: University of British Columbia.

Baron, R. A. (1992). Criticism (informal negative feedback) as a source of perceived unfairness in organizations: Effects, mechanics, and countermeasures. In R. Cropanzano (Ed.), *Justice in the work place: Approaching fairness in human resource management* (pp. 155-170). Hillsdale, NJ: Lawrence Erlbaum.

Bemmels, B. (1996). Exit, voice, and loyalty in employment relationships. In D. Lewin, D. J. B. Mitchell, & M. A. Zaidi (Eds.), *The human resource management handbook* (pp. 495-509). Greenwich, CT: JAI Press.

Bond, M. H., & Smith, P. B. (1996). Cross-cultural social and organizational psychology. *Annual Review of Psychology, 47*, 205-35.

Brockner, J. (1992). The escalation of commitment to a failing course of action: Toward theoretical progress. *Academy of Management Review, 17*, 39-61.

Cheng, J. L. C. (1989). Toward a contextual approach to cross-national organization research. In S. B. Prasad (Ed.), *Advances in international comparative management* (pp. 3-18). Greenwich, CT: JAI Press.

Cheng, J. L. C. (1994). On the concept of universal knowledge in organizational research. *Management Science, 40*, 162-168.

Farrell, D. (1983). Exit, voice, loyalty, and neglect as responses to job dissatisfaction: A multidimensional scaling study. *Academy of Management Journal, 26*, 596-607.

Garland, H. (1990). Throwing good money after bad: The effect of sunk costs on the decision to escalate commitment to an ongoing project. *Journal of Applied Psychology, 75*, 728-31.

Hirschman, A. O. (1970). *Exit, voice and loyalty: Responses to decline in firms, organizations, and states*. Cambridge, MA: Harvard University Press.

Hirschman, A. O. (1976). Some uses of the exit-voice approach—discussion. *American Economic Review, 66*, 386-91.

Leung, K., & Wu, P. G. (1990). Dispute Processing: A cross-cultural analysis. In R. W. Brislin (Ed.), *Applied cross-cultural psychology* (pp. 209-231). Newbury Park, CA: Sage.

Lewin, D., & Peterson, R. B. (1988). *The modern grievance procedure in the United States*. Westport, CT: Greenwood Press.

Lonner, W. J., & Berry, J. W. (Eds.) (1986). *Field methods in cross-cultural research*. Beverly Hills, CA: Sage.

Messick, D. M., Bloom, S., & Boldizar, J. P. (1985). Why we are fairer than others. *Journal of Experimental Social Psychology, 21*, 480-500.

Parker, L. E. (1993). When to fix it and when to leave: Relationships among perceived control, self-efficacy, dissent, and exit. *Journal of Applied Psychology, 78*, 949-59.

Petty, R. E., & Cacioppo, J. T. (1986). The elaboration likelihood model of persuasion. In L. Berkowitz (Ed.), *Advances in experimental and social psychology* (pp. 123-205). New York: Academic Press.

Redding, G., & Wong, G. Y. Y. (1986). The psychology of Chinese organizational behavior. In M. H. Bond (Ed.), *The psychology of the Chinese people* (pp. 267-295). Hong Kong: Oxford University Press.

Roberts, J. T., & Coleman, D. F. (1993). *Predictors of exit, voice, loyalty, and neglect*. Paper presented at the Administrative Science Association of Canada, Lake Louise.

Roongrerngsuke, S., & Chansuthus, D. (1998). Conflict management in Thailand. In K. Leung & D. W. Tjosvold (Eds.), *Conflict management in in the Asia Pacific*. Singapore: Wiley.

Ross, M. H. (1988, October). Political organization and political participation: Exit, voice, and loyalty in preindustrial societies. *Comparative Politics, 20*, 73-89.

Rusbult, C. E., & Farrell, D. (1983). A longitudinal test of the investment model: The impact on job satisfaction, job commitment, and turnover of variations in rewards, costs, alternatives, and investments. *Journal of Applied Psychology, 68*, 429-38.

Rusbult, C. E., Johnson, D. J., & Morrow, G. D. (1986). Determinants and consequences of exit, voice, loyalty, and neglect: Responses to dissatisfaction in adult romantic involvement. *Human Relations, 39*, 45-63.

Saunders, D. M., Sheppard, B. H., Knight, V., & Roth, J. (1992). Employee voice to supervisors. *Employee Responsibilities and Rights Journal, 5*(3), 241-59.

Simonson, I., & Staw, B. M. (1992). Descalation strategies: A comparison of techniques for reducing commitment to losing courses of action. *Journal of Applied Psychology, 77*, 419-26.

Singelis, T. M., Triandis, H. C., Bhawuk, D. P. S., & Gelfand, M. J. (1995). Horizontal and vertical dimensions of individualism and collectivism: A theoretical and measurement refinement. *Cross-Cultural Resesarch, 29*(3), 240-75.

Staw, B. (1976). Knee-deep in the big muddy: A study of escalating commitment to a chosen course of action. *Organizational Behavior and Human Performance, 16*, 27-44.

Thomas, D. C., & Au, K. (1998). *Impact of national culture on the behavioral response to exchange variables.* Paper presented at the Inaugural Conference of the Australia-New Zealand International Business Academy, Melbourne, Australia.

Tjosvold, D. (1982). Superiors' incorporation of subordinates' information in decision making. *Journal of Applied Psychology, 67* 189-93.

Tjosvold, D. (1992). *The conflict-positive organization: Stimulate diversity and create unity.* Reading, MA: Addison-Wesley.

Tjosvold, D. (1998). Cooperative and competitive goal approach to conflict: Accomplishments and challenges. *Applied Psychology: An International Review, 47*, 285-342.

van de Vijver, F., & Leung, K. (1997). *Methods and data-analysis for cross-cultural research.* Thousand Oaks, CA: Sage.

Westin, A. F. (Ed.) (1981). *Whistle blowing.* New York: McGraw Hill.

Withey, M. J., & Cooper, W. H. 1989. Predicting exit, voice, loyalty, and neglect. *Administrative Science Quarterly, 34*, 521-39.

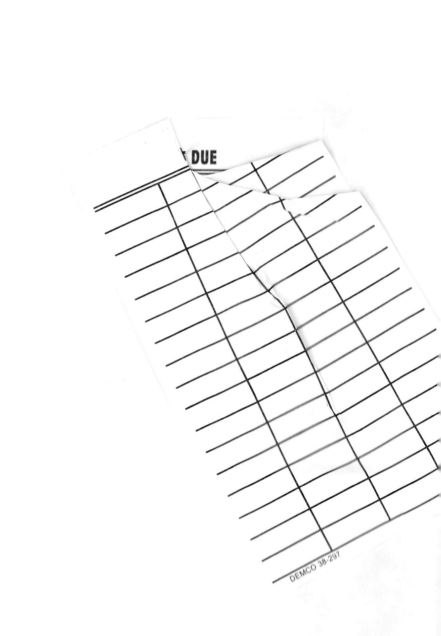

DUE

DEMCO 38-297